IN EXILE FROM ST P

In Exile
from St Petersburg

The Life and Times of Abram Saulovich Kagan
Book Publisher, as told by his son
Anatol Kagan

Adapted and edited by
Michael Atherton

Brandl & Schlesinger

Cover and book design by Andras Berkes-Brandl

First published by Brandl & Schlesinger in 2017
PO Box 127 Blackheath NSW 2785 Australia
www.brandl.com.au

 A catalogue record for this
book is available from the
National Library of Australia

ISBN 9780648176404

Printed by Bennetts Printing, Katoomba

I have striven not to laugh at human actions, not to weep at them,
nor to hate them, but to understand them.
Baruch Spinoza

CONTENTS

A Note on the editor
Professor Emeritus Michael Atherton

Following research in literature at the University of NSW, Michael studied music at the University of Sydney and the University of New England and completed a doctorate in music an cultural history at the University of Technology Sydney. He played early music in the Renaissance Players (1974–1980); joined Rivendell as a music therapist (1978–80) in the team of Professor Marie Bashir; pioneered cross-cultural music in Sirocco (1980–6); and directed his own ensemble, Southern Crossings (1986–93). He continued to perform internationally for Musica Viva following appointment in 1993 as the Foundation Chair of Music at Western Sydney University.

Michael is an expert in the ethnomusicology of musical instruments and sound making objects in Australia and the Asia-Pacific. He composes music for the concert hall, film, television and radio. In 2008 he was the featured composer in the Aurora Festival, with five world premières. He is a Fellow of the Royal Society of Arts, Manufactures and Commerce. Other awards include a Centenary Medal (2003) for service to the community. In 2009 he co-edited *Music of the Spirit: Asian-Pacific Music Identities*. Michael is also a member of SynC, an electroacoustic duo with Garth Paine. Performance highlights include: New Interfaces for Musical Expression (NIME), New York, June 2007; and NIME/Agora Resonances, Paris, 2006. Michael's most recent book is *Musical Instruments and Sound Producing Instruments of Oceania* (2010). He retired from Western Sydney University at the end of 2012 and was honoured with the title, Emeritus Professor, for his distinguished contribution to teaching and research in the field of music and service to the University over many years.

Acknowledgements

This book has gone through several transformations. It began with a son's desire to write a biography of his father for family, friends and those interested in academic research on specific topics on Russia, in particular book publishing. Anatol had access to interviews given by his father to Professor Raeff, which he translated and edited. The original translation remains with Anatol's wife, Dawn Kagan, in Sydney. As Anatol began working on the interviews, adding his own text, Dawn became his tireless typist and proof-reader. She knows the manuscript inside out from the working and reworking undertaken by Anatol, and has remained ever ready to read my own work in the final presentation.

Along the way, between 1997–1999, Ms Leone Palermo, my personal assistant at the University of Western Sydney helped me re-format the manuscript. Anatol then revisited the text on and off until 2006, when we produced photocopies for friends and family.

We are grateful to all those who have read the first manuscript and offered comments. Included are: David Hills, Frank Harvey, Bart Plunkett, Bob Gould, Peter Kagan, Natalie Kagan, Catherine Kagan, Irene Guttman, Dr Pamela Tinslay, Harvey and Stephanie Sowerby, Dr Nancy Wickham, Dr Alf Liebhold, Len Loker, Bob Fastovsky, Bruce and Trixie Harvey, Professor Ivor Indyk, Hall Greenland, Dr Dorian Thorpe and Simon Reeves. Assistance with Russian names and a translation of poems was provided by Professor Alexandra Y. Aikhenvald, Dr Nonna Ryan and Anna Klimova.

In 2011, Melinda Jewell, a research assistant, moonlighted on *In Exile from St Petersburg*, while working with me on music research projects. Melinda helped me reduce the original manuscript after I decided to emphasise Abram's memoir *per se* by reducing the amount of Anatol's commentary and foregoing many of his footnotes. The current version is 30,000 words shorter than the original manuscript.

Preface

In Exile from St Petersburg is an annotated memoir of Abram Saulovich Kagan (1889–1983) in the context of the events that governed his life, with annotations and biographical interpolations by his son, Anatol Abramovich Kagan (1913–2009), my father-in-law.

Abram Saulovich never wanted to leave St Petersburg, or Petrograd, as it was called at the time when he was exiled. It was there that he founded the publishing company, *Naooka i Shkola* (Science and School), the first of several, and where he joined Petropolis, the publishing company that became the main focus of his activity in Berlin after his expulsion from his homeland. *Petropolis*, the Greek word for "Peter's City" was named after Peter the Great who founded St Petersburg in 1703, replacing Moscow as the capital of Russia, until 1918 when Moscow assumed that role again, this time as the capital of the Soviet State, which replaced the former Empire of the Tsars. Four years earlier, at the outbreak of the WWI in 1914, the German-sounding St Petersburg was changed to the Russian Petrograd, only to be changed to Leningrad, after the death of Lenin.

St Petersburg became the centre of culture and a font of progressive thought. Petrograd was the site of the October Revolution, which hoped to change the world and lay the foundation for a rational, brotherly human society. But, even before Lenin's embalmed body was placed into the Mausoleum and Petrograd was renamed Leningrad, the Revolution was perverted by Stalin and his successors, who, as it was put by

Trotsky (next to Lenin, the most prominent leader of the Revolution) "abused their power in such a way as to prepare an explosion of the whole system, which may completely sweep out the results of the Revolution".

And this was indeed what happened in 1991, seventy-four years after October 1917. The process which was set off by what has become known as *Perestroika* (Restructuring) was derailed and did not lead, as was thought by some, to a Socialist Renewal, but to the restoration of Capitalism at its worst. Symbolically, Leningrad was once again re-christened, and today the hero-city, which had withstood the 900-day Siege by the Nazi armies, bears once again the alien Teutonic name that it had under the Tsars.

In the years preceding the Revolution and those immediately following it, Abram Saulovich was an active participant in the cultural life of St Petersburg-Petrograd before he was expelled from his homeland.

In 1922, while on board the *Preussen*, a German ship taking him and a group of writers, academics and other members of the intelligentsia into exile, he was approached by a fellow female passenger making the rounds of the *expulsanty* as they were known, to write down a few words in her autograph book. Abram Saulovich wrote: "I would be happy to return to my homeland under changed conditions". However, he did not live to seize that opportunity, for he died two years before the launching of *Perestroika*, and thus, this oldest of Russian book publishers to survive the Revolution, remained in exile until his death.

Following the death of Abram Saulovich in December 1983, the New York based Russian newspaper *Novoye Russkoye Slovo* (*New Russian Word*), of 8 December 1983, published an obituary written by Andrey Sedykh, in which Abram Saulovich was referred to as "… one of the most noble representatives of

14

the Russian-Jewish intelligentsia". It was ironical that Abram Saulovich, who was deeply steeped in Russian culture and was never connected with anything that could be remotely related to specific Jewish cultural pursuits, was posthumously awarded that accolade which, no doubt, was meant to be complimentary. However, the bestowing of that accolade must give pause to some thought: What is a "representative of the Russian-Jewish intelligentsia?" How does such a person differ from an intellectual who is merely "Russian"?

To be able to answer this, we have to look first at the condition of the Jews in Russia, the old Tsarist Russia that gave rise to the Russian-Jewish intellectuals of Abram Saulovich's generation.

Russian Jews were subjected to many forms of official discrimination and residential limitation, including forced exile. They were confronted with endemic anti-Semitism and suffered state-sponsored pogroms in which they were singled out as scapegoats for whatever troubles were besetting the community.

Before the Revolution the majority of the Russian Jews had to live within the *Pale*, which comprised mainly the Western and Southern part of the Russian Empire. They were not allowed to engage in agriculture, they were excluded from government jobs and were not allowed to accept employment in major industrial enterprises. The Jews of Tsarist Russia had some limited and conditional avenues of advancement in contrast with the future horrors in Nazi Germany, where the Jews were at first excluded from all walks of life within the German community, to be eventually subjected to extermination, only limited by the capacity of the ovens in the concentration camps. Thus, for the Russian Jews, there was a way out of the confines of the *Pale* to those who underwent Christian baptism, or were able to obtain tertiary education (which was only possible within a restrictive quota system), or achieved success by attaining a certain rank in the hierarchy of commerce, e.g. "Merchant of the First Guild". But such advancement was not available to the majority of the Jews, and besides, it did not stop anti-Semitism.

While in the twentieth century Nazism has displayed the most obsessive, cold and systematically genocidal form of anti-Semitism, it must not be forgotten that the old Russian Empire contained some particularly nasty aspects of that reactionary manifestation many years before Hitler. It must be remembered that pogrom is a Russian word denoting "destruction" and "massacre", but having a specific meaning in Russia to characterize the organized terrorist acts against the Jewish population perpetrated by reactionary elements with the participation of criminals. The organization that was generally connected with the instigation and perpetration of the pogroms bore the name of The Union of the Russian People, and was generally referred to as the Black Hundreds, the precursors of the Nazis and Fascists, and their present-day imitators in Russia such as the members of the Pamyat' (Remembrance) Society.

Michael Atherton
October 2017
Sydney

Introduction

Abram Saulovich was an extraordinary man. Not only was he extraordinary in his intellectual capacity, organizing genius, ability for intensive work, efficiency, stubbornness, toughness in adversity and in possessing a prodigious memory, but also time and time again he found himself in extraordinary historical circumstances, and he met countless extraordinary people. He lived an intensive life containing enough events to fill several life spans. He was a publisher in Russia, Germany, Belgium and the United States. The books he published comprised quality literature ranging from art and esoteric poetry to politics and psychoanalysis. He was also politically active during the stormy period of the Russian Revolution.

He lived a long life punctuated by adversity. As a child he was not allowed to start school because of a religiously discriminating quota system that applied in Russia in those days. When he was eventually admitted to high school and had reached senior grade, he was expelled for supporting his Polish fellow-students in their struggle for national independence.

He had to continue his studies on his own since he was excluded from enrolling at any other high school. After having topped the final school examination as an external student in a different part of Russia, where his expulsion from a high school was not known, he managed to enter university at the age of sixteen. He graduated in three different disciplines: Mathematics, Law and Economics.

Having reached the position of Professor of Economics in his early thirties, as well as having launched a publishing company in Petrograd, he was jailed on trumped-up charges, and was exiled after being confronted with the certainty of being executed unless given hospitality in a different country. Having started a new publishing enterprise in Germany, but ironically retaining a Soviet passport which however disallowed return to his homeland, he was expelled from Germany shortly before the outbreak of the Second World War. After again establishing himself as a publisher, this time in Belgium, he had to flee ahead of the advance of the German army. He was interned in Vichy France, and eventually succeeded in coming to the United States where he again set up a publishing company, this time in New York, where he founded the prestigious firm International Universities Press, Inc.

From the above one can conclude that much can be written about Abram Saulovich. This for me seemed to be reason enough to justify the writing of his biography. But this was not the only reason. There was also something akin to a strong desire for atonement: for over the years, Abram Saulovich and I had had disagreements and furious arguments, both personal and political. Often, when I recognized in him some trait which I saw in myself, and which I did not like, I felt particularly hostile to him.

It could be argued that to write one's father's biography from a desire for atonement is not a good reason for undertaking such a task, since it would be difficult to take a detached view of one's subject when one's emotions are so openly displayed. But then I do not intend to take a detached view of Abram Saulovich. I remain as unrepentantly partisan as ever in respect of our disagreements, although I fully intend to try to understand their nature.

Writing the biography was, of course, not just to satisfy my personal need. It was also for the readers out there in the world, and I had to ask myself: "Who will those readers be?" In the first place there will be my relatives and friends. After that there would be persons concerned with academic study and research on specific topics, most likely book publishing. In fact, research in this respect has already been undertaken by Ms Susan Cook-Summer of Columbia University, who delivered a paper at the Fourth World Congress of Soviet and East European Studies, in July 1990, in Harrogate, England: "The Petropolis publishing house and A.S. Kagan". Ms Cook-Summer and I, to our mutual benefit, exchanged relevant information regarding Abram Saulovich's publishing activity.

Furthermore, I thought that apart from relatives, friends, and some academics, there should be other sympathetic (or possibly hostile) readers, who would be interested. What precisely would interest these most diverse types of readers?

Abram Saulovich's *Memoirs*, which are the core of my narrative, abound with mentions of names of people prominent in various fields, as well as of book titles and of historical events, which may be just so many names to the uninitiated. Those interested in book publishing may be interested in the specific subjects of the publications. As for historical events, these may have been forgotten or misinterpreted, or their memory has become a matter of indifference. Thus there arose the question as to how much to add to Abram Saulovich's *Memoirs* by way of explanation?

I consulted Professor Marc Raeff of Columbia University, where Abram Saulovich's *Memoirs*, books, and archival materials are preserved in the Bakhmeteff Archive. Professor Raeff replied by quoting the maxim: *"On s'engage, et puis on voit"*, attributed to Napoleon, and also adopted by Lenin. Napoleon had in mind: "Engage in the battle, and see how it evolves". Lenin applied that maxim to the Russian Revolution, and no matter what its eventual fate, there was a lesson to be learnt (and has still to be learnt!).

My aim was much more modest, but I found the maxim just as useful. I had to imagine what would be the reaction of the various kinds of readers to the material contained in Abram Saulovich's *Memoirs*? How much of their contents would the readers follow? For example, there is mention of historical events. Now my youngest daughter, Catherine, had the following comments accompanying her results in History on her High School Certificate: "Catherine is a dedicated historian". But then I found that the comment was actually the result of my rather persistent interest in her studies in this subject, and once the parental pressure was gone, history had become for her somehow irrelevant. And what about other people who have no family member keen on history? Yet without some knowledge of the historical scene, it would not be possible to fully appreciate many aspects of Abram Saulovich's activity. Thus, some choice of informative material had to be made. The reader may not agree with my choice, but he or she at least will be induced to consider the issues involved. And, history apart, I believe that the many writers, philosophers and artists mentioned in Abram Saulovich's *Memoirs*, should be more than just so many names.

Whether I have overdone the task of making relevant explanations, I do not know. I still remain in some doubt as to whom the biography should be addressed? I imagine that most people will be interested in some of the subjects, but I do not think that many people will be interested in all of the subjects. Some may avidly take in the narrative about some events, but be bored to distraction by other sections of my effort at biography, which is the outcome of a creative urge, and not of a wish to write a best-seller by making the marketplace my criterion. Anyhow: "*On s'engage, et puis on voit*".

As stated earlier, I do not lay claim to any impartiality. On a number of occasions I state my own opinions, and, at times I make critical remarks about Abram Saulovich's attitudes. The reader will also notice, by my choice of quotations, that I take sides with certain protagonists.

To a large extent the following narrative consists of a translation of extensive sections of the *Memoirs* which are otherwise used as "raw material" for the biography, together with the transcript of a number of tapes on which are recorded interviews between Abram Saulovich and Professor Raeff, as well as further tapes containing interviews I had with Abram Saulovich back in 1977, and a series of notes by him dealing with the Petrograd period. All this is supplemented by my own recollections, and I shall also figure in the story as a participant in various situations. The reader will notice that, in a way, I too am "in exile from St Petersburg".

An example of a typical pogrom was that which occurred in Kishinev (now the capital of the newly formed Republic of Moldova), in April 1903, when, in the course of two days, the pogromists looted and destroyed more than 1,500 Jewish homes and shops, slaying forty-five Jews and injuring hundreds more. But the worst pogroms were to occur during the Civil War, and were perpetrated by the White Army, which, during the final years of the struggle, massacred thousands of Jews, holding them responsible for the Revolution. Only the Holocaust surpassed, at least quantitatively, the outrages against the Jews committed by the White Army.

Present day Russian reactionaries who have emerged as one of the less pleasant results of the freedom of expression brought about by *Glasnost'*, proclaim as of old, that all the misfortunes that have befallen the Russian people are the result of a "Judeo-Masonic Conspiracy" against them. But so far they have not managed to organize any pogroms, in spite of all attempts to turn back the wheel of history in that unfortunate land now known as the Commonwealth of Independent States, a conglomerate characterized by the implacable hostility of its members towards each other which, in some places, has spilled into tribal warfare.

It must be noted that the infamous forgery known as *The Protocols of the Elders of Zion*, a document outlining a purported plan for nothing less than complete world domination by Jewry, acquired a particular significance as the centrepiece of anti-Semitic propaganda in pre-revolutionary Russia. *The Protocols* were used by the old regime in its very death throes, when copies of the "document" were handed out to the troops of the White Army.

The historian Christopher Andrew argues that there is a strong probability that *The Protocols*, which he calls "perhaps the most influential forgery of the twentieth century", are the work of Pyotr Rachkovsky, who made a career as the head of the Foreign Agency of the Tsarist political police (Okhrana) at the end of the nineteenth century. Rachkovsky combined that activity with that of a highflyer in Paris society and a very successful speculator at the Paris Stock Exchange. Rachkovsky's specialty was forgery.

Many Jews resigned themselves to accept discrimination in all its ugly forms, as the natural order of things, as something in a way given by God to his "Chosen People". In the main this was the basis of the culture of the Ghetto. But millions of Jews emigrated, especially to the United States where the Statue of Liberty was beckoning. At the same time, as pogrom was a Russian word, the concept of Zionism was native to Russia. The Zionists set before the Jewish masses living in miserable conditions inside the *Pale*, the vision of a Jewish homeland. This homeland was to be established in *Palestine*, that is, in a land, which the Jews had left long ago, which was inhabited by other people, where the immigrants and the State, which they were to establish, would become pawns of the major powers. This would give rise to insoluble conflicts and a possible world conflagration, but this was still in the future. In the meantime, the dream of the "Promised Land" and the old Passover motto, "Next year in Jerusalem", was to become real.

However, there were also those who confronted discrimination as a challenge, as something to be overcome without the indignity of baptism and without having to leave their native land. Abram Saulovich belonged to this particular group, which included those who threw in their lot with the Russian people. Many intellectuals were attracted to the Marxist vision of a harmonious society to be established throughout the world. Marxism spread more rapidly among Jews than any other ethnic groups. Anti-Semites have often pointed to the relatively large number of Jews among the leaders of the Russian Revolution. Indeed, many Jewish intellectuals had espoused the Leninist proposition of a World Revolution, towards which the Russian Revolution was to be the first step.

The political spectrum displayed by the Jewish intellectuals comprised all shades, but the term "political" is too narrow to describe the whole amplitude of intellectual endeavour, the general characteristic of which was a complete absorption in, and identification with the Russian intelligentsia. This intelligentsia was rooted overwhelmingly in the middle classes, which in Russia never grew to the same dominant position in society, as was the case in the advanced countries. And it is to that type of intelligentsia that Abram Saulovich belonged, that is, during his formative years, for he was only thirty-three years old when he left Petrograd in 1922.

Transferring his activity as a publisher to Berlin where he brought out both Soviet and Russian émigré literature, he thus remained in the forefront of Russian culture in a foreign land. The Nazis put an end to this, as they put an end to the unique Russian émigré culture centered in Berlin, where it flourished particularly in the early twenties. After being a fugitive and a displaced person, Abram Saulovich finally established himself, again as a publisher, in New York where, after several ventures, he established the International Universities Press, Inc. This company published books devoted to psychoanalysis, which was quite a different field of intellectual endeavour from that to which he had devoted himself in Petrograd and Berlin, but which he tackled with the same dedication. The subject of psychology had also figured among the books, which Abram Saulovich had published in Russia and Germany.

Anatol Kagan
June 2000
Sydney

Abram Saulovitch Kagan, 1914, aged 25.

PART ONE

RUSSIA
1889–1922

Chapter One

Childhood

I, Abram Saulovich Kagan[1], was born into a well-to-do Jewish family on 20 April 1889[2], in a small township by the name of Lyady in the Moghilev Province of Belorussia[3].

My father, Saul Natanovich, was an exceptionally kind, responsive person. He was not devoid of some public spirit. He was not religious, but took part in many Jewish concerns[4], and he did this from an inner conviction and not from a wish to show off from a position of loftiness[5].

My father was a very well read and passed on the love of books to me. I developed a passion for books from an early age. My mother was completely absorbed in her care for the children. She was a wonderful housewife, but did not let one day pass without reading the newspaper, both Russian and Yiddish. She regarded my father as an unquestionable authority in all spheres. She considered him to be infallible, and took great care of him. My father treated my mother irreproachably and kept her informed about all his business affairs. But if there was some unpleasantness, he concealed it, and spoke about it only when it was past or had been favourably resolved.

I loved my mother very much, but my father was also my friend from my earliest years. He always brought me books from his frequent trips. My parents never suppressed my will, and in my actions I always considered how they would look at them. Of course, I followed my own road, but this inner attachment to the family saved me from many mistakes. For example, I felt no urge to seek different company, as is often the case with boys. If somebody undesirable intruded, I attempted to avoid him or her.

My father owned stores of petrol and kerosene in various towns[6]. Their number gradually increased, and the business grew. He stockpiled, with great surpluses, oil products for a whole year, and paid for them as he sold them. By the end of the contract year, the accounting was carried out regarding the surplus. According to the contract, he was either paid the difference between the purchase price and that on the date of the contract's expiry, or he had to make an additional payment. Of course, there was an element of speculation in all this, but as far as I can remember, the difference was always in favour of Saul Natanovich.

My maternal grandfather [whose surname was Fainberg] owned an estate in Lyady, like a regular landowner. Grandmother, grandfather and my parents lived in the main building[7], together with the children. There were two of us, my sister and I. Apart from the inhabited rooms, there was a whole suite of rooms just for show, which were filled with wonderful antique red timber furniture of enormous value. These rooms were accessible, but they were not used, and were kept exceptionally clean. Apart from this, there was a separate building in the yard, where my uncle, whose name was also Abram, and his family lived.

Then there was a building for the servants, of whom there were countless numbers. Only my sister's nanny lived in the main building. Then there were huge stables and accommodation for carriages. When I was a little child and would not go to sleep during the day, a carriage with two horses was prepared, and the driver, Yegor, drove my nanny and me out of the township, until I went to sleep. My mother often reminisced about this.

Saul Natanovich Kagan, with daughter Rosa with her baby son Jacob, 1914.

A perfectly wonderful garden joined onto my grandfather's mansion. There was an abundance of all kinds of fruit and berries. In autumn, jams were prepared with special solemnity. Cucumbers, tomatoes, apples and pears were marinated. There were enough provisions for the entire family for the whole year, and the following autumn the surplus was given away to anyone who wanted it.

Grandfather Fainberg was a unique person. He was of enormous height, with a broad and thick beard. He did not look Jewish. He was a really rich, self-made man, without education, but he built railroads and communicated with people in high places. God only knows how he carried out all the calculations and estimates, but the Control Commission confirmed his work, the trains travelled on the rails without crashing, and the stations did not collapse. In other words, everything was fine.

Grandmother was slim, beautiful and of tall stature. She spoiled us utterly. When we used to move back into town, Grandmother also went with us. Grandfather was always on the move, and when he came into town [Vitebsk] he lived with us, and, without fail, gave me and my sister a "Gold Imperial" (at that time 15 roubles = $7.50 US).

Grandfather had an exceptional wine cellar in his Lyady mansion. Hard liquor was kept maturing for dozens of years. What this was for was unknown, for no one in the family used to drink. Only at Passover was wine consumed, and this was purchased. Sometimes Grandfather drank a glass of hard liquor, but this was more for show.

One of my first childhood memories was of the fire, which burnt down Grandfather's mansion. We all sat in the street among our belongings, and I looked in terror and wonderment at the blazing building. This happened during the night, and everything assumed an aspect of unreality. We were given shelter by Rabbi Shneerson[8], a well-known Hasid[9] who lived in a building similar to Grandfather's. People flocked to him from the various ends of Russia in search of miraculous healing, and everybody brought their own offerings of thanks, which was, of course, not monetary.

We stayed with Shneerson until the re-erection of our [Grandfather Fainberg's] mansion, but I have not retained any memories of this period, except for my fear of the huge beard of the rabbi.

We rented an apartment in town [in Vitebsk]. We moved fairly frequently, each time to larger accommodation, until we acquired our own home: a house that used to belong to an aristocrat who had squandered his fortune. It was one of the best houses in town, situated opposite the Red Cross building in a quiet residential street with good houses.

We stopped travelling to Grandfather's in summer, rented a dacha [summer house] in the environs, and used to travel out there with the whole family, with Nanny and servants. We had our own carriage. I learned to ride horseback from early childhood, and often without a saddle.

During the first year of our being on vacation in the environs of Vitebsk, my little sister Manya, when swinging on a maypole, got tangled up and hit her head against the pole. She lost consciousness and died several days later from cerebral inflammation. This was my first encounter with death. My sister's death affected my mother terribly, and my father sent her to Alushta, in the Crimea, to recuperate until autumn.

I remained the only child for several years. Then my sister Rosa was born, and a year and a half later, my brother Misha. Rosa was an exceptionally beautiful girl.

Chapter Two

School

I can remember in detail my first great upset. I was being
prepared to enter the preparatory grade of the gimnaziya in
Vitebsk[10]. I had just had my eighth birthday. One could not be
admitted before that age. I had passed the examination with "full
fives", which corresponded to A's, and I was convinced that I
was amongst the percentage norm set down for Jews[11]. A uniform was tailored for me. A cap with a coat of arms and a broad
leather belt were purchased, and even a gala uniform frock coat
with silver buttons and a white silk lining, was tailored. Everybody congratulated me and brought presents.

How great was the shock when, at the very beginning of
the school year, the information was received that I had not
managed to make it to the percentage[12]. I fainted, apparently
due to nervous shock, and could not remember anything after
that[13].

After I had fully recovered, I began to study with a group
of boys who had also failed to enter a *gimnaziya*[14]. The teacher
was a certain Staroselsky. We studied from morning until 1.00
pm. Staroselsky not only instructed us, but he also was in
correspondence with schools in various regions of Russia. He
made inquiries as to where there were vacancies for Jews,
arranged matters with the parents, and placed one boy after
another. His group was being continuously replenished, and
there were even some who studied for many years, right up to

the Matriculation Certificate, for which one could sit as an external student. Apart from this, I began to take regular lessons in both German and French.

My German teacher, Fräulein Emilia, taught at the Girls Gimnaziya. She was the daughter of the pastor, and she also had three sisters, all of whom were teachers. I went to Fräulein Emilia at the pastor's home. I can remember its cleanliness even now. During the lessons I was treated to tea with homemade cakes.

My French teacher was a Madame Osoline, who also taught at the Girls Gimnaziya. She was a real French woman, very imposing. Her husband was a brilliant officer, who also spoke perfect French[15]. Sometimes, instead of a lesson, they invited me for dinner, and the three of us talked French. This was more useful than the lessons[16].

At the age of 13 I started at Pultusk Gimnaziya (in Pultusk, near Warsaw)[17]. I can remember the building of the gimnaziya. At some time in the past it had been a Jesuit college. The classrooms were spacious, the ceilings and windows were high, there was a huge gymnastics room, the corridors were wide and long, everything was chemically clean, the floors were waxed so hard, and they were slippery. Of course, there were no such amenities as bathrooms, and once a week each class in turn went to the public baths, which resembled the Turkish variety. Most of the students were Poles, and there were several Orthodox Russians. Almost all the Poles were not from the township, but were the sons of landowners of the surrounding area, and they all lived in different boarding houses, several dozens in each. The Russians were sons of Russian officials, since the whole administration in Pultusk, as well as in the whole of Poland, was Russian. The Jews, there were fifteen of us in the whole gimnaziya, lived in two separate boarding houses: eight students lived in one, and seven students lived in the other, and the latter was the one in which I settled down.

The gimnaziya was a State high school. It was a civilian, not a military school, but everything was run on military lines. The uniform was, of course, obligatory: a black shirt, buttoned to the top, a wide belt with a shiny white buckle. The full dress uniform, which reached below the knees, was dark blue, with shining silver buttons down the front, and a standing-up collar with silver ornamentation. (These days I am in favour of a uniform for school pupils: there is no differentiation between rich and poor, only that for some, the material and cut could be better, but similar to the others). No speck of dust was allowed on the clothing, the boots had to shine. Everybody's hair had to be cut short, some had a crew cut, others a parting. Before the lessons the Supervisor stood at the door of each classroom and carefully scrutinized the students as they entered, and for the smallest laxity the mark for behaviour was reduced.

There was a break at midday, and we had a snack in the yard, or went to the one and only café in town. Everything was cheap and clean. At the end of the lessons we had gymnastics. The teachers were officers in the local garrison. We were put through some real military drill (except that there was no instruction in the use of arms).

On holidays we marched through the town behind a military band, the Principal and Gymnastics teacher in front, the Form Master (an additional role played by one of the teachers) ahead of each class. We marched in our uniforms, to the sound of commands, not any worse than soldiers. In winter and on cold days, we marched in our grey double-breasted greatcoats, which had two rows of shiny buttons. Once a week we had dancing lessons, which were also obligatory, and, as the school was not coeducational, some of the boys had to take the place of the girls. The class as a whole went on picnics and also to the ice rink, with the Form Master in charge. We were not allowed to go out into the street after 7.00 p.m. To do so was strictly forbidden, nor were we allowed to go out singly. We were allowed to visit the confectioner's shop, but there was always one of the Form Masters there. The Supervisor often called in at the boarding house after 7.00 pm to check that everybody was present, and he made an entry into a special journal which was kept in each boarding house.

In my grade[18], apart from myself, there was another Jew, a Pole, overweight and of very limited capabilities, but very musical. He played the violin.

I was given one of the desks furthest from the front. The atmosphere was highly anti-Semitic. I was called "Yid", and when I walked past, attempts were made to push me, as if by accident. During a lesson, almost on the day following the beginning of the term, someone called out to me "Yid". I flew into a rage and flung a heavy inkwell at the offender, covering him with ink and apparently causing him physical pain. I was called up before the Principal who attempted to find out why I had done that, and who the culprit was who had called out "Yid". I explained why I had acted the way I did, but would not give the name of the student who had directed that derogatory term at me, although it was clear who it was. I was put into the "lockup" for two weeks. "Lockup" was a high-sounding designation, for it simply meant being detained in the classroom until dinner, where I did my homework and some reading. Then the Supervisor came and took me to the boarding house. The punishment was withdrawn after one week. The Form Master remarked that I had been studying well from the very first day, that I was attentive, and that my behaviour in the classroom was exemplary.

After this incident, the attitude to me in the classroom changed radically, and even a good relationship with my fellow students was established[19]. This was largely promoted by my setting out to study excellently. I was transferred to one of the front desks. I was always the first to finish the written work, and managed to throw notes to my colleagues with a solution to problems, or the synopsis of literary themes. I assisted my fellow students unselfishly.

Already during the first semester I became the best pupil and remained so until I left the gimnaziya. I knew much more than my fellow students, especially in mathematics and literature, so that I could even assist colleagues in higher grades, and I acquired a reputation of being a "know-all". In addition, my reputation among the students was strengthened by yet another circumstance. "Russification" was carried out very energetically, and within the walls of the gimnaziya it was forbidden to talk Polish. This was strictly adhered to, even though ninety-five per cent of the students were Poles. The Polish students talked with each other in whispers and avoided using Russian. They spoke Russian in class with an accent, even in the upper grades. Polish lessons were not even obligatory for the Poles, although they attended Polish lessons on principle. All the others, including myself (I was considered a Russian, since, officially, I was born in St Petersburg), left the classroom on these occasions. I decided to master the Polish language, and one day, instead of leaving, I said to the teacher that I would like to remain for the lesson. The teacher, a Pole, said that I must ask the Principal for permission. He could not give me permission on his own, and he did not advise me to apply for such permission. I still went to the Principal, received a good telling off and a categorical prohibition to attend Polish lessons. For my impertinence he made me copy, five times, a large passage from Caesar, which I was to bring to him the next morning.

I continued to study the Polish language on my own, and, already after a short time, I could recite by heart large passages from Mickiewicz, the Polish equivalent of Pushkin, to the astonishment and shame of my colleagues, who learnt their language only formally and for political reasons.

In spite of the military drill and the stern discipline, I have retained pleasant memories of the gimnaziya. In my boarding house I made friends with all my colleagues, helped the young ones, and often the older ones. A serious atmosphere became established. As Jews, we understood well that achievement was the guarantee of enrolment at universities or tertiary institutes. We were happy about our achievements and saddened when someone fell back, and we tried with all means and without sparing time, to urge on the one who had fallen back. We even brought out a little monthly journal, a handwritten one, of course, for in those days there was not even a hint of a typewriter, and one of the students (the dullest among us, but one who had an exceptionally beautiful and even handwriting) spent whole days copying our "manuscripts". I can remember the name of this student was Finkelkraut. He was two years older than me and two grades ahead, a tall lanky fellow whose homework I used to do, and whose mathematical problems I used to solve, and whom I asked to at least study well, so that he could not be accused of having someone else do his work for him.

Our boarding house had an exceptionally high reputation at the gimnaziya, in accordance with our achievements, and we were held up as an example to others.

My relationship with the Poles also became friendly, and I was often invited on weekends to one or other estate[20].

One Easter I visited the estate of the parents of one such school friend and some highly placed Russian official called on the landowner on some business matter, and stayed for dinner. The landowner's wife, the children and relations, took their places at the table. The dinner was festive and solemn, but the landowner himself dined separately in his study with the official, and not with us. Poles considered it not permissible for Poles to sit down at the table with Russians, who were called "Muscovites", or to generally have Russians as acquaintances.

After two years at the gimnaziya I was expelled as a student activist and returned home[21]. My parents were very upset, and I too was depressed. I had become as one with the gimnaziya and my colleagues.

My father again started talking about sending me abroad. I insisted that I should be left at home, that I would study on my own and would prepare myself for the examination for the Matriculation Certificate, which meant preparing myself to cover the entire gimnaziya curriculum. I had to conceal not only the fact that I had been expelled from a gimnaziya, but that I had even attended a gimnaziya at all.

I studied assiduously on my own. I took lessons only in languages, firstly because I wanted to know languages myself, and secondly, at the insistence of my father. He took a critical view of my chances of passing the examinations, since I had to sit for them in all the subjects in all eight grades. It was not enough to pass the examination; it was necessary for me to receive excellent marks, for otherwise I could not qualify for university study.

I prepared myself for the examinations in two years of intensive work. I then began to make enquiries as to where to go to sit for them where my expulsion would not be discovered, for in such a case I would not be admitted to the examinations[22].

In the train[23], in the same carriage, there travelled two persons much older than myself, who also intended to sit for the examinations. One of them, who had failed in Novgorod-Seversk during the previous year, knew the town. After leaving our belongings at the station, we went in search of accommodation. There was not even a hotel in the town, only some furnished rooms. On the street we encountered a Cossack, who enquired what we were looking for? We told him, and the Cossack said that he could accommodate one of us, and picked me. I was decently and cleanly attired, had city manners and spoke a pure Russian, while my fellow travellers were something akin to present-day hippies.

I settled in at the Cossack's house. His wife used to feed me abundantly [literally: "as if to fatten me for slaughter"]. Their place was absolutely clean. I set my parents' mind at rest. My hosts became so used to me that they started to insist on wanting to adopt me, for they had no children of their own. When I told them that I was a Jew, they did not want to believe me, but did not change their attitude towards me.

I never had such exceptional conditions for work. When conversing, my hosts kept their voices down to whispers. Since it was summer, I could also work in the garden, and when it was hot, my hosts used to bring me a jug of *kvass* [Russian horehound]. I cannot remember how much I paid them, but it was quite a negligible sum. I believe that they were losing on me, out of the kindness of their hearts.

Apparently I made a good impression on the examiners. I had a military bearing, I held myself with dignity, did not interrupt, and listened attentively.

The written examinations were the decisive ones. I passed them all with top marks, and as for the oral examinations, these were not difficult at all. After the teachers already knew about my marks for the written examinations I was not picked on, but was almost prompted.

After the last examination, the Principal called me and said that there had been no meeting of the School Council yet, but that I had passed all examinations brilliantly, and that the Council, without a doubt, would issue me with the corresponding diploma. He wished me success for the future.

Before going back to my Cossacks, I went to the telegraph office and informed my parents. I had top marks in all subjects, and I could expect to go to the University. I was sixteen years old.

Chapter Three

The Revolutionary Year

1905 [A.S.K. 16 years old]

After passing the examinations I spent the summer at the dacha of my parents. During that summer I made the acquaintance of Genya and her friend Sonya. Genya's parents lived at the same place, and Sonya was her guest. I used to meet them, but at that time I was little interested in girls. This was the time of being engrossed in socio-political tasks. Young people almost one and all, especially the Jewish youth, had joined the revolutionary movement[24]. I considered myself a Social Democrat Menshevik, a Bundist[25] (the Jewish Social Democrats), although I could not speak Yiddish (but I could read it). I read the Yiddish paper *Der Wecker* (*The Awakener*) until it was banned.

I read a huge quantity of books so as to get myself prepared to take an active part in the movement and to become a comprehensively educated person. Reading programs were passed from hand to hand, and how much there was of this, both literature and art, journalistic material, philosophy and science! It was considered obligatory to master all this to be a conscious activist. Of course, only a few persons mastered all this. I was among them[26].

In respect of literature, I systematically read both Russian and foreign classics, considering that what we had studied at

43

school was dead weight. I also read pre-classical literature such as Derzhavin, Kantemir and Kheraskov. Of foreign literature I will mention Shakespeare, Goethe, Heine, Byron, Flaubert, Balzac, Zola and, of course, Ibsen and Hamsun. All this was in Russian translation. Then, of course, there was current literature. And then critiques: the utterly boring Skabichevsky[27], then Belinsky[28] and the very primitive Pisarev[29].

In order to be a "conscious Social Democrat" it was necessary to know not only Materialism but also Idealism, which had been "appropriated" by the Social Revolutionaries. Mikhailovsky was obligatory, and I knew his essay "What is Progress?" almost by heart. Then there was Chernyshevsky with his novel, *What Is to Be Done?*[30]

Beltov's (Plekhanov's pseudonym) *About the Monistic View of History* was considered a handbook, a kind of catechism. In it Marxism was expounded in a very simple manner, with unbelievably polemical fervour and with derision of all who thought otherwise.

It was necessary to become acquainted with the precursors of Marxism, in particular with Feuerbach and even with Anarchism, such as the books of Bakunin, and, of course, Stirner's *The Only One*. It was necessary to know Hegel, since from him came Dialectics: "thesis, antithesis and synthesis". Timiryazev's *The Life of Plants* and his opposite number, Chelpanov's *Brain and Soul*, were obligatory as examples of the Marxist approach – the counterweight of the primacy of matter to the idealistic superstructure.

I forgot to mention the "whale": Karl Marx's *Capital*. The first volume of *Capital* had been translated into Russian and was freely sold[31].

Generally, one must say that although censorship existed, and people continuously complained about it, that it could in no way be compared with that of the Bolshevik epoch, when in fact all freedom of expression was eradicated. The majority of the enumerated books were available for sale, and were even available in municipal and private libraries.

While all this literature took up much time, youth nevertheless asserted itself. I was a passionate player of croquet, in which I was considered the best player, and always came first in competitions. I loved to ride on horseback, to the terror of my mother who only calmed down when I returned the horse. I rode a bicycle, and even took part in bicycle races. I swam well, I probably would have also dived from a diving board, but at that time these did not exist [sic]. I can remember when, after many, many years, in 1935, we were at the Lido in Italy, and I went for a swim, Tolya was amazed that I swam, and that I swam very well[32].

I would like to recall still another episode that took place in that summer. A wave of anti-Jewish pogroms rolled across the country. The Bund equipped me with a revolver, which I remember was a Smith & Wesson[33]. I did not know how to shoot, and was as scared of the revolver as of fire. During the night I kept it under my pillow, while during the day I tucked it away somewhere so that my mother would not see it. I used to go as far as possible into the forest with a friend, and practise shooting at a target. We learned how to shoot and thanked heaven when we no longer had to do so. The pogroms passed us by.

Chapter Four

University

[A.S.K. 16–20 years old]

I passed my matriculation examination and told my father I intended to study at a university in Russia. It wasn't possible to enrol at a university under the age of eighteen but the Dean of the St Petersburg University, Professor Grimm, recommended that I should apply to the Ministry of Education for enrolment in the Faculty of Law at that University.

After six weeks, the Ministry advised me, as he put it, "to study some more", since under age, but directed me to the Department of Pure Mathematics at the Faculty of Mathematics at Kazan University, which apparently was available as a venue for those who could not be admitted elsewhere.

One of the young girls whose acquaintance I had made during the vacations, told me that her married sister lived in Kazan, and that she would write to her about me, and they (the sister and her husband) would help me to get settled. They turned out to be charming people by the name of Shneerson [not related to the earlier mentioned Shneerson]. They lived outside of town in Arskoye Pole, a thickly wooded suburb of Kazan consisting of detached houses.

Shneerson was a "permanent student", a fairly usual phenomenon in those days. He had to earn his living and had a good job in a bank. He studied at the Faculty of Law, which did not require obligatory attendance at lectures, and he passed his examinations little by little.

The Shneersons had two charming children – girls seven and eight years old. The wife was sweet, friendly, and a very good singer. (I should mention that one of her sisters was a soprano, and sang in important roles at the Berlin Opera.)

The Shneersons received me very well. I had come only for advice as to where to find accommodation, but they insisted that I stay for dinner, and pressed me to live with them until I found a room. They obtained accommodation for me at a friend of theirs, Korostelyov, also a "permanent student", a philologist who made a living by giving lessons. He had a wife and an infant. He was the President of the Council of Elders at Kazan University, and through him it was easy for me to obtain entrance into the students' milieu.

I had a separate room at the Korostelyovs' place. They did not interfere with my life. I lived as if I was at home. Breakfast was brought to me in my room. I had my other meals at the university canteen.

The Korostelyovs often invited me for supper, and in this respect they competed with the Shneersons. They refused to accept any payment and accepted presents only after long arguments. Of course I paid for the room. The furniture was spare: a bed with a mattress, a table (not a writing desk), two chairs, a wash-stand with a basin and ewer, a bookshelf, a simple clothes stand – and that was all.

My hosts' furnishings were not much better, but for their child there was everything.

The toilet had a flusher, which was rare in those days. As for bathing, I went once a week, as did everybody else, to the public baths, which could be described as "Turkish", similar to those in Pultusk[34].

The Korostelyovs were pure Russian people (i.e. not Jewish). They were open-hearted and devoid of any hypocrisy. He was the son of a priest, she was the daughter of a teacher, and both were studying to become teachers.

In regards to the university in the past the Kazan University was one of the best in regard to its Physico-Mathematical Faculty. Its fame was linked with the name of Lobachevsky, the founder of modern mathematics[35]. His monument now stands in front of the University, but in my time there were no outstanding luminaries there.

One could prepare oneself fully by following textbooks without attending lectures[36], which were read as one would read minutes, and the textbooks were those, which were used at the St Petersburg University. I still attended some of the lectures, namely on "Differential and Integral Calculus", "The Theory of Numbers", and "The Theory of Probability". The point was, that if you could see how the professor carried out the calculations on the board, it was easier afterwards to master the textbook. While there were no workshops, the professor sometimes asked whoever wished, to prove a theorem, and I was often among the ones who were willing to do so.

I got to know Professor Alexander Alexanderovich Vassilyev during one of the lectures, which he delivered on "The Theory of Numbers". He was capable of winning the interest of the students by his love of the subject, in spite of the dryness of it. He often asked me to carry out the calculations and bring them to a satisfactory conclusion.

On one occasion, after Vassilyev had praised me, he asked me to follow him into the staff room. He had become interested in my studies, and I told him candidly that I was dreaming of studying political economy. He said that in his opinion I was fairly good at mathematics, and that after finishing the course at the Physico-Mathematical Faculty, I should specialize in statistics at the Law Faculty, and then choose as my speciality Mathematical Statistics, which had a great future in the insurance business, in particular in connection with "The Theory of Probability".

After this, my first acquaintance, I did not miss a single lecture of Vassilyev. I talked to him fairly frequently after the lectures. But one fine day, Vassilyev was appointed to membership of the State Council, and left for St Petersburg. (Part of the State Council was appointed by the Tsar, part came from the Estates, and part from the Universities.) He took leave of me, recommending that I should not forget his words, and reminded me that should I move to St Petersburg, he would assist me to the full extent of his abilities.

My life in Kazan proceeded very quietly. Although I had joined the University Branch of the Social Democratic Party (noblesse oblige!), I did not take an active part and concentrated on study.

The food at the University canteen was quite acceptable, and most of the students, and not only those without means, used to eat there. Those who had no means obtained books of vouchers for meals from the Society for Assistance to Students, and this was very tactfully arranged so as not to humiliate them: such books were held by all students, but nobody knew who paid for them and who did not. The prices for meals were laughable. For example: for 12 kopeks (6 US cents) one could obtain a plate of borsch or soup (one could get an additional serving) and two meatballs with fried potatoes. Kissel (a jellylike dish) was 3 kopeks (1.5 US cents). Coffee, tea or milk was 2 kopeks (1 US cent). Prices at that time in Kazan were generally low: for 50 kopeks (25 US cents) one could have a complete dinner at a restaurant[37].

At the age of eighteen I was admitted to the Faculty of Law in St Petersburg, what I had always longed for[38].

I began to attend lectures assiduously, both at the Faculty of Law and at the Historico-Philological Faculty. The Faculty of Law was, in its composition, the best in Russia. Tugan-Baranovsky taught there, and I did not miss a single one of his lectures. I took part in the workshops, although these were not obligatory. Professors such as Lossky and Lapshin taught there, and I came close to many of them, in particular, to the last two mentioned. I was even befriended by them, and later I published their books[39].

Nikolay Onufriyevich Lossky had married a Stoyunina, whose mother was the Principal of the Girls Gimnaziya named after her. This was the most progressive gimnaziya. Its teaching staff was excellent. In the home of Lossky–Stoyunina I was like one of the family. The old lady Stoyunina treated me as if she was my mother, and during my visits, she used to embrace me and kiss me on the forehead.

During one of my first examinations, namely that in Statistics[40], something happened to me, which determined my future scientific career. On the Examination Board were Professor Emeritus Kaufman, Professor of History of Economics I.M. Kulisher (later a friend of mine and one of the authors whose books I published), and Antony Yosifovich Bukovetsky, an economist-theorist.

The examiners sat at separate tables, and it was left entirely to chance as to who would examine you. Everybody hoped to be able to avoid being examined by Bukovetsky who was very strict. Statistics was a secondary subject for us. Many students confined their study to memorizing a synopsis of this subject. Bukovetsky knew that synopsis well, and always caught a student who had not studied from the basic work, the book by Kaufman, which, according to its size, was very impressive.

Fate had it that Bukovetsky was to be my examiner. He started to ask questions aimed at revealing whether I had confined my studies to the synopsis. I do not know what prompted me, but I told him that he should ask me questions of substance, and not try to catch me out as if I had prepared myself by using the synopsis only. He became furious, and raised his voice as to how I dared to talk like that to a professor! But, to demonstrate his impartiality, he invited Kaufman and Kulisher from the adjoining tables to hear me out, and they all examined me in turn. I answered everything. Twice they did not agree with my answers, but I insisted on my conclusions, and in the end they had to admit that my conclusions were correct. I passed with triumph. Professor Kaufman asked me how I had acquired such knowledge as would do honour to a scientist? I indicated that I had studied at Kazan at the Department of Mathematics of the Physico-Mathematical Faculty, and that I was considering choosing Mathematical Statistics for my specialty.

I obtained the highest mark: "Highly Commended". The examiners shook my hand, and Bukovetsky asked me to meet him in the staff room during the break. In the course of our meeting he explained that he had become furious over the answers of the preceding student who had not even mastered the synopsis, and thus he had poured his ire over me, for which he apologized. He said that he would like to maintain contact with me, and invited me to his home for dinner. This incident brought us together in a firm friendship, and thanks to him my academic career was secured. Later on we met in each other's homes, and Genya [my mother] became friendly with his wife, who was a teacher. The examination determined the whole of my future.

This first conversation with Bukovetsky went as follows[41]:

"You know what? Let us be friends."

I replied, "with pleasure". And we really became friends.

He said, "I am a professor at the Institute of Agriculture... I lecture on Political Economy. I will need an assistant, would you agree to take that position?"

I replied, "It is too soon to talk about this. When I finish university, then we shall see".

Bukovetsky hoped that I would agree.

"We have not a single professor on the staff that is an anti-Semite", he said. "I am not an anti-Semite... perhaps it (the appointment) could be arranged".

Chapter Five

Settling Down in St Petersburg

[A.S.K. 21–24 years old]

From Petersburg I started a lively correspondence with Genya. She had enrolled at the Medical Faculty at Berne, Switzerland, where she went with her friend Sonya. Medicine was not to Genya's liking, and she decided to return to Russia to enrol in Petersburg at the Women's University. I spent the summer at a resort not far from Vitebsk, where Genya's parents also stayed. Sonya also returned from Berne for vacations at her parents' place.

In autumn, Genya and I went to Petersburg, where she enrolled in the Historico-Philological Faculty of the Women's University. One of the professors at that university was N.A. Kotlyarevsky, who later became my partner in the publishing company *Naooka i Shkola*.

Not attaching any great significance to a formal marriage, for we were both radicals, we still decided to get married. Firstly, we did not want to upset our parents. Secondly, there were technical reasons: Genya's study course was no entitlement for residence in Petersburg. It was necessary to obtain a certification of employment from some industrialist to secure the right of residence. Such certification would be valid only for a short period. From time to time there were checks on whether a person was really engaged in industry, and it was necessary to bribe the police. In brief, to study without residential entitlement was made difficult.

And thus we got married. To our parents' sorrow, we did not have a "proper wedding" (a religious wedding), but went to the Registry. We arranged a dinner, which was attended only by my parents, my brother Michael, my sister Rosa, Genya's two brothers Boris and Shneir, and her two sisters Yokha and Vera, and of course, the two of us. The only guest outside the family was Sonya, who had come to Petersburg especially for that occasion.

The problem of residential rights was now resolved, because I had such rights [both as a student and also as the son of a "Merchant of the First Guild"] which were extended to the wife and progeny.

The passing of an examination in Latin was required at the Historico-Philological Faculty at the Women's University [in English-speaking countries this would correspond to the Faculties of English and History], and this was also the case for the Medical Faculty [in Berne] for Sonya. But neither Genya nor Sonya [who was still in St Petersburg] had finished the gimnaziya with ancient languages. I gave them lessons, since I knew Latin perfectly, and they passed their examinations very well, after which Sonya returned to Berne.

Genya and I lived a full life in Petersburg. I worked tirelessly, while she attended her study course. We went to concerts, theatres and museums. In summer we went either to her parents in Vitebsk, or to Finland, or to the environs of Petersburg, to Pavlovsk or Tsarskoye Selo.

I took part in political activity only to the extent that I would not sever my connections with my comrades. I was a registered member of the Menshevik faction of the Social Democratic Party, but I concentrated mainly on study, and "consumed" an incredible quantity of books[42].

I completed my studies and having passed the examinations, I first of all enlisted as a "Solicitor's Assistant". In order to become a solicitor it was necessary to hold the grade of "Assistant" for five years. Yet after this, Jews were not admitted as solicitors. "Assistants" also had no right to independent practice, apart from defence of criminal cases, for which no fees were allowed. But it was permissible for the "Assistants" to settle down as legal consultants of solicitors, and thus to conduct the affairs of their employers[43].

As a student who had passed all university examinations, I still had to submit a thesis, and after its acceptance, the student would have achieved the grade of "Candidate", e.g. "Candidate of Law". I picked as the subject of my thesis The Municipalisation of Industrial Enterprises.

The choice of this theme was a very bold one. It must be taken into consideration that this was during the Tsarist regime, and that the radical element did not predominate among the professors. But my point of view was very definite: tramways, gas and electricity services, all should be owned by the municipality. A trend towards this was already becoming evident at that time, but in Russia those services were operated in the majority of towns by large Belgian and German firms[44].

My thesis was accepted without changes, and now, if I had not been a Jew, the way was open to the academic activity of which I was dreaming.

In this period our first apartment for Genya and myself was in Khersonskaya Street. We lived there for two years, not in luxury but in sufficiency.

Tolya was born in 1913, and he had a nanny, such a nanny as is described in old novels: tall, portly, elderly. She was like a member of the family. She treated the boy with great love. She carried herself with great dignity. When Genya was away studying, Nanny took charge of everything. She kept the cook in terror. She used to smoke, never in the nursery, but in the kitchen, and she always rinsed her mouth after smoking, so that there would be no "tobacco spirit". She became ill with angina pectoris and could work no longer. I took her to the station and obtained for her a berth in a sleeping carriage, to the great surprise of the passengers. [Such mixing of Upstairs, Downstairs was not acceptable in pre-revolutionary Russia.] We maintained her until the end of her days.

Chapter Six

First World War and Involvement in Publishing

[A.S.K. 25–28 years old]

According to a dispensation – as the oldest son – I was not called up for [active] military service[45]. And, upon presenting myself, I was enrolled in the Second Reserve of the Home Guard, which was called up only in wartime, and was to serve after all the other Reserves. I had no desire to take part in the war as a volunteer with a privilege of enrolling in an Officer's School, which, in any case, was not permitted to Jews, and, since I did not want to volunteer, I enrolled at the Medical Faculty of the Psycho-Neurological Institute in Petersburg. Due to my having previously attended the Physico-Mathematical Faculty, I had many credits that qualified me for studying the new subject. At the Medical Faculty I got as far as Anatomy, but at the sight of corpses on which I had to work, I could not overcome my revulsion, and thus my medical career terminated.

When, in the course of the war, the threat of being called up to the Front became almost real, I joined the Military Industrial Committee. Having a science degree, I had the right to wear a military uniform with a captain's tabs, of which right I did not avail myself.

At the Military Industrial Committee I met many Left-wing activists. However, strange as it may be – side by side with professional public servants there was a large number, even a prevailing one, of Left-wing elements, mainly Mensheviks, but I cannot recall a single Bolshevik[46]. There I made the acquaintance of Gvozdyov, the future Minister of Labour in the Provisional Government, and of Boris Osipovich Bogdanov, of whom I shall speak later.

I began to become interested in social issues. Departmental work did not take up much of my time, and I was able to continue my scientific studies. I did not lack materially, my parents never refused me anything, but I endeavoured to stand on my own feet.

The idea of choosing a scientific career did not leave me. During one of my meetings with Professor Antony Yosifovich Bukovetsky, whom I have already mentioned, and who held the Chair of Political Economy at the Agricultural Institute (which was later changed to "Agricultural Academy"), the latter suggested that I abandon the idea of a university appointment for the time being, and join the Institute as his assistant.

Since, in the whole of the Institute, there was only one Jew amongst the professors, Professor B. D. Brutskus (he actually joined after the Revolution when the quota system limiting Jewish staff was abolished), and since the gravitation of Jews towards the Institute was nought (I had not met a single Jewish student there), the Government did not entertain the idea of the threat of Jewish dominance. I wrote an application, which I handed to Bukovetsky. He referred this to the Council of Professors, which elected me without a single protest, and my position was confirmed. I was beside myself over this result. At the Institute, and later at the Academy, I was well received, and was soon elected Science Secretary[47], and then Deputy Rector.

While Science Secretary at the Military Industrial Committee I noticed the curious situation of illegal literature, that of Mensheviks, Bolsheviks and Social Revolutionaries, published in large quantities. This took place almost in full view, and it is remarkable that the police could not discover it, especially since such literature was printed openly in the majority of cases, and not in illegal printing establishments. The reading of the galleys was an honorary job. I remember how I happened to proofread one of Lenin's brochures. I was amazed at his careless, clumsy style[48].

His language was so coarse, so horrible. But my corrections were accepted without any objections. These corrections were not about the essence of the argument, but in respect of the repetition of words, or of the same thing repeated clumsily and needlessly.

Also at this time I became involved in bringing out books on self-education, one of which was the so-called *One Thousand Words in German*. I do not think that I would approve of such a book of self-instruction in the German language today. But not all self-education material was of such doubtful character and much of this kind of literature published at that time was of a high standard. Thus before the First World War, the publishing house of Sytin deployed an immense publishing activity of great educational significance, and this applied to Sytin's programs for self-education, which became textbooks for the young generation.

Before the First World War, the publishing business was developing slowly but uninterruptedly. It comprised not only fiction and belles letters but also various fields of knowledge. The tempo of development of publishing accelerated shortly before the war, and many publishing companies could be ranked among the finest European ones. The same process took place in the printing business. The printing firm of Golike and

Vilborg occupied an exalted position. It used to publish exclusively finely illustrated books, many of them multi-coloured, which, considering the technology of that period, represented the pinnacle of achievement. One could name, for example, the following publications: *Gore ot Uma* ["*Woe from Wit*" – the classical play by Griboyedov], *Queen of Spades* and *Livre de la Marquise* with illustrations by the artist Somov.

Other publishing companies were: Marks, Karbasnikov, Wolf, Sabashnikov, Soldatenkov, Granit, Brockhaus and Efron, Saykin and Mir.

Brockhaus and Efron published an encyclopedia, the first one to achieve great fame in Russia, and they were also known for luxurious publications of foreign classics. Mainly Russian classics were published by Granit. Wolf and Karbasnikov also brought out many editions of Russian classics, both in single volumes as well as in multi-volume editions. One-volume editions of the classics were also published in the capacity of prizes intended for scholastic achievements. Multi-volume editions of the classics, e.g. Leo Tolstoy, were brought out both for the broad public and in luxury editions. The publishing house of Marks played an important role in the disseminating of classics through its weekly magazine *Niva* (*Cornfield*). Its supplement contained texts of the Russian classics. At the same time these classics were printed on special paper and were widely distributed. The immense significance of this educational influence deserves the highest appreciation. Saykin published a youth magazine *Priroda i Lyudi* (*Nature and People*) and, following the example set by Niva, brought out free supplements containing writings of foreign authors suitable for young people.

One cannot avoid mentioning such substantial publications as *Russkoye Bogatstvo* (*Russian Wealth*), *Vestnik Yevropy* (*European Herald*), and the art journals: *Apollon, Mir Iskusstva* (*World of Art*),

Starye Gody (*Old Times*), *Stolitza i Usadba* (*Capital and Country Estate*).

Vestnik Yevropy (*European Herald*) was one of the oldest journals. It encountered problems when communications were disrupted during the war[49].

Chapter Seven

The Revolutionary Year 1917 and the Budding Publisher Becomes the Politician

[A.S.K. 28 years old]

When the February Revolution broke out in 1917[50], I went on the very first day to the Tauride Palace, where the Soviet of Workers and Soldiers Deputies was being established[51]. There was the impression that the whole of Petrograd was streaming towards the Palace. I do not speak just of Shpalernaya Street, where the Tauride Palace was situated, but all adjoining streets were packed with people, with a preponderance of military units. As usual, the State Duma was sitting in the Palace, and all entrances were being guarded.

I got into the Palace by some miracle. There was unbelievable disorder. Soldiers stood, sat and lay everywhere. A short distance to the right of the main entrance a corridor led to the offices of the State Duma, and a guard was mounted there. But the large vestibule, the General Assembly Chamber, and the series of rooms along the sides were occupied by the "revolutionary" crowd. The Soviet of Workers and Soldiers Deputies was being organized by way of registration of delegates.

Almost as soon as I entered the Palace, I met Boris Osipovich Bogdanov[52]. He asked me not to leave, for "I would be required".

Meetings of soldiers and workers took place in the General Assembly Chamber. There were appeals for elections in the workers' districts and military units. Addresses were given by Chkheidse, Bogdanov, Gvosdyov and others. The speeches were moderate, there were no Bolshevik slogans. All the time there were appeals for "revolutionary" discipline and order. There was no arbitrary violence. Different departments and offices of the Soviet of Workers and Soldiers Deputies sprang up as if by the wave of a wand. The question of passes was regularized, and some order was established, though far from ideal.

The Soviet was actually created spontaneously, and not on the basis of any elections. I do not even speak of democratic elections. It was somehow formed in a haphazard manner. Still, there was the attempt to bring about some sort of order regarding elections, as to how many workers had the right to elect one candidate, and the same went for the soldiers. The peasants formed the Soviet of Peasant Deputies, which consisted almost exclusively of Social Revolutionaries. But their leadership formed part of the Soviet of Workers and Soldiers Deputies.

Somehow, immediately after the Revolution, there was formed the so-called "Other Towns Department" attached to the Soviet of Workers and Soldiers Deputies. Bogdanov suggested to me that I should become the Secretary of this Department.

Bogdanov says to me: "Would you like to be Secretary?" I say to him: "I have no mandate. I am even an unofficial member of the Party. I was in the Party as a student..." – "Well", he says, "this does not mean a thing... Have I got a mandate? And all of them, do they have a mandate?"

They also put some Bolshevik onto that Committee, but he was mostly absent, so that generally the Credentials for the First Congress were issued by me.

The "Other Towns Department" was in contact with the whole of Russia (i.e. outside of Petrograd.) The old power in the townships and in the villages was not elective. But the first step was an instruction that the former Presidents of the Local Councils should be placed at the head of the Administration. This immediately caused some confusion in many localities. In many cases these persons had been removed, and democratic elections had been undertaken in accordance with the famous "foursome": general, direct, equal and secret voting. In many places the Administration was appointed by the local Soviets of Workers Deputies. An inexhaustible stream of deputations from all corners of Russia started to make its way to the "Other Towns Department". Complaints were submitted, which required immediate attention.

The "Other Towns Department" was comprised of Bogdanov, Liber, Gorev, Zaslavsky and Kantorovich, who were all "Defencists" [Mensheviks who stood for the continuation of the war], and of Avel Safronovich Yenukidze and Shalva Zurabovich Eliava who were Bolsheviks. Bogdanov was the life of the Department, but he was so occupied by the affairs of the Executive Committee [of the Soviet of Workers and Soldiers Deputies], that he could not attend many meetings, and I reported to him later about all that took place, so that he would be informed and could take the necessary action in case of disagreements.

The Department thus consisted mainly of "Defencists". Zaslavsky, who after the Communist overthrow became a rabid Bolshevik, an inveterate leader of the "godless", who devoured "soft-bellied intellectuals", stood then on the extreme Right-wing: for the "war to the victorious end" and for the restraining of the Communists. An extremely acidic person, who later on was to take his place with the same passion in a different camp.

I became friendly with Yenukidze and Eliava. Yenukidze was a Bolshevik right from the beginning, whilst Eliava was an "Internationalist". Both were exceptionally decent people. Yenukidze was a simple person. He always wore a soldier's uniform, was extremely tall and had red hair. He was a pure Georgian, and had great respect for the President of the Soviet of Workers and Soldiers Deputies, Chkheidse, a Menshevik, and by this he called forth some suspicion among some members of his Party. Yenukidze always talked about not having had a proper education and was pained by it.

The labours of the "Other Towns Department" were limitless. There was no sphere in which it would not be concerned. For example: the sending of Military Commissars to the Front. Of course, they travelled in the name of the Government, but the Soviet of Workers and Soldiers Deputies both elected as well as confirmed them. The first one to be sent by the Department was Linze. He was a modest young man, a mathematician by training, aflame with the wish to serve his homeland. He was a "Defencist" and was depressed by the collapse at the Front. His fate was tragic. Apparently he was not reticent in his speeches, and the soldiers literally tore him to bits.

The second Military Commissar was also a "Defencist", Anatoly Dubois. He was handsome, stately, as if destined to be an officer. He was a man of good manners and education. He escaped Linze's fate, and later, during my exile abroad, I used to meet him in Berlin.

I cannot avoid mentioning two more Commissars: Savinkov and Moiseyenko. Both were Social Revolutionaries, and the initiative in their appointment came not from the Soviet of Workers and Soldiers Deputies, but from the Government, with the Soviet being obliged to give an additional warrant. Both impressed me not as Social Revolutionaries, but as cutthroats who were capable of anything. Both of them were insignificant [sic]. Moiseyenko, I did not know at all, I only knew that he was a terrorist and was a member of the "Fighting Group" of the Social Revolutionaries. As for Savinkov, he was known as the author of a very successful book, *Kon Bledny* (*The Pale Steed*)[53]. Both were in a great hurry to go to the Front. Since Chkheidse's signature was missing on their warrant, I went with them in search of Chkheidse who was attending one of the meetings[54].

What later became of Moiseyenko, I do not know, but Savinkov worked in the War Ministry. He was a wilful man. He took part in the White Movement and participated in the Yaroslavl revolt. Finally he fell into a trap set by the Bolsheviks and perished.

The Director of Administration [of the Central Executive Committee] was Broydo, a Menshevik "Defencist". He was a very nice and decent man, but he spent all of his time at meetings, while the Administration was in disarray and became gradually filled with Bolsheviks. The time for the calling of the Congress of Soviets of Workers and Soldiers Deputies, and the first elections was approaching, and it was necessary to be on the alert. Bogdanov suggested that I should join the Administration, which I did.

At first, it was necessary to sift through the office staff. The Secretary was Olga Davidovna Kameneva, Kamenev's[55] wife, Trotsky's sister[56]. It was natural that everything that was happening became immediately known to the Bolsheviks. Kameneva was a completely unbalanced, tasteless and foolish person, who fancied herself an actress. The administration of Theatre Affairs was concentrated in her hands. Of course [sic], nobody took any notice of her opinions, and complete chaos reigned there, yet she was still the boss. It was necessary to remove her without causing any commotion[57].

One day I somehow found Kameneva in conversation with Stalin, who was completely unknown at that time and did not distinguish himself in any way. Stalin was an insignificant man wearing a soldier's uniform. I only knew that he was an inflexible Bolshevik. I did not take any notice of him at that time. I met him accidentally two or three times. Later on, he was always in the Petrograd Committee that was in a separate wing of the building and was the headquarters of the Bolsheviks.

Gordon, who had organized the Bolshevik Printers Committee, also worked in the office. He too had to be removed, for all the correspondence was in his hands, and God only knew to whom he sent it. His removal was successfully achieved, and he was replaced by Yevgenya Moiseyevna Dalina.

Zurits, a "Menshevik-Internationalist" who had arrived from Copenhagen, and who subsequently went over to the Bolsheviks and made a career amongst them (he was even appointed Ambassador to Berlin, succeeding Krestinsky), became Secretary of the Central Executive Committee. Both he and Krestinsky, were liquidated in the purges during the reign of Stalin. Zurits was a complete nonentity without a backbone, but "where there are no fish, a lobster is a fish". [Russian proverb]. He could speak German, and had a fine appearance. His sister, Yevgenya Zakharovna Zurits, an old maid who was sickly and could hardly cope with the minutes, was his secretary.

Somehow it happened that Chkheidse's stamp was entrusted not to Zurits, who was Secretary of the Central Executive Committee, but to me. I used to affix Chkheidse's stamp and ratify it with my signature.

Nikolay Semyonovich Chkheidze [the Menshevik President of the Soviet] did not trust anybody. He and I became friends. His stamp was under lock and key in my drawer. When a paper was to be signed, he initialled it, and I then applied the stamp to it.

With the arrival of the "Menshevik-Internationalists" in the Central Executive Committee, the "Defencist" faction began to weaken, and the threesome of the "Defencists": Gots, Liber and Dan, had to fight for their positions. The disputes increased with the arrival of Trotsky who had not gone straight over to the Bolsheviks. The debates in the Central Executive Committee continued indefinitely, Trotsky alone could speak for hours, not to mention Lenin. But Trotsky had an outstanding oratorical talent, while Lenin, using rough sentences, hammered away at the same thing, repeating himself endlessly. Both Lenin and Trotsky were leaning on the Petrograd Committee, in which they applied their line with exceptional energy.

The Petrograd workers were increasingly going over to the Bolsheviks, while the Central Executive Committee was, in general, Menshevik. The Plenum consisted of representatives of different regions of Russia, where Bolshevism had not yet penetrated to such an extent.

It was imagined that the system would be capitalist, with democratic representative institutions elected according to the so-called "foursome" (the general, direct, equal and secret electoral right), with a responsible ministry and so on. And with regard to a guarantee of liberties, one went as far as the absurd. (I will, for example, mention the Duma Deputy, who insisted seriously that the right to hold meetings should extend to railroad reserves!). Generally it was axiomatically considered in our midst, that according to Marx, Socialism was only possible in the most developed countries[58]. To jump over to that system in such a backward country as Russia was impossible. Capitalism was considered to be a historical stage, which was completely unavoidable, but that it had only to be poured into a democratic framework to industrialize the country and to open the road towards Socialism.

Right from the beginning the responsible active Mensheviks had a feeling of doom. Nobody believed that a democratic regime would finally be established. But danger was perceived not from the Left, but from the Right. Everybody was afraid of the "General on the White Steed" who would crush the Revolution... The danger was threatening from quite a different direction: the Bolsheviks acted with impunity, without any restrictions, up to the calling for an armed uprising. In spite of this and also the agitation by the Bolsheviks among the workers, especially those in Petrograd and Moscow, the spreading of Bolshevik propaganda among the soldiers at the Rear and at the Front and the July uprising in Petrograd organized by Trotsky – all these were not taken as warnings. Except for the Menshevik leadership, workers were already dominated by the Bolsheviks.

I can vividly remember the July uprising headed by Trotsky. It was suppressed on the same day after it had hardly been born. Only an insignificant part of the Petrograd garrison had been swayed by propaganda, the vast majority was on the side of the "Defencist" Soviet of Workers and Soldiers Deputies, to which it had expressed its loyalty. Upon the first appeal by the Soviet, the troops came out against the workers loyal to Bolshevism and an insignificant section of the soldiers. It did not even come to any shedding of blood. All motorcars were confiscated by the Soviet, and were issued only to members of the Soviet for the purpose of addressing army units. No one could obtain a motorcar without my signature.

The Bolsheviks, headed by Trotsky, retreated. I can remember how I was passing through the emptied hall of the Soviet, and was amazed to see there Yury Steklov, a prominent Bolshevik. He was *Pale* and scared. Steklov was a giant with a broad thick beard and a substantial stomach, who looked more like a well-fed bourgeois. He said to me that, frankly, he was scared to go out into the street. He spent the night on a couch in one of the halls of the Soviet.

It would seem that this uprising should have brought the Soviet to its senses, but, strange as it may seem, no repressions followed. Nobody was arrested, and, after a short time, Trotsky turned up again as though nothing had happened. Of course, the *rector spiritus* was Lenin, but he, as it so often happened with him, was in hiding, and all appeals came from Trotsky. Having been orientated against a mythical Right, and not seeing the danger of Bolshevism, appears as a completely unexplainable short-sightedness when one looks back.

Apart from the Menshevik leaders, the workers were already in the grip of the Bolsheviks. In the Petrograd Committee of the Soviet, the Bolsheviks comprised a huge majority, and the Mensheviks and Social Revolutionaries had great difficulty in speaking there as they were often met with booing, and none of their resolutions were carried.

I would like to point to the following fact: Trotsky took shelter during this uprising in the very centre of town, in an apartment in the same building where I lived one floor below Yevgenya Zakharovna Zurits, the sister of the Secretary of the Central Executive Committee. I found this out from her personally, and she made no secret of it. The question is: what would I have done if I had found out in good time about Trotsky's whereabouts, and not after he was already walking about freely? Would I have reported this to the Presidium of the Soviet? I have no doubt whatsoever that Trotsky would not have been arrested, and, what is more, I believe that certain members of the Presidium knew of his whereabouts and reckoned that to arrest him would be a blow against the Revolution and would only be to the advantage of the Generals. All this was some kind of delusion: the spectre of the "General on the White Steed" who would crush the Revolution, became the obsession of the activists of the Revolution. It was a conclusion from a simplistic understanding of the historical process[59].

The fear of a coup from the Right, and the absence of a fear of the Bolsheviks became even more pronounced after the July uprising. There followed the Moscow State Conference. Almost the whole of the Central Committee repaired to Moscow for this gathering. Only Komensky, who was entrusted with issuing an appeal to the population, which he composed together with me, actually remained in Petrograd. In reality there was no need for such an appeal. There was no one to be soothed – a calm before the storm had set in.

Then there was the Democratic Convention in Petrograd. I was the Secretary of the Menshevik Party at that gathering. And finally, the October days burst out upon us.

Chapter Eight

Civil War and Life
after the Revolution

After the October overturn, the "Committee for the Salvation of the Motherland and the Revolution" still continued to exist. Then a bloody liquidation was unleashed. But there was as yet no systematically organized terror, and many of those who had been active during the Revolution succeeded in saving their lives and retired to a different activity, for example, the establishment of cooperatives.

I withdrew to my publishing activity and to scientific work, which I had relinquished earlier. Somehow, I succeeded in withdrawing without being noticed. Perhaps it was because a connection between me, as an officer of the Soviet of Workers and Soldiers Deputies, and the publisher and scientific worker had not been established, as if these were two different individuals.

After the Revolution we lived in our second apartment in Spasskaya Street [today, Ryleyeva Street, called thus after one of the "Decembrists". The apartment was in the building in which Trotsky was supposed to have been hiding after the July Days] [60]. The old baroness who used to live there had left for her estate and transferred the apartment to us. The accommodation was exceptionally good with all comforts, and we paid only a very modest sum for the furniture. But what was more important than all else, was that the baroness passed on to us her house-keeper, a German woman, some thirty years of age, unmarried, who turned out to be a treasure. Mishelina Davidovna spoke an educated German and also spoke Russian. She treated Tolya exceptionally well[61]. During the Civil War years she was quite irreplaceable. When food started to become scarce, she managed to find everything so that we did not suffer any hardship. We were even able to invite visitors no less than once a week[62].

At one stage one of the most prominent and talented Mensheviks, Mikhail Isaakovich Liber, hid in our apartment. We allotted him the room of our little son Tolya, who was very scared of him because Liber had a huge black beard, the like of which could rarely be seen. Whenever Tolya saw him, he used to hide behind Mamma's or my back[63].

After the October Revolution there was no end of turn-coats, amongst them the prominent Menshevik Khinchuk. [Later he became Soviet Ambassador in Berlin]. The process of the turning of outspoken anti-Bolsheviks into stooges of Bolshevism, began rapidly. For example, such an inveterate enemy of the Bolsheviks as Zaslavsky, who could not find sufficiently sharp enough invectives against the Bolsheviks, and who only spoke of suppression by force, became a rabid Bolshevik, and assumed a position at the head of religious persecutions[64].

Further Liber's brother, a pure man, went over fairly soon into the Bolshevik camp. What induced him? I do not know. He was not at all a careerist. Rafes, a prominent member of the Bund (the Jewish Menshevik organization) also went over to the Bolsheviks. The October days passed. The "heroic" army looted the wine cellars, the slogan "Rob what has been robbed" was a great success[65].

Factories as well as banks were nationalized. Nationalisation brought about a complete stagnation of production, especially in the beginning. In the banks all safes were broken into and emptied, including mine. No bother was taken to inform the owners of the safes so that they could be present at the opening.

House Committees, elected by the tenants, were formed in each building. We also found ourselves members of one of these. The function of these committees was not defined. Essentially, it consisted of collecting rent and of guard duty at the gates at night. This was previously the duty of the caretakers, who now had become assistants of the militia. Everybody, without exception, had to undertake guard duty, except the sick and decrepit old people. It was forbidden for one person to take the place of another. Thus Genya had been detailed to guard duty, and the caretakers watched that there was no substitution. But what could a woman do against hooligans? Of course, I maintained guard duty together with Genya.

Soon there began a curtailment of living space in apartments[66]. Our building in Zhukovskaya Street was inhabited by people who had lived there for many years: doctors, lawyers, professors and teachers. There was no friction whatsoever between us. Above us lived an officer of royal descent. He was supposed to have been the illegitimate son of the Grand Duke Nikolay Nikolaevich, and his surname was Nikolayev (those born out of wedlock were generally given the name of the father). We did not betray him, but he and his wife remained completely without any means of support. In winter they heated the stoves with their antique furniture and with parquetry which they removed from the floor. The tenants used to bring them food. One fine day, he and his wife finally vanished somewhere.

Various credentials were obtained to avoid the curtailment of residential accommodation. For example, on the door of my study there was a certificate to the effect that I was a professor, and that I required a separate room for studying. On the doors of the huge drawing room which had four windows and a balcony and which was filled from floor to ceiling with books and a butterfly collection (the property of N.A. Kotlyarevsky), there was a notice stating that the library was under the patronage of the Academy of Sciences, that I was responsible for it, and that no books whatsoever could be removed.

Other tenants made similar arrangements, and in our building there was no compulsory resettlement. Some tenants increased the population ratio by bringing in their relatives.

Searches were always carried out late at night or at dawn. Electricity was usually turned off in the whole block when a search was to be carried out in some apartment. On such nights, one hardly slept, expecting uninvited guests. And since electricity was sometimes turned off due to the inadequacy of the power supply, sleepless nights were many.

However, life continued somehow, and an impression was created that it had fallen into a groove, though, it is true, full of unexpected dangers. I returned to my scientific and publishing activity.

For a long time the Government did not interfere with the life of the universities and institutes. All professors continued to be elected and not appointed. The Councils of Elders were, as of old, the favoured representatives of the students. After the Revolution, students' representatives were admitted to sessions of the Council of Professors. As far as I remember, there were no conflicts.

Being on the staff of an institution of tertiary education made everyday life considerably easier. Scientists began to receive rations through the ARA (American Relief Association), and soon the "House of Scientists" was established, to which the scientists owed practically everything. We dealt exclusively with it, and not with the provision shops. My ration was fairly impressive, for I, as the Administrator of the Institute, was included in a specially privileged category. Money had lost almost all its purchasing power, and if it was not for the ration, things would have been very difficult. The ration did not allow for luxurious living, but we had enough to eat. Sometimes they issued horse meat or rabbits, and we exchanged these for other products with the inhabitants of the surrounding villages, as was done with other products which we received in our rations but did not use. We received material of good quality for suits, but all of the same grey colour, so that all were dressed alike, even the women. We also received footwear, but here there were many difficulties, e.g. one often received shoes not comprising a pair, such as two shoes for one foot, or one shoe of one size and one of another size. I cannot remember that I wore shoes received in the academic ration.

Politics were put aside. My academic activity continued for a fairly long time under the Bolsheviks. We were left in peace, but we felt that sooner or later the storm would break. I had no clashes either with the professors or with the students. We were completely autonomous and, even after the arrival of the Bolsheviks on the scene, we were, in the beginning, left alone. We defended our autonomy. Nobody was delegated to us, and we accepted appointments to our staff only in accordance with scientific merit. Clashes started when an attempt was made to force onto us some professor renowned for his right-wing convictions but who subsequently went over to the Bolsheviks. We black-balled him.

Then a so-called "Workers Faculty" was established. This was for workers who were to be coached to enter a tertiary institution. For this, they had to pass an examination before a special commission formed at every such institution. As the Deputy Rector, I was already a member of this commission. Of course, there were students of the "Workers Faculty" who were worthy enough to enrol at a tertiary institution, but the huge majority were completely unprepared — they were "straight from the plough". I can remember, there was a question at the examination: "Who wrote *Eugene Onegin*?" The student answered: "It is superfluous to know this for agriculture". Or to the question: "Who was Turgenev?" there followed the answer: "A landowner, an exploiter". Or to the question: "Which works of Dostoevsky are known to you?" — Answer: "I know that he was a reactionary".

Chapter Nine

Naooka i Shkola
(Science and School)

[A.S.K. 28–33 years old]

The book business had attracted me for a long time, and my university acquaintances encouraged my idea in every way. I wanted to create a publishing company, which would not just pursue profits, but would be an establishment based on ideas, which would serve the interests of the community[67]. After lengthy negotiations, I decided to establish a cooperative, in which an active part was taken by a number of academicians. First there was Nestor Alexandrovich Kotlyarevsky, whom I had met through Genya when she was a student at the Women's University, where Kotlyarevsky used to lecture. At that time he was the Director of the Alexandrinsky Theatre, where his wife, Pushkareva-Kotlyarevskaya, was an actress. Then there was Professor Lev Platonovich Karsavin, whose lectures on Catholicism I used to attend for some reason. Next was Professor Yury Petrovich Novitsky, who had been transferred to Petrograd from the Kiev University and was lecturing on Criminal Law. Furthermore there were the Professors Alexander Liverievich Saketti, Nikolay Onufrievich Lossky and many others. The directorate of the cooperative was formed by Kotlyarevsky, Karsavin, Novitsky, Alexander Alexandrovich

Krolenko (a lawyer who left shortly) and myself. The cooperative was called Cooperative of Professors and Educationalists – *Naooka i Shkola* (Science and School).

At first we rented a small office on the corner of Liteyny Prospect and Basseynaya Street, but shortly afterwards we moved to larger premises, comprising a series of rooms in the building on the opposite corner, facing both Basseynaya Street and Liteyny Prospect[68].

The members of the cooperative were experts in various disciplines, which were to be the subjects of the books proposed to be published. I concentrated on the philological disciplines and on the history of literature. A particularly useful member when launching the cooperative, was Nestor Alexandrovich Kotlyarevsky, one of the heads of its administration, who previously had been connected with the highly respected publishing company owned by Stasyulevich. This company was headed by Mikhail Mikhailovich Lemke, known for publishing the book *Sto Dney v Zarskoy Stavke* (*One-hundred Days at the Tsar's Head-quarters*). Before retiring, Lemke concluded an agreement between Stasyulevich and *Naooka i Shkola*, according to which all works by Kotlyarevsky were passed on to the latter, and it was to publish all further books by him. After the death of Stasyulevich the company, which he owned, came to a standstill, and the whole of its stock was taken over by *Naooka i Shkola*. Both the new and re-published books which had been brought out by Stasyulevich and which were now taken over, enjoyed a huge success.

A special role was played by Yekaterina Dmitrievena Knaz, who was born Baroness Nolde, and who was well known in educationalist circles. She used to be the principal of a girls' gimnaziya, and was at the head of an education committee through which *Naooka i Shkola* supplied schools with textbooks, and also acted in an advising capacity, which was very appropriate at that time. The most popular primer was *Zhivoye Slovo* (*The Living Word*), created by the prominent philologist Ostrogorsky, who, incidentally, was a relative of the expert on Byzantine culture of the same name. Another expert in this field was Zhebelyov, who was also a member of the *Naooka i Shkola* cooperative, complementing its array of experts. Being connected with many other educational councils, *Naooka i Shkola* supplied schools generally with textbooks by other publishing companies, so that its trading department prospered.

Apart from the premises on Liteyny Prospect, *Naooka i Shkola* had a branch on Vasilyevsky Island, which was managed by my wife and Yekaterina Knaz.

The publishing business began to develop very successfully, especially after I relinquished my administrative position at the Agricultural Academy[69]. However, I continued calling there to give lectures.

In the beginning I published *Posledniye Stikhy* (*Last Poems*) by Zinaida Gippius. This book, although it did not enter into our program at all, was published as a favour to N.A. Kotlyarevsky[70]. The latter played an important part in the Pushkin House, which was a branch of the Academy of Sciences. We undertook to publish a monthly journal, *Irida*, under the editorship of the Secretary of the Pushkin House, Alexander Fomin. This journal was solely devoted to literature. By the way, the name of the journal gave me the idea to call our daughter "Irene" which is close to Irida, Greek for "rain-bowed" (cheerful).

Also I introduced into Russia the psychologist William James[71], who was hitherto unknown there. Professor Ivan Ivanovich Lapshin translated James' *Principles of Psychology*, which was immediately accepted at all institutions of tertiary education, and one issue after another was sold out.

The publishing company became a centre for scientists and social activists, who crowded in large numbers in the huge reception room of the company where they made appointments with each other. There was no respite from offers to have books published. On Wednesdays, some ten or twelve people used to meet for dinner at my place. Genya was an excellent hostess, and I know of no case when someone refused an invitation.

Strange as it may seem[72], this was the time of the flourishing of the publishing activity. Commercial publishing companies such as Wolf and Karbasnikov were closing down. But whoever could, were changing their companies into cooperative ones, and, in spite of the existence of a strict censorship, books were being published in unprecedented numbers, many of which were of a non-Marxist character. *Naooka i Shkola* published books of a predominantly philosophical, non-Marxist type[73] (works by Lossky, Karsavin and Lapshin, or works on economics, for example, by Kulisher)[74]. A book which was sold in large quantities was Professor Derzhavin's *Grammar,* which was accepted in a majority of schools. But when the Chancellor of the University was dismissed and Derzhavin appointed to that position, which appointment he did not decline, I had the temerity to reject his book (to discontinue its further publication), and this went by without any consequences for me.

Chapter Ten

The Beginning of Petropolis

[A.S.K. 31–33 years old]

One beautiful winter's day, a modest, plain girl, all frozen, with red hands (as if frost-bitten), came to my office and asked me to grant her an interview. She was Raissa Noevna Blokh, a student at the Historico-Philological Faculty and a disciple of Karsavin, which meant that she specialized in the Middle Ages. She had come upon Karsavin's recommendation. The case was this: her brother Yakov Noevich and Grigory Leonidovich Lozinsky, both university professors, had formed a book cooperative which was buying up antiquarian books and had decided to launch themselves into publishing[75]. The name of the cooperative was Petropolis. And thus she had come on behalf of her brother and Lozinsky to invite me into the cooperative, since they had no publishing experience, whilst I had both the experience and the capability. (At that time I was managing the best printing establishment in Russia). [About this see later.]

I made the acquaintance of Blokh and Lozinsky, and I liked them very much. We formed the management of Petropolis, which consisted of Blokh, Lozinsky and myself. Lozinsky was an irreplaceable chairman. The activity of Petropolis did not clash with the activity of *Naooka i Shkola* and was devoted exclusively to poetry, literature and art. After a short time, the authors who were engaged became closely linked with the publishing company. Actually, Petropolis was our hobby, and the material aspect did not interest us. For example, we published Lope de Vega, Ben Johnson etc., where one could certainly not expect any profit. Among the poets we published Anna Akhmatova, Gumilyov, Mandelstam (we published his *Tristia*), G. Ivanov, Adamovich and Kuzmin[76]. The books had great success, and each new publication strengthened our popularity. Among the artists, we were close to Dobuzhinsky, Annenkov, Altman and some others.

My wife and I made friends with the Blokh family (mother, sister and wife) and we became almost as one family.

When interviewed about the establishment of Petropolis in 1981 by Professor Mark Raeff, that is eight years after writing about the establishment of Petropolis in the memoirs, I said that the visit from Raissa was in 1917, before the October Revolution. In the beginning of 1917. You see, my memory... She says, Professor Karsavin sent her. What about? She is Karsavin's pupil, she has a brother, Blokh, he is a professor and is about to launch a publishing company together with his friend Grigory Leonodovich Lozinsky. They are inexperienced, they don't know how to go about it etc. Could I meet them? I met them, Blokh and Lozinsky. Lozinsky was a specialist on the subject of Italian literature. And Yakov Noevich was a specialist on the Renaissance. They had organized the purchase and sale of antiquarian books... At that time... the February Revolution... people had begun to come and go. Some... many for example left for the newly established university in Saratov, some went abroad, making use of the circumstance that they were born, say in Latvia, or Estonia, or Germany, that they were actually not born in Russia... and also native Russians could leave relatively easily. And they liquidated their libraries, while others, who did not consider leaving at all, were acquiring whole libraries and individual books.

They [Blokh and Lozinsky] worked without remuneration, only the secretary, who worked full time, had to receive a salary. The secretary was Nadezhda Alexanderovna Zalshupina. And then the Professors Lozinsky and Blokh began to publish works which, at that time, seemed completely impossible... Henry de Regner, Epicäne [not clear on tape]... some volume about Cervantes etc. We decided to launch a publishing company to bring out mainly fine literature. And composed of three persons. That is Yakov Noevich and Lozinsky, the three of us. I was to take charge of printing and, generally of everything, Lozinsky was, so to speak, our chairman, and Yakov Noevich was to conduct negotiations with authors etc. I concluded the contracts with the authors. Our first author was Akhmatova. As for the pricing of books, we decided to considerably increase the prices of antiquarian books so as to be able to pay author's fees. We did not allocate any salaries to ourselves, but of course the authors had to be paid, and our first author was Anna Akhmatova. We started with Anno Domini. After we had received Anno Domini — there came Gumilyov. We published his *Ognennyi Stolp* (*The Fiery Pillar*) and *Kostyor* (*Bonfire*). Then there came authors in infinite numbers. We published Georgi Ivanov, Mandelstam, Sologoub, we were very selective. For example Adamovich was accepted by us with great difficulties. We had argument upon argument until he, so to speak, did not win, but we still published him[77].

Chapter Eleven

Further Publishing Ventures
in Petrograd

I also took on the management of other publishing companies. Naum Borisovich Glasberg, a major entrepeneur, left Russia, and he passed on to me the large publishing company *Ogni* (*Flames*), which in turn, had taken over the company *Gryadushchi Den* (*The forthcoming Day*). The well-known humanist, Senator Koni, was in charge of *Ogni*. The catalogue of the two companies was huge. What *Naooka i Shkola* published in popular form as introductions to specific subjects, *Ogni* brought out as works of an advanced and specialized nature. Thus *Ogni* produced some quite remarkable series of books on historical subjects, e.g. *Catholicism* by Karsavin. For its part *Gryadushchi Den* brought out a luxurious five-volume work on Richard Wagner, also books on Machiavelli and Savonarola. There were also works on literature, for example, the *History of Russian Literature* by E. Liadsky.

But the most important circumstance was that the printing establishment of Golike & Vilborg, which had belonged to a group of oilmen operating the company Mazut, of which Glasberg was the Director, was left in my care. This was the best printing house in Russia, and even in the whole of Europe. Luxurious multi-coloured books were published by it, e.g. *Pikovaya Dama* (*The Queen of Spades*) by Pushkin, with illustrations by Alexander Benoit and a richly illustrated publication of *Gore ot Uma* (*Woe from Wit*) [Griboyedov] and of *Eugene Onegin* [Pushkin]. Also, among others, there was a book that was quite exceptional in its luxury, *Le Livre de la Marquise*, illustrated by Somov. The last mentioned work was in two variations, with the same multi-coloured illustrations, but one issue, consisting of one hundred numbered copies, had additional illustrations which were very explicit (part of the Marquise's clothing had been removed).

Of course, Golike & Vilborg had been nationalized, but this firm was still under my care[78]. Its technical manager was Skamoni, an outstanding expert of the printing trade. My relationship with him was very good, and I managed to publish my so-called "luxury" publications in his printing establishment.

The following incident highlights the climax of publishing activity at this time. At the head of the State Publishing House stood Yonov, a protégé of the all-powerful Zinoviev (Yonov was the brother of Zinoviev's wife). He was an utterly extravagant person, who had no knowledge whatsoever of the printing trade, but who deemed himself to be a connoisseur of books and a patron of the arts. Yonov felt flattered that he worked with scientists, and everybody came to him as if to seek his advice. But, thanks to him, the sway of censorship over my publishing company almost completely disappeared.

Blokh and I conceived the idea of publishing a book which was completely out of character with the times: *Ex Libris of Russian Artists*[79]. Who would be the owners of libraries possessing *ex libris*? Those, of course, who were far from being proletarians. We talked Yonov into ordering an *ex libris* from an artist, and included it into the book which had already been put together, asking only that he should permit it to be published in the printing house of Golike & Vilborg. He not only gave his permission but participated actively, and in all ways exerted pressure on the printing establishment to speed up the setting and printing[80].

КНИЖНЫЕ
ЗНАКИ
РУССКИХ
ХУДОЖ
НИКОВ

Ex Libris of Russian Artists, St Petersburg: Petropolis, 1922.

On choosing authors for publication I was the definitely political individual [within the management of Petropolis]. Lozinsky was non-political, and Yakov Noevich was also completely non-political. Why did we not have Blok? I could not forgive him for the *Twelve*. We could have had him, but I did not want this. Why could we not have Yesenin? We could, but we did not take him, and we also did not take Mayakovsky[81]. It took great effort to refuse them without insulting them[82].

Anatol's personal ex libris plate.

I published several books under my own name, simply out of my love for art. They included a luxurious edition of Derzhavin's monograph[83], a complete edition of Pushkin's *Gavriiliada* (under the auspices of the Pushkin House[84]), an edition of the unpublished works of the poet Delvig (a contemporary of Pushkin) edited by Yury Verkhovsky, and a monograph of Pisarev. Out of friendship for the writer Iretsky I published a luxurious edition of his *Tales*[85].

One day, N.S. Gumilyov, with whom I was closely acquainted, came to my publishing company. He had a poem, "Ditya Allakha" (*Child of Allah*), published in the journal *Apollon* [a high quality art journal]. I reprinted a certain number of copies for distribution, and he introduced me to the management of the journal. I purchased all of the very large stock of reproductions and turned these into albums which sold out in the shortest possible time[86].

Tolya was still a small child. We enrolled him at the kindergarten attached to the *Shidlovskaya Gimnaziya*. This kindergarten was based on the Montessori system. The parents took part in the work of the kindergarten and the *Gimnaziya*[87]. The drawing teacher was the well-known artist Tatiana Gippius, who was the sister of the poetess Zinaida Nikolaevna Gippius, the wife of the writer Merezhkovsky. One day she showed me her drawings for an alphabet in which each letter corresponded to some object, animal or bird, and I immediately offered to publish it. I printed ten thousand copies of this alphabet. It was a great success and was sold out in a short time.

As the commercial publishing companies closed down, or to be more precise, as they were nationalized, the number of cooperative companies in Petrograd, as well as in Moscow, increased[88]. By the way, the Bookshop of Writers was formed in Moscow, in which writers of renown and public figures like Boris Zaitsev, Osorgin and Melgunov took part.

Private publishing firms continued to still exist for some time after the October days. Such major publishing companies as *Karbasnikov*, *Wolf*, *Sytin*, were very soon nationalized. Smaller firms, for example *Sabashnikov*, continued to exist, but were changed into cooperative companies and joined our union of cooperatives. After my forced departure from Petrograd in 1922, there still existed a number of firms like mine, although I cannot tell precisely for how much longer. And this was perhaps the "golden age" for private companies. Former Mensheviks, Social Revolutionaries and other members of the intelligentsia, all rushed into cooperative organizations which multiplied on a large scale, and within the shortest time. These cooperatives were also the best consumers of books, and the publishing companies began to exist for the needs of these cooperatives.

It was also then that publishing firms, which previously had a specific image, expanded their publication of books in their specific fields. Books that were specially adapted for the use of the peasant population, for workers, for tradesmen and so on, found an incredibly large market. For example, I can point out from my own experience before my departure, that Perelman's book *Entertaining Physics*, was bought up in its entirety before its publication by one Moscow cooperative, so that I had to order a new edition immediately. I have no idea what the cooperatives made of such publications as, for example, those of *Sabashnikov*, who used to publish works by Euripides and other such works. But the cooperatives bought up these editions and the publishing companies supported this, not from any particular consideration, but simply because people were buying "just in case", irrespective of whether there was a demand, or not. There were publishing firms such as *Na Zachatke Znaniya* (*At the Rudiments of Knowledge*), which began to publish literature on topics connected with schools, and they endeavoured already to put forward the "October Line" of behaviour, so as to save themselves. Derzhavin's *Grammar* was immediately adopted and distributed in hundreds of thousands of copies. At that time I used to publish the reader *Zhivoye Slovo* (*The Living Word*), and I could hardly cope with bringing out one edition immediately after another. Where did all these books go? How could such a demand suddenly arise from neither this nor that, was very hard to say[89].

I would also like to mention that the cooperative publishing companies had established a court of arbitration. The following persons were members of this court: Senator Walter, whose brother was the Dean of the Agricultural Academy, S.A. Pergament, who was my superior at the Academy, Solomon Yosifovich

Ginsburg, who was the Legal Adviser of the State Bank (already in Soviet times), and Yekaterina Fleishits the first woman lawyer.

I can remember the case of *Brockhaus & Efron* in which Pergament and I took part, with Walter presiding. *Brockhaus & Efron* was one of the largest publishing firms in Russia. How the firm escaped nationalization during the first years, I do not know. The shareholders vanished somewhere, there remained only a certain Perelman, and the publishing firm was acquired by a certain Iglitsyn. I was acquainted with Iglitsyn. He was a very active person. I was quite amazed that he had managed to acquire such a large publishing firm. But he was in possession of all the documents, and when Perelman requested arbitration, the case was decided in favour of Iglitsyn.

It is of interest that in those days (I don't know in what year it was, but it was still much before 1921–1922) people thought not of liquidating their businesses, but of the possibility of continuing them[90].

In Petrograd we organized the *Soyuz Kooperativnykh Izdatelstv* (Union of Cooperative Publishing Companies). Ferapont Ivanovich Vityazev, who was the head of the publishing company *Kolos* ("Ear": of rye, wheat etc.), became its president and I became its vice president.

Kolos published books of a Populist orientation (a position taken by the Social Revolutionaries). In the field of sociology, Kolos published the work *Kollektivnaya Refleksologia* (*Collective Reflexology*) by the eminent psychiatrist and scientist, Bekhterev. [Incidentally, Professor Pitirim Sorokin, a university friend of Abram Saulovich, and who later lectured at Harvard, was also connected with *Kolos.*]

Vityazev and I conceived a very risky idea: we composed a memorandum addressed to the Council of Peoples Commissars, regarding the necessity to denationalize the printing establishments. In a completely formal, non-polemic tone, we set out to prove:

- that with the existence of a preliminary censorship, the need for nationalization fell away;
- that the printing establishments had been headed by very experienced people, who had been replaced by non-specialists;
- that the nationalization of the printing establishments had created chaos in the printing business;
- that the printing establishments had been amalgamated, and that this was done in such a way as to cause an unbelievable confusion;
- that printing types had been mixed up;
- that the machines could not be maintained;
- and finally, that printing establishments were dropping out of commission one after another.

We were so bold as to print the memorandum in twenty copies, in a very elegant form, in the printery of *Golike & Vilborg* of which I had taken charge. Of course, this was done secretly, and the printing establishment was not mentioned. Vityazev and I signed the memorandum personally[91].

I have already indicated earlier that I was on good terms with Yenukidze. At that time, he was Chairman of the Central Executive Committee of the Supreme Soviet. I travelled to Moscow and, at first, got in touch with the earlier mentioned Moscow Cooperative, Bookshop of Writers, which approved our step, and then I went to the Kremlin in order to submit our memorandum directly to the Council of Commissars through Yenukidze, so that it would not go astray. Avel Sofronovich [Yenukidze] received me immediately and promised to pass on the memorandum to the correct destination, but he also expressed the opinion, that the Council of Peoples' Commissars considered nationalization a cornerstone of the Communist program, and would not agree with our arguments, and there could even be some "consequences" for the initiators.

I returned to Petrograd. We were waiting impatiently for an answer from Moscow, but an answer was not forthcoming. It was likely that a negative comment had been made on the memorandum, and that was as far as it would go. But the affair could have turned out badly both for Vityazev and myself, as well as for the Union of Cooperative Publishing Companies. Also an investigation could have been started to track down the printing establishment in which the type had been set, and also to track down the typesetter, the printer, etc.

Chapter Twelve

The Last Years in Russia

(The Fate of Yenukidze)

One is amazed how one could continue with such an intensive activity as I had been carrying on under the Soviet regime, or how I could continue my academic activity, as well as that in connection with publishing companies and journals and my contact with people. All this amidst continuous arrests and liquidations!

It was a strange time, a terrible time, and yet people somehow adjusted themselves. Some people left Petrograd, or had themselves transferred to the backwoods, believing that life would be better there. Others went abroad, and, in this respect, it was strange that people were allowed out, or were allowed to go abroad on some assignment. For example: Lozinsky [one of the three partners of Petropolis] left allegedly on an assignment to the Sorbonne University. Actually, he had no such invitation to the Sorbonne, yet he went, and later became a lecturer there. But life asserted itself. We did not think of leaving. For us to do so seemed foreign. What would it mean to leave our Motherland? This was some kind of patriotism, and this was quite natural.

A member of our management, Yury Petrovich Novitsky, a university professor, a politically harmless person, did not turn up at the office one day. He had been arrested, implicated in the "Case of the Churchmen" and was hurriedly shot. Nikolay Stepanovich Gumilyov was arrested and shot, yet only on the day prior to his arrest he had called on me at the publishing company.

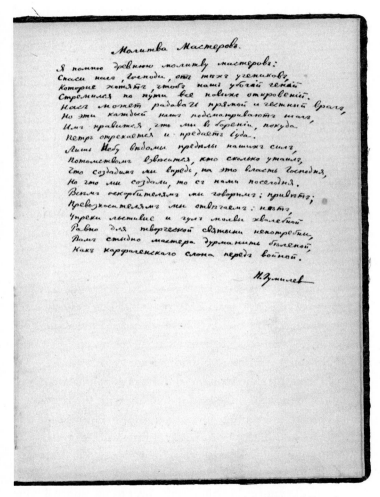

"Molitva Masterov" (Prayer of the masters) by Nicolai Gumilev – hand-written in Abram Saulovich's autograph book.

Life proceeded in its own way under the Bolsheviks. I had no feeling of fear, perhaps fear was only subconscious. But there was no end of sad surprises. Genya's sister Vera was married to Prince Vyazemsky, a charming young man, handsome, with wonderful manners, and a person with the kindest of hearts. Vera arrived at our place one morning before dawn, and announced that he had been arrested during the night as a former officer. Enquiries were initiated, and it was revealed that he died in prison from typhus[92].

There were also unexpected incidents: as I was returning late at night from some meeting, a detachment of soldiers stopped me, together with a number of passers by, on the corner of Morskaya Street and Nevsky. The soldiers demanded that in the morning we should come to the outskirts of the city (at the end of Vasilyevsky Ostrov) to dig trenches. They gave us notices, which threatened the sternest possible measures in case of our non-appearance. My protestations to the effect that I was connected with many institutes did not help, but since our names and addresses had not been recorded, I, of course, did not put in an appearance.

But somehow life went on. We used to meet with an enormous number of people, receive visitors and call on acquaintances. We often visited the Blokhs. There we would meet the poet Kusmin, who used to settle himself at the piano and sing little melodious songs with his nasal but pleasant voice.

I cannot forget the wonderful dinners at Sabina Savelevna Gessen's, which were quite out of keeping with the times.

There were evening functions in the "House of the Litterateurs" and in the "International Literature" rooms.

In summer we lived in Pavlovsk, renting a whole house. We became friends with the well-known ballet critic Andrey Yakovlevich Levinson. He often came over to us, especially one summer when his wife and daughter went to her relatives in

Siberia where living conditions were easier. They both visited us in Petrograd.

Yelena Isaakovna's father, Grinberg, lived in Finland. He made an arrangement with a certain Finn for an illegal entry into Finland. Grinberg gave a letter to the Finn, in which the whole procedure was described in detail. The Finn was arrested by the Soviet authorities at the border and the incriminating letter was seized. The Chekists turned up at the Blokhs and, not knowing which one of the female members of the family was mentioned in the letter, wanted to arrest all three just to make sure i.e. Yelena Isaakovna, Rayusha and Dora Yakovlevna [Yakov Noevich's wife, sister and mother]. They left the mother, but Yelena Isaakovna and Raya were taken to the Cheka. The situation was very serious. This was the time of the well-known Tagantsev affair, the shooting of Gumilyov and the "Case of the Churchmen".

Yakov Noevich called on me in despair. Without a doubt, the women were under threat of being shot. Lesser "crimes" had been punished by shooting. In addition, the case fell into the hands of Agranov, one of the most bestial investigators who had executed, in droves, a large number of people. Incidentally, he was also the investigator of the intellectuals subjected to exile. I had a slight hope of saving Rayusha and Yelena Isaakovna by turning to Yenukidze, who at that time was the Chairman of the Central Executive Committee, and with whom I had had a good relationship in the past, in spite of holding completely opposite political views.

Genya and all around me were against my trip to Moscow to see Yenukidze, lest I fall into a trap myself. But I left for Moscow without hesitation[93]. Yenukidze received me cordially and he even embraced me. His huge office was equipped with items taken from some palace. I told Avel Safronovich [Yenukidze] the purpose of my visit, and without hiding anything, explained to him the particulars of the Blokh affair. He did not attempt to refuse his help, and said that for me he would do the impossible. He ordered breakfast for me, consisting of tea with rusks and honey (instead of butter) and a piece of cheese, and asked me to wait. He left, locking the study with me inside. He returned in half an hour or after a somewhat longer period, and said I could leave, and also that the Blokhs would be released the next day. He embraced me again. I returned to Petrograd and immediately called Yakov Noevich. Towards the evening Raya and Yelena Isaakovna were actually released[94]. Yenukidze himself was shot later during the infamous purges[95].

Chapter Thirteen

The Case of the Churchmen; Arrest, Jail and Expulsion

[A.S.K. 32 years old]

We spent the summer vacations in the environs of Petrograd and in Finland, in Sestoretsk, Pavlovsk and Oylilo. In Pavlovsk we became closely acquainted with the artist Konashevich and his wife, and with the well-known ballet expert Andrey Yakovlevich Levinson, about whom I have already written.

It was just after coming back from Pavlovsk in the summer of 1922, that uninvited guests came to visit our apartment late in the night. The Chekists were not very rude, only curt, and did not engage in conversation. Without presenting a warrant for arrest, and even without a search, if one should not count making the rounds of all the rooms of the apartment, they took me to the Gorokhovaya [place of custody], without even granting me the possibility of taking anything with me[96].

In the place to which I was taken, there were two large rooms with two tiers of bunks on all sides. There I found a huge and very mixed crowd. I was pleased to see people who were close to me among those who had already arrived and were arriving all the time: Karsavin, Lossky, Lapshin, Iretsky, Khariton, Ostrovsky, Zamyatin, Brutskus, Odinzov, Izgoyev, Selivanov and others. Nobody knew why they had been arrested.

I was miserable, the dirt was impassable, the bedbugs in an infinite quantity. I settled down on one of the bunks with Karsavin. One could not even think about sleep. One simply fell into a stupor due to weariness. Amongst us there was also such a representative of the Russian nobility as Count Valentin Platonovich Zubov, who, at that time, had pretended to be a Bolshevik. Karsavin, who was an extremely witty person, never called him anything but "Your Excellency" or "Your Radiance", or "Count by the grace of Marx", which induced Zubov to fury. As it turned out, Zubov, who held the position of President of the "Institute of Arts" in his own palace, was accused of selling his own paintings, and his arrest had nothing to do with ours.

Anatol, aged 11, exiled with his father, often drew and painted their memories of St Petersburg.
(Courtesy: Bakhmeteff Archive, Columbia University)

He did not produce the impression of a real magnate. He was a descendant of Platon Zubov, the lover of Catherine the Second [Catherine the "Great"]. But if his great-grandfather had been like him, he would not have been Catherine's lover. He was puny, small, shorter than me[97], and very carelessly dressed, but he had a very intelligent face. How he got into our midst was a mystery. Zubov was a very wealthy man. He had inherited the Zubov palace on Konnogvardeysky [Horseguards] Boulevard. In it there was a remarkable gallery, and in order to save it, he passed the gallery on to the Bolsheviks on the condition that an "Institute of Arts" would be organized there, of which he would be the director. And this is what had taken place. In 1912 Zubov had founded the All-Russian Scientific Research Institute of Art Science.

I had never met Zubov before, I met him for the first time in Gorokhovaya. Karsavin, who stood next to me, asked him jokingly: "What is your Communist Radiance doing here?" He was, according to his response, accused of being a fake, of not being a genuine Communist, and of intending to export his pictures abroad – and for this he was arrested.

I do not know what happened to him later, but I met him again in Berlin. He had married his disciple, a student, the daughter of a very well known Jewish physician. Zubov turned out to be a very nice person, and our families used to meet frequently.

He died fairly recently [about 1980]. He was an exceptional art expert... quite exceptional. But he was like that from the cradle, so to speak... he was born into such an environment. He was well known in the Berlin galleries, in the Italian galleries and elsewhere.

When arrested no thought could be given to eating, as the food was repulsive, and the two days spent in the Gorokhovaya were for us a voluntary or compulsory fast, apart from what some of us were able to pick up at home and had divided up in a brotherly way.

We were at a complete loss as to why we had been arrested, but by the composition of those present, one could see that all were from the circles of the intelligentsia, especially of the circles of the academics. Most of all, I was frightened that I had been drawn in because of my political activity, but the composition of those arrested bore evidence that there was a connection with the University and with publishing.

On the day following our arrival at the Gorokhovaya they began to call us up singly for questioning. Every one of us was very afraid of such questioning. With us there were sailors who were also under arrest, and who returned from questioning cruelly beaten up, with bleeding noses, disfigured faces and bruises all over their bodies (they washed their wounds naked in the common wash room). This was not the case with us.

Our interrogator was Agranov, who was notorious for his cruelty. Later he was liquidated by Stalin[98].

Agranov questioned us in a stereotyped fashion, making absolutely absurd accusations in respect to White Guard activity, aid to General Yudenich during his advance on Petrograd etc[99].

This every one of us expected least, for none among us was implicated in anything like it, so that there was no need for us to reply in detail to the accusations. There was not a single fact, which had to be denied, and all this nonsense was categorically rejected. We were not kept long at the interrogation, perhaps everyone for half an hour. There was no particular politeness, but there was no physical violence in respect of any of us.

We were completely perplexed as to what case the Bolsheviks were preparing. No definite charges were laid against us, and after two days we were transferred into a proper jail on Shpalernaya Street, where we were accommodated in cells for two or three persons each. Generally, we could choose with whom we wanted to be confined, but did this without drawing attention to it: we lined up in two rows, and mechanically arrived at the cell with the person of our choice.

As I had wished, I found myself in a cell with Lev Platonovich Karsavin, my friend and business partner. In the cell there were two iron bunks with thin mattresses, a wash basin with running water (cold only), a toilet (fortunately not a bucket) also with running water, and a steel panel fixed to the wall, which acted as a table when dropped. The window was very high, much above human height. There was a small window (a peephole) in the steel door, through which the warden could see into the cell. On the ceiling there was a lamp, which was lit and turned off by the warden at night. He lit the lamp several times during the night to check the prisoners through the peephole.

First of all, Karsavin and I undertook to clean the cell and ourselves. We soon got rid of the bedbugs, and cleanliness was established. We made sure not to leave any crumbs, so as not to attract rats or mice. Our cell became the model one.

Every day we were taken out into the prison yard for a half hour's walk. We could communicate with each other. The wardens stood at a distance and could not listen in. Since we still had not heard from our relations, we were not able to get any news. The weekly prison bath, with an abundance of hot water, was a great delight.

After some time, permission was given for the receiving of parcels, and this was a great relief, for the prison food was uneatable. Then personal visits from relatives began, and Genya came with Tolya, who was still quite a young child.

In spite of the complete uncertainty about our destiny, Karsavin and I endeavoured to distract ourselves by making ample use of the prison library. In its time, many political prisoners had been in that prison, and many had left their books when they were released. There was a choice to suit every taste.

I got busy with French classics: I remember we received some small volumes of Alfred de Musset, and we recited the poems to each other. This, of course, distracted us.

Some young man was brought in to share our cell for a short time, and he possibly thought that we were not quite normal to indulge ourselves with poetry in such a setting. But Karsavin and I devoted even more time to this, for it was dangerous to talk in the presence of a stranger. It was possible that he was brought in on purpose, as a spy.

At night it was often scary. From somewhere there were wild shouts, and occasionally one could hear shots. This would mean, as was explained to us by the warden, that someone was summoned for questioning with "laying on of hands" or "being put into waste" [translation of idiomatic Russian expression for "being shot"]. We had made friends with the warden, and he even passed on notes to our relatives. I also used to supply him with *Botkin Powder* (a powder against indigestion, which probably corresponded to *Alka Seltzer*), which Genya included in our parcels.

Finally, they started to call us up singly to the interrogator and again repeated the same charges. None of us signed the report of the interrogation, and no one slandered another. We were informed that we were charged with "treason". According to the legal code of that time, this was punishable by expulsion from the country, but if this could not be effected, then the next measure was execution. We were all in a depressed condition, yet we still were in command of ourselves and maintained a decent bearing. We learned that arrests among professors and the intelligentsia had taken place in Moscow and in other cities, and that these arrests were widely known.

The German Government, through its Ambassador, Count Brockdorff-Rantzau, declared that it was prepared to accept us and would issue the corresponding visas into Germany, and that the Soviet Government had agreed to release us. But we were not told anything, and we continued to sit in jail. It was from relatives who came to visit us that we learnt of our forthcoming expulsion to Germany.

The interrogator also summoned Genya and told her that I would be expelled, but that I did not want to take her with me. The same was told to the wives of some others, including the wife of Karsavin. It cannot be explained why the interrogators had to stoop to such mockery – maybe it was personal sadism.

Finally they began to call us up to the interrogator who informed us that we would be expelled abroad forever, and gave us a paper to be signed regarding our agreement to be expelled with wives and children. We were told that we would be released shortly before the very departure, that the passports provided with a visa of the German Consulate would be handed to us in the prison, and that we would be given a couple of days to liquidate our affairs.

Many began to apply for a release before the appointed time. Genya was given by Bukharin a personal letter to Zinoviev, to the effect that he, Bukharin, was prepared to vouchsafe for me until the expulsion, and that he was taking full responsibility for me. Bukharin played an important part at that time, and Genya was convinced that I would be released on the spot[100].

Genya went to the Smolny to Zinoviev, to whom Bukharin's letter was addressed. Generally it was not easy to obtain an audience with this potentate, but Genya's announcement that she had a message from Bukharin had a magical effect. Zinoviev immediately received her. He read Bukharin's letter, turned as red as a lobster and flew into a rage. He tore the letter into small shreds, declaring that in Petrograd he was the boss and would not permit his business to be interfered with, and that I would be released when everybody would be released.

As it turned out, two succeeded in being released before the appointed time. These were the writer Zamyatin[101] and the economist Ostrovsky.[102] Zamyatin went abroad after a year, but Ostrovsky died from a heart attack still before our departure. He was very stout and nervous. He was a direct descendant of the well-known dramatist Ostrovsky[103].

We were all released some ten days before our departure. Cares began. It was necessary to collect some financial means so as not to be penniless upon arrival in Germany. It was, of course, useless to take Soviet money, which was completely devalued, and it was necessary to transfer everything to foreign currency.

M. Ginsburg, whom I knew very well. Both of us had taken part as arbitrators in a number of cases, especially in the sorting out of complicated relationships in the well-known publishing company of Brockhaus-Efron. His assistant, Yekaterina Fleishits was one of the first women lawyers in Russia. She helped us to change the Soviet money into dollars and English pounds, which was a risky undertaking. Some of us had some foreign currency. Also something was obtained from the sale of belongings for such currency. (By the way, on arrival in Berlin, it turned out that some of the dollars were counterfeit.) Many had some valuables, even though modest ones: diamonds, pearls, etc. The question arose: how could we take all this with us? We did not doubt that we would all be subjected to a body search at the departure, but we were fortunate, as I shall describe later.

In the German Consulate, where we had to fill in our papers, we were treated with exceptional attention. It transpired that we were to be sent to Stettin on the ship *Preussen*. I do not know on what grounds, but the Soviet Government paid First Class fares for our passage. Such miracles do happen!

When we were finally released, we were amazed that our friends and acquaintances did not shun us, but expressed their sympathy with us in all sorts of ways. It could be said that in my apartment the doors were never closed. Among others, we were visited by the artist Yury Annenkov, who, at that time was close to those in power. He was not even scared to write some touching lines in my autograph album[104]:

> I regret, dear Abram Saulovich, that I cannot make you a drawing which would be much more appropriate here than these helpless lines.
>
> But if I am much stronger in drawing than in words, then my feelings towards you remain equally warm whether by pen or by pencil.
>
> Briefly, I thank you for the book, I embrace you for the farewell, I wish you luck, I kiss you firmly, and hope that our work together will not end with *Portraits*[105].

When taking leave we embraced.

The Consul introduced the representatives of the expellees, including myself, to the Captain of the ship who offered his services. We were to collect from everybody money and valuables, which did not take up too much space, and place these into a trunk. We were to make a list as to what belonged to whom, and to deliver the trunk to the Consulate from where it would be taken to the Captain directly on the ship in the guise of "Diplomatic Luggage". It did not take long to convince us, and we began to feverishly make the rounds of everybody and, in a short time, the trunk was delivered to the Consulate. Nobody was held up, and everything went well. The Soviets did not notice anything. "Every man has a fool in his sleeve" [Russian proverb].

Before the very departure we were given a reception with speeches and good wishes, at the home of one professor.

Finally, the day of departure arrived. We did not believe until the very last minute that we would be allowed out. When we embarked, a delegation of students farewelled us on the wharf.

We did not doubt that we would be searched, and when embarking everybody was frisked (a female agent was allocated to the women). Tolya had a small toy bear from which he did not want to part. He had been given it when he was only one year old, and it was in a rather worn condition. The agents poked it from all sides, and in spite of Genya's and my entreaties and of Tolya's tears, they cut the bear's stomach to make certain that nothing was hidden inside. The boy could not be pacified for a long time and kept on sobbing. Genya found some cotton and sewed up the place where the bear's stomach had been cut.

We made ourselves at ease in the cabins which were comfortable and spacious and were fitted with all conveniences.

After we had passed Kronstadt, and had entered neutral waters, the Captain invited representatives from amongst us, Karsavin, Odintsov and me, to his cabin, congratulated us, and gave us possession of the trunk which had been sealed with a diplomatic seal. All the contents were intact, and an offer for a reward was rejected by the Captain as an undeserved insult. He became quite furious, and we had to apologize to him for quite a long time. He was an old sea wolf, a genuine Prussian with extremely conservative views, but in the end he invited us to dinner at his table, and we had a drink for general good health.

Жалею, дорогой Абрам Саулович,
что не могу сделать Вам рисунок,
который был-бы здесь много уместнее,
нежели эти беспомощные строки.

Но если в рисунке я более
силен, чем в слове, то чувства мои
к Вам остаются одинаково горячими
и под пером и под карандашом.

Одним словом, я благодарю Вас
за книгу, обнимаю Вас на прощанье,
желаю счастья, целую крепко и надеюсь,
что „Портретами" не закончится
наша совместная работа.

Юрий Анненков

19/XI 22
Питер.

Yury Annenkov's parting words a few days before Abram's
expulsion, hand-written in Abram's notebook.

PART TWO

THE FIRST EXILE
1922–1938

Chapter Fourteen

Towards a New Beginning and Russia's Second Capital

The trip on the *Preussen* left a vivid mark on my memory. The majority of us were accompanied by our families. All of us were good friends, and we grew even closer to each other during the journey. I was, of course, already bound in close friendship with Kotlyarevsky and Karsavin. One of our fellow travellers was Maria Nikolaevna Stoyunina, Lossky's mother-in-law. She was the founder and director of the well-known *Gimnaziya of Stoyunina*, which was one of the best high schools in Russia, known for its progressive teaching methods, and from which many well-known female activists and educationalists had graduated. Maria Nikolaevna thought highly of me. I was a frequent visitor at the Losskys, and when they moved to Prague I used to visit them there as a matter of course.

On our way to Stettin we had already discussed, in the common lounge of the ship, the question of creating a new publishing company in Berlin. Amongst us were members of the management of my company, *Naooka i Shkola*, Kotlyarevsky and Karsavin. Then there were Lossky and Lapshin, who were close to Karsavin. We even indicated a number of books intended for publication, which I later carried into practice. We decided that, upon arrival, we would bring in authors from other exiled groups, especially from Moscow: Berdyaev, Frank,

Stepoon and Vysheslavtsev. I remember that apart from this mainly religious-philosophical group, I also wanted to attract Prokopovich and Kuskova. Actually, I wanted to achieve, in general, that which I had been doing in Petrograd.

On the ship, there travelled as a private passenger the well-known playwright Yevreinov, with his wife, a very lively and intelligent person. She made the rounds of all of us expellees, and asked us to write a few words in her autograph album. I wrote that I would be happy to return to my homeland under changed conditions. Part of her *Memoirs* were published in *Novy Journal* [*New Journal*] 1955 No.40, where she quoted my words[106].

After a three-day voyage without special incidents, we arrived in Stettin. From there our group made its way by train to Berlin. In Stettin we were met by our relative David Yefimovich Kagan (my great-uncle) who had already prepared a room for us in a guesthouse on Rankestrasse, in Berlin, while he took Kotlyarevsky, who travelled with us, to the apartment of one of our other relatives.

Upon arrival in Berlin we went our own ways, but kept in touch as to each other's whereabouts[107]. After a short time we called a meeting of exiles for the purpose of becoming acquainted with each other, for there were exiles not only from Petrograd and Moscow, but also from other cities[108].

The "expulsanty" Russian exiles in Berlin.
(Back row far left) Abram Saulovitch Kagan; (front row far right)
Eugenia "Genya" Samueleva Kagan (nee Entin); (front centre)
Anatol "Tolya" Abramovitch Kagan, aged 10.

Chapter Fifteen

The Russian Publishing Scene in Berlin; Petropolis Transplanted; The Berlin Kagans and Obelisk

In the beginning of our life in Berlin we lived in a guesthouse in Rankestrasse, then the relatives offered us the apartment of Boris Yefimovich (another of my great-uncles), on Wieland-strasse, while he moved to an apartment in Schlüter Sstrasse. Then they built an additional story on a building on Lützow-platz for my family and for another relative. There was no talk about any rent. We lived on Lützowplatz for several years, and when we expected the birth of our second child, Irene, we moved to a wonderful apartment on Barbarossastrasse.

We arrived in Germany at the beginning of inflation. David Yefimovich bought the furniture for our apartment. By the time the order had been carried out there was practically nothing to pay. I had unlimited credit with my relatives. I bought paper with cheques to be presented in six months, and when the paper arrived, it was almost for free and lasted for countless numbers of books[109].

To begin with, I had to make myself familiar with the situation regarding Russian publishing and book trade in Germany, which meant, specifically, in Berlin. The picture that presented itself to me was quite amazing. The publication of Russian books was in full bloom.

Raissa Blokh, *Moy Gorod* (*My City*), published in Berlin by Petropolis (1928).

It was hard to believe, but for some time there were more Russian books published in Germany than there were German books. I did not believe that until I was convinced by the statistics of the *Börsenverein des Deutschen Buchhandels* (Stock Exchange of the German Book Trade).

I rented a room for the publishing company[110] in a building adjoining my relatives' office, *Nitag* [in Kleiststrassse] but worked at night, mostly at home, and then in the Petropolis office. At first the Petropolis office was in a small room on Uhland-strasse[111], then the combined Petropolis and Obelisk office moved to a half-basement room which, however was very comfortable, in a building belonging to the Kahans [originally Kagans] on Schlüterstrasse[112]. From Schlüterstrasse we moved to Joachimsthaler Strasse, and finally, we moved to Meinecke-strasse, where we stayed until we left Germany.

The management of *Obelisk* consisted of two persons: David Yefimovich Kahan and myself. *Obelisk* was a GmbH [i.e. a Limited Company][113]. Petropolis was a shareholding company, and the management consisted of the Blokhs, Grinberg and myself. Grinberg left after some time. At first he went to live in Finland and finally established himself in London.

In my publishing company, *Obelisk*, I concentrated mainly on books on philosophy and on religious-philosophical literature. One of the first was the republishing of the book by my close friend N.A. Kotlyarevsky *Nashe Nedavneye Proshloye [Our Recent Past]*, which went somewhat beyond my program. Then, one after another, were published: Berdyaev's *Filosofiya Neravenstva [The Philosophy of Inequality]* and *Smysl Istorii [The Meaning of History]* by the same author, S.L. Frank's *Vvedenye v Filosofiyu [Introduction into Philosophy]* and *Zhivoye Znanye [Living Knowledge]*. There followed N.O. Lossky's *Obosnovanye Intuitivizma [The Justification of Intuitionism* − i.e. the belief that primary truth and principles relating to ethics and metaphysics are known directly by intuition], F. Stepoon's *Zhizn i Tvorchestvo [Life and Creativity]*, I. Lapshin's *Estetika Dostoevskovo [Dostoevsky's Aesthetic]*, then a book by Vysheslavtsev about Dostoevsky and a book by Alexanderov on Soviet economy. In particular, I would like to mention the anthology, *Sophia*, which contained articles of a philosophico-religious character by the main representatives of this trend[114].

Chapter Sixteen

Travels in Europe

When I used to go travelling in connection with the affairs of the firm, I travelled for fairly lengthy periods and visited a number of countries.

There was a large market for Russian books. Apart from the German market, there was a great demand for Russian literature in the countries which previously comprised parts of Russia, like Poland, Latvia, Lithuania, Estonia, as well as in some of the centres of Russian emigration: in Paris, Prague and Yugoslavia, in the far away North and South America, in Canada, even in China and Japan. Large numbers of Russians were everywhere in European countries, e.g. in Finland, Great Britain, and even in Italy and Sweden. There was a good Russian market in Czechoslovakia. There was also a large market in the Far East: in China, in Harbin, where there was the well-known publishing house of *Churin*, as well as in Shanghai.

It was one thing to publish books, and another to distribute them, especially in view of the spread-out nature of the Russian reading public. Russian people, outside of Soviet Russia, were spread out over the whole world, and were not yet, as now, assimilated in any great measure with the population of those countries among which they found themselves.

Large firms outside Russia established Russian departments, as mentioned earlier. But the "Achilles' heel" was the absence of a distributive apparatus. It must be noted that some such agencies did exist, but they were established without any experience, often without any means, and under a great risk, due to ignorance regarding the credit-worthiness of the clients. In the beginning we entrusted the distribution of our books to the publishing company *Obrazovanye* (Education), but we soon became convinced of its complete worthlessness. We changed to the firm *Russian Book Export*. However, this firm did not exist for very long, and went bankrupt. This was accompanied by great losses to us.

It was then that I decided that we should establish a distributive apparatus ourselves. I devoted my efforts towards achieving this objective by making use of my connections in the literary world wherever I could do so. I began to travel all over Europe with this in mind, but in remote countries I chose to work through firms which had proved their high credit rating.

My travels greatly enlarged my circle of acquaintances and strengthened old connections. These journeys did not have the appearance of business trips, but in essence they were just that. The publishing company could hardly have done without them.

Prague

My first trip was to Prague and made a great impression on me. On one hand, there was the ancient city with outstanding buildings of remarkable architecture; the picturesque Hradschin, with its palace where the President lived, and private buildings which did not offend the eye and which were inhabited mostly by people of the intellectual professions. A wonderful river, with a remarkable bridge and park at one end. Then the Vaclavske namesti, having a commercial, but also a somehow special character, and terminating with the wonderful building of the

Museum, where a musical clock played in some charming way, but I cannot remember whether it was every hour, or more frequently.

Amongst all this antiquity, there emerged some kind of, I would say, "Americanism": an unusual ebullience and energy. Just consider, for example, the Bata works. This firm produced shoes and galoshes in the American fashion, outstanding by virtue of their good quality, but at an exceptionally accessible price. The factory was situated in a separate township, where houses with all conveniences had been built for the workers and the clerical staff. I do not know how many houses there were, but in any case, thousands, and they became the property of the workers after being paid off. There was the possibility of extending the payments over a number of years by monthly deductions from the wages, such deductions being modest so as not to burden the borrowers or get them into debt. A special department store had been established, where the workers and clerical staff could obtain everything at cheaper prices. But there was no compulsion to buy at that store. The employees took part in the profits of the enterprise. There were schools which prepared the cadres of the future workers and clerical staff. Where else could one find enterprises of such range?

Life in Prague was very comfortable. Here, for example, one could get shoes repaired whilst waiting. In Prague, you could get the suit that you were wearing, cleaned and pressed in half an hour, whilst you waited in a comfortable cabin.

I stopped at the popular hotel *Axa*, which was affordable to people of medium income. It also had a Turkish bath and massage rooms, several restaurants and a large swimming pool. What is this if not an American fairy tale?

After an inspection of the sights of Prague, I began to do the rounds of my acquaintances and friends. Sergey Nikolaevich Prokopovich and Yetakerina Dmitrevna Kuskova received me most cordially. With them lived a friend of Yekaterina Dmitrevna, the already aged Zvereva.

The Prokopoviches lived in Hradschin, in a very cosy building. They introduced me to the "Russian bias" of the Czechs. The Czechs very generously welcomed Russian scientists and the intelligentsia generally. Russian scientific institutions had been established, and Russian scientists were maintained by the Czechs, who encouraged all kinds of cultural activities.

Zemgor (a cultural organization) extended its activity. The Countess Sophia Vladimirovna Panina published *Russkiy Ochag* (*The Russian Hearth*). The Slavonic Library was generously replenished with Russian books.

I visited the Prokopoviches more than once, both during my first visit to Prague, as well as during the following ones. In Berlin I had paid my dues to my scientific interests by founding, together with Sergey Nikolaevich Prokopovich, the journal *The Economist*. This journal was the organ of *The Economist's Cabinet* established by Prokopovich. I continued to publish the journal until Prokopovich, together with *The Economist's Cabinet*, moved to Prague. Soon I started to supply books to Sergey Nikolaevich's Cabinet, and I came to an agreement with him regarding the publishing of his new books. Apart from the journal, I also published a number of books on economics.

Professor G.V. Vernadsky had also settled in Prague. He established the *Eurasian Publishing Company*, and asked me if I would like to take part in it. Vernadsky, whose book on Novikov I had published in the beginning of my activity in Petrograd, introduced me to his colleagues, and among these to P.P. Savitsky. I became a publisher of the group of Eurasians[115]. I established the most friendly relations with Savitsky, and became his and Vernadsky's publisher.

The Losskys received me as one of the family. They lived very modestly but pleasantly. The whole family was united in friendship. Stoyunina was charming (Stoyunina was Lossky's mother-in-law, and the former Principal of the Girls' Gimnaziya named after her). Lossky undertook to write a number of books, and I was to be his publisher. At the Losskys I met, for the first time, Pyotr Petrovich Savitsky, who invited me then and there to his place. Savitsky and his wife, father and mother, all lived together. What immediately struck me was the profoundly religious nature of the family, including their observation of formal religious rites, churchgoing, etc. It was the same with the Losskys. Pytor Petrovich knew about me from Professor Vernadsky and wanted to secure my cooperation and active participation in the publishing of a number of books of the *Eurasian Publishing Company*, of which he was one of the inspirers. I had a number of meetings with him and Vernadsky, as a result of which I became their publisher. I established a very friendly relationship with them.

I visited *The Russian Hearth* of Countess Panina. Attached to it was a library, and I offered my services to supply it with books. This was eagerly accepted. Countess Panina said that she had a project for me, but that it was still necessary to think about it, and that she would get in touch with me about it later. As it turned out afterwards, it was the case of publishing the biography of her father, Petrunkevich, a well-known democratic activist. But she feared that I would decline, since it was anything but an attractive proposition from a financial point of view, and she wanted first to make sure of the influence on me in this regard of such people as Propokovich[116]. She told this to me herself, later on. Of course I published the book.

I became friendly with Professor Bem. As I mentioned earlier, he used to publish anthologies of Dostoevsky. I took over the publishing of these. I established a friendly relationship with him to our mutual benefit. In Prague, Bem organized a circle of poets called *Skit*[117], and when I visited Prague I was a welcome guest of those poets and was held in great esteem by them. They felt flattered to be in my company since I used to publish books of outstanding poets in Petropolis. Among the poets was Alla Golovina, a charming person. I published a collection of her poems. Golovina's husband was a wood sculptor, who was as charming as his wife. He made me a present of one of his sculptures which, unfortunately, was later lost when leaving Berlin.

In Prague I also made the acquaintance of Sergey Yosifovich Gessen, the son of Yossif Vladimirovich Gessen. He was a well-known educationalist. He had published a number of books and was a professor at the Prague University. He was the son of Yossif Vladimirovich from his first marriage with a Kalmyk woman, with whom he lived when he was in exile in Siberia. Sergey Yossifovich also looked like a Kalmyk, although he had traits of his father. He was married to the daughter of Minor, the once well-known Social Revolutionary. Sergey Yossifovich had two children, but although he was an educationalist, he could not bring up his children properly, and they made a very sorry impression. The house was very untidy. He and his wife were very hospitable people, but she was a very poor housewife. The food which she served up was unpalatable, however one had to eat out of politeness. I do not know what became of Sergey Yossifovich later. I only know that he moved to Warsaw, divorced his wife and married for a second time.

Also in Prague, and as I mentioned earlier, there lived with the Prokopoviches the now elderly Zvereva, who was known by her activity in the field of education in Russia. She was corresponding with Bervy, a well-known woman champion of popular education, who lived in Canada. For a long time Bervy had the idea of publishing a work on the spreading of education in Russia. She wrote to me in Berlin on the recommendation of Zvereva, enquiring whether I would be interested in publishing her work in the Russian language. A lengthy correspondence ensued, which took on a friendly turn.

Zvereva's book was published under the title *What to Tell the Children*. It was a success, and called forth very laudatory reviews. Finally I made an agreement with Bervy. I published the first volume of her work in Berlin, and the second volume in Brussels to where we moved after Berlin. These books represented an irreplaceable source for the study of popular education in Russia at that time.

By the way, I should mention that, when in Russia, I was seriously interested in the question of education. Attached to the publishing company *Ogni*, in which I took a very active part, there was a specially established "School Commission". In it, a very active part was played by the well-known social activists: Kaydanova and Kapitsa. The latter was a charming woman, the mother of the nuclear scientist, who was then still a very young man.

I visited Prague often, not less than three times a year. Prague turned out to be a wonderful market for books. In this respect my connection with the Prague scientists and institutions turned out to be very useful. Every time when Genya and I went on holidays to Karlsbad or Marienbad or the High Tatra, I did not miss the opportunity of calling on Prague.

Warsaw

Among other countries I visited Poland on two occasions. Poland was an excellent market for Russian books. Our representative there was the firm *Dobro*. In Poland we supplied not only books for companies for which we had the agency, but also books from Soviet Russia, books on science and literature, and also antiquarian books which we imported in large numbers.

Before travelling to Poland, I used to correspond with Professor Kulakovsky, who was lecturing on Russian literature at the Warsaw University. He was the son of the well-known Russian academician, Julian Kulakovsky. He had access to Polish literary circles. We became closely acquainted during the short time that I spent with him in Warsaw. He suggested to me to publish a book of contemporary Polish poets in the Russian language. The Polish government was warmly disposed to this project and promised to pay the expenses of the translation into Russian. The task was not easy. This should be explained by the fact that Kulakovsky was a poet himself, and some of the Polish poets knew the Russian language well. I was received courteously at the Ministry of Education and at times they even spoke Russian to me. (I understand Polish when it is spoken, but I do not speak Polish myself. Whilst at the Gimnaziya I was interested in Polish literature and read its classics in the original. I can even now recite Mickiewicz from memory.)

At the Ministry we agreed on a translation, but undertook the publication of the book at our own expense. I spent almost all evenings together with Kulakovsky, and we had heart to heart talks. He extended to me Warsaw's hospitality, and we visited the small cafés with their *couleur locale* where Polish poets and literary people used to meet. I did not encounter any hostility as a Russian, although I feared that this could be expected, due to the extreme Polish nationalism. The book came out under the title of *Contemporary Polish Poets*. The book was a success, if one takes into account that the size of the *émigré* market was not large for such publications. All reviews were full of praise.

Deviating somewhat, I would like to mention the following: In Russia I was one of the prominent acquirers of books. When one of my firms acquired whole libraries, with the aim of selling these as separate volumes in our shop (either *Naooka i Shkola* or Petropolis), I had, of course, the opportunity to put aside for my

Abram's wife, Eugenia "Genya" Samueleva Kagan, Berlin, c. 1930.

own library, books which interested me. Among some of these happened to be the book of poems by the famous Polish poet Mickiewicz which had a personal inscription on the title page, addressed to no lesser person than A.S. Pushkin, to be sure, in Polish. Such a find had an enormous cultural value, linking two poet geniuses of two Slavonic countries. I was greatly tempted to leave the book in my library, but finally decided to present it to the library attached to the *Pushkin House* of the Academy of Sciences. I informed the then president of the Pushkin House, Kotlyarevsky, as well as its member, the Academician Mavsolevsky and the Secretary Fokin, about my intention. They were pleased about this acquisition, and directed an official letter of thanks to me in the name of the Pushkin House. I did not regret having done this without any remuneration.

Baltic Cities

From Warsaw I went to Vilnius, the city which, at one time, was the capital of Lithuania[118]. I had nothing to do there from a business point of view, but I wanted to inspect the city from which so many activists in the field of Jewish culture had come. Besides, I had an assignment from my relatives to inspect the printing house of the *Widow of the Brothers Romm* (this is what it was called), which my relatives had acquired in the past.

The city made a pitiful impression. There were almost no new buildings. The old buildings had become decrepit and were obviously not being repaired. The roadways were broken down, cabbies with scruffy horses and with vehicles in a similar state. In the streets I could hardly hear any Polish spoken, but mainly Yiddish, and sometimes Russian more often than Polish.

What made a great impression on me was the printing establishment of the *Widow of the Brothers Romm*. It was conducted not on a commercial basis, but from the love of books.

The books published were exclusively religious, amongst which the first place was taken by the *Talmud*. Then there were bibles of various sizes, and prayer books for festive and non-festive days. *Shass*, the Vilnius *Talmud*, was well known all over the world where there were Jews. After the Berlin printing works, I was dumbfounded: all these books, including the many volumes of the *Talmud* were set by hand. Whoever has seen a *Talmud* would understand what a "labour of Sisyphus" it represented – the different kinds of lettering, the artistic spacing of the basic text and of the interpretation. The employees of the printing works were fascinating. They consisted mainly of elderly men with broad, thick beards. They worked wearing their hats or *yarmulkes*. They ritually washed their hands before meals and intoned the corresponding prayer. The working day was long, and there, in the library they performed the *minkha* and the *maariv* (morning and evening prayer). Ten men required for a *minyan* (quorum) were always present. I witnessed how one of them happened to drop a book on the floor, whereupon he lifted the book and kissed it reverently. I need not mention that affixed to all doorjambs there were *mezuzes* (scrolls containing the Ten Commandments), and the employees, when entering, touched the *mezuzes* with the palms of their hands and then kissed the point of contact.

Lithuania, which I visited more than once, presented a peculiar picture. With the declaration of independence, Kovno, or in Lithuanian, Kaunas, became the capital[119]. It resembled a large town within the *Pale*, which in effect it was. Although the official language was Lithuanian, and I had studied it well before visiting the city, I could literally not hear a single word spoken in Lithuanian, but could only hear Russian and Yiddish. The President at the head of the Government was a former assistant professor at the Petrograd University.

In Kovno there lived my close friend and partner, Professor L.P. Karsavin, who had been exiled together with me from

Russia, and with whom I had shared the prison cell. He was Professor of History at the Kovno University, and although he could not speak a single word of Lithuanian when he arrived in Kovno, he not only mastered the language in the shortest time, but delivered lectures in Lithuanian, published his works in that language, and even became an authority in the field of style and syntax of Lithuanian – its innovator. Karsavin was an exceptionally gifted and talented person, with an enormous knowledge both in historical as well as in philosophical disciplines. As I have written earlier, we used to read Alfred de Musset and other French poets, together, to keep up our spirits in the prison cell. I was very proud of his friendship, and while in Kovno, I was daily his guest[120].

Stankevich, another acquaintance who was from Petrograd, also lived in Kovno. He too was a professor at the Kovno University. He was an assistant professor whilst in Petrograd. He held a ministerial position under Kerensky.

Professor Karsavin with sister, Karsavina.

Russian social life in Kovno and in Lithuania generally, was very lively. Russian theatre performances and lectures were daily occurrences. The reading public was Russian or Russian-Jewish. There was Boleslavsky's[121] large Russian firm, *Literatura* and then *Mokslass*. The latter had the agency for Soviet books, and, at the same time, sold foreign books (i.e. Russian books published outside the Soviet Union). Since *Literatura* did not want to order Soviet books from its competitor *Mokslass*, we used to supply these books to *Literatura*, while *Mokslass* had to reconcile itself with this, for it depended on us in respect of the supply of foreign publications.

Belyatskin, a Petrograd lawyer who had been considered one of the greatest experts on civil rights in Russia, also lived in Kovno. I met him for the first time in Kovno, although I had already heard of him in Petrograd, where, at the Seminar on Civil Rights, both Professor Walter and Professor Pergament often held up Belyatskin's interpretations as examples. He too had a leaning towards Russian literature, which he knew excellently, and had a penchant for writing novels. One cannot say that they were bad, but they did not rise above the bounds of mediocrity. After I had become acquainted with Belyatskin, he tried to persuade me to publish those novels. We agreed that I should publish them under a different firm's name, rather than mine, where I felt only "master works" (I am joking half-seriously) could be published.

Several times I was in Latvia, where my father was then living.

Riga made a very good impression on me. Russian social life was in full swing there. A large daily, *Sevodnya* [*Today*] was published in Riga. One of its editors was Boris Osipovich Khariton, with whom I was on friendly terms. In Petrograd he was the head of the *House of Litterateurs*, which I used to visit almost daily, where I often lunched and where I did not miss a single literary evening. Khariton had also been one of my prison mates at the time before our expulsion from Russia. *Sevodnya* could be placed on the same level as the papers published at that time in the European capitals. To be sure, *Posledniye Novosti* [*Latest News*, published in Paris] was more serious in a political sense, but the newspapers in the Latvian language could not be compared in any respect with *Sevodnya*. I used to spend a lot of time in the editing office, exchanging local news and those from Berlin and Paris.

In Riga there was a large firm, that of Mrs Ettinger, who was one of our clients. She was an educated person, and her bookshop was like a salon, where the members of the Russian intelligentsia rubbed shoulders.

My university friend, Maxim Yakovlevich Lazerson, was a professor at the local university, and was the leader of the Jewish group in the Latvian parliament. He was considered to be a prominent social activist. Our friendship was renewed later in New York, when he migrated there.

In Riga there lived a prominent Russian lawyer, Oskar Osipovich Gruzenberg, who was well known in Russia for his role in political cases, especially the Beilis' case[122].

Gruzenberg was, without doubt, a very talented orator, but he was insanely vain. He expressed the wish to see me, and we met. He suggested to me that I should publish his *Memoirs*, and even wanted to take part in the expenses. His *Memoirs* did not suit the character of my publishing company, and I, very politely, and with many compliments, declined to publish his book. My refusal amazed him so much that he exclaimed: "How is it that you do not want to print me, Gruzenberg, for I am none other than the famous lawyer known to the whole world!" Later on he had his book printed in Paris, at his own expense. The book was a complete hymn of praise of himself, and I was pleased that I had not taken it on.

I cannot desist from telling the following anecdote regarding Gruzenberg. This was already during the Revolution. My wife and I were invited to dinner at the home of Yossif Mikhailovich Kulisher. As we were about to sit down for the meal, Anna Semyonovna, Kulisher's wife, said that she would like to show me something that would interest me. She led me to the front door landing. Exactly opposite was Gruzenberg's apartment. On his door there was a notice: "Visiting hours cancelled due to my appointment as Senator". I must remark that he had been appointed Senator some time ago[123], but the notice still remained affixed – what vanity!

When coming to Riga I usually visited Estonia, actually only Reval, which has since been changed to Tallinn, the capital of Estonia. Reval was a most beautiful city, remarkably clean, and while new buildings were absent, the old ones were carefully preserved, and there were many monuments of olden days.

While in Riga one could make oneself understood by practically everyone, if not in Russian then in German, but it was harder to converse in this way in Reval, for the Estonians, after their oppression by Tsarist Russia, had become rabid nationalists and declined to speak Russian, even if they knew that language. Yet there were strata of Russians and Germans, and both these minorities maintained their culture. The Yurev University (now the Dorpat University, it was thus called even before the attainment of the independence of Estonia), subject to a strong German influence, had become the national university of Estonia.

In Reval there was a Russian book firm which was well established. It was run by one of our clients and the firm ordered books through us. I used to be welcomed there in a most hospitable manner.

My associate in exile, Leonid Pumpyansky, was the head of a concern utilizing the peat deposits of Estonia for fuel and for obtaining different derivatives. He was married to a typical Russian by the name of Olympia Kharlamonovna. She was the niece of the writer Romanenko[124], who was well known in his time. If I am not mistaken, she was the daughter of a priest.

There was another acquaintance of mine, Carl Lunz, an Estonian. He had worked for some time in my publishing company in Petrograd. He had graduated from the Law Faculty of the Petrograd University. When Estonia became independent, he became the Secretary of the Estonian Embassy in Petrograd. He unselfishly rendered services to his acquaintances. He used to receive newspapers and magazines through the Embassy and he sent them to me, so that I always had fresh editions of *Berliner Tageblatt*, *Vossische Zeitung*, *The London Times*, etc. After reading these, I passed them on to my friends, and they circulated them further. It is strange that the Bolsheviks did not take any notice of this, in spite of all their surveillance. Later, Lunz turned up in the Estonian Ministry of Foreign Affairs at Reval[125].

Chapter Seventeen

Copyrights for Soviet Writers

Completely beyond understanding was the fact that, in spite of me being exiled as a "political criminal", the connection with Soviet Russia was not broken[126]. Manuscripts continued to arrive without interruption, some even through the Soviet Embassy. All writers who arrived in Berlin, or, for example, were passing on their way to Paris, invariably called at our publishing company, offering manuscripts. Thus came Nemirovich-Danchenko and brought us the manuscript of Stanislavsky's *Moya Zhizn v Iskusstve* [*My Life in Art*] which we published[127].

Fedin came with the manuscript *Bratya* [*The Brothers*], which we also published. Others who came and whose books we also published, were Tynyanov, Ehrenburg (who at that time was a rabid Bolshevik[128]), Vera Inber and many others[129]. They brought not only their own manuscripts, but also those of others. Some even left in our account, money which they did not want to take back to Russia. It could be said that all more or less known Soviet writers were published by us. This was advantageous for them, for being published by us established their copyright under the Berne Agreement[130].

Thus everybody came to pay their respects, and it is strange how they got away with all this contact with a "political criminal".

A strange situation came about when the first editions of books of such a huge country as Russia were published abroad.

In such a way, for example, Ehrenburg was able to sell the film rights of some of his works to Hollywood, which he could not have done had his books been first published in Russia. It is hard to conceive how all this came about so smoothly, since obviously anti-Communist books were published in my other publishing companies. For example: Larson's *On Soviet Service*, Aronson's *Red Terror*, works of S.N. Prokopovich, books by Nikolayevesky, Gul, and so on.

Meyerhold arrived with his company. He asked us to help him, and we printed the program of his performances, which comprised a whole brochure. We also met his actress wife, who was a charming person. We went to all his performances. He was talented, without a doubt, although I was not an admirer of all his extravagances. The success of his performances was moderate[131].

There were some terrible moments. Pilnyak sent us his book *Krasnoye Derevo* (*The Red Tree*). We published it. Then, either in *Pravda* or in *Izvestya* there appeared a notice about the arrest of Pilnyak. And there was the deposition given by Pilnyak that he had not given the book *Krasnoye Derevo* to Petropolis, but that Petropolis had stolen it in some fashion, by the intermediary of its agents. Of course, we could not respond to this... I had received that book in the Soviet Embassy, directly from the Secretary! And it was written on the envelope: "To Kagan, or Y.N. Blokh – from the author (Pilnyak)". Petropolis had been in correspondence with Pilnyak and had a contract with him concerning the publication of two of his books. These were subsequently published in the Soviet Union. But Pilnyak got into trouble and could not be saved.[132]

Yakov Noevich Blokh, professor of languages, Berlin, 1930.

Chapter Eighteen

Mayakovsky

One fine day Mayakovsky came to our office. I was not one of his admirers, and, what is more, I could not stand his poetry[133]. I knew him already in Petrograd, where he used to call on me with his mistress [Lily Brik][134]. She was a charming woman. Her library consisted exclusively of books of erotic content, but this was not reflected in her behaviour. Her husband was a *litterateur*, who made a good impression. He was well mannered, but in literary circles it was said that he was a GPU informer... *mariage à trois!*

Vladimir Mayakovsky behaved arrogantly, even impudently. He was arrogant in everything. Perhaps his arrogance was intended to cover up shyness. This is how cowards, in order to cover up their fear, turn out to be heroes on the battlefield.

He announced himself: "I am Mayakovsky!"

Yakov Noevich and I received him. He had brought us the manuscript of his play *Klop* (*The Bedbug*[135]), and insisted that we should hear it through on the spot. He asked for it to be published, stating that we would "immediately become famous"! Both Yakov Noevich and I replied that we first had to read the play. After insisting that there was no point in reading it, that he was a "luminary", that nobody had ever spoken to him like that, and that he was bestowing a great honour on us by his offer, he suddenly stood up, walked to the door of our office, locked it, and literally forced us to listen to him reading the entire play.

This was in the middle of the day, in the middle of all the work. We were not impressed by the play, possibly partly because we were revolted by his behaviour, partly by the raised voice and the whining tone with which he was reading the play. We still did not give an immediate reply, as he had insisted, and later, after consulting with each other, we declined to publish it. There were no bounds to his indignation. He dropped phrases like: "What – you reject Mayakovsky?!" but we remained adamant.

This was the end of our relationship with Mayakovsky. As is well known, he committed suicide[136]. There were many versions regarding this act. Unrequited love, general disappointment with life… but perhaps the most likely reason was that he was suffering from syphilis in a rather grave form, and the drug Salvarsan did not help. Penicillin appeared only many years after his death[137].

Chapter Nineteen

Bukharin the Sponsor

I have already mentioned that Bukharin wanted to vouchsafe for me when I was in prison. We had never thought alike, we were on two opposite poles, but he was a decent person and wanted to help me during the beginning of my life in Berlin. He was the head of the publishing company *Ekonomicheskaya Zhizn* (Economic Life) in Moscow, and commissioned me to translate Keynes' *A Tract on Monetary Reform*[138].

The translation was published as one by A.S. Kamenetsky (the name of my maternal great-grandfather), for my real name could not be given. The book contained many tables. I wrote the headings and data by hand, but the publishing company did not deem them worthy of typesetting, and thus the handwriting was reproduced as it was in the original.

Bukharin was "liquidated" later, but this was in no way for indulging a "political criminal"[139].

Chapter Twenty

Leon Trotsky and the
Alter Egos of Petropolis

One day a young man came into my publishing company. He had fair hair and no particularly outstanding features. His surname was Sedov, which at first, did not mean anything to me. He referred to my son, with whom he was acquainted through the *Technische Hochschule*, at which they were both students[140]. This young man turned out to be none other than the son of Leon Trotsky. The aim of his visit was to offer me his father's autobiography, *My Life*, for publication. There was no end to my amazement, for Trotsky was precisely the individual who had instigated the expulsion of the academics, including myself, from Russia.

I frankly stated this to Sedov, asking him why he turned especially to me with an offer to publish his father's autobiography? A long conversation ensued between us. It turned out that his father had become just as much a *persona non grata* as I was. I accepted the book for publication[141].

However opposed my relation to Trotsky's political activity had been, he had played a great part in the political life of Russia.

As a personality he was abominable. I had made his acquaintance already in Petrograd. His sister, Olga Davidovna Kameneva, worked in the Secretariat of the Soviet of Workers Deputies. She was, in general, a foolish person who fancied herself to be an actress, and since she was Trotsky's sister and Kamenev's wife, she believed herself to be above all who were around her. We succeeded with great effort to have her leave the Secretariat, where she was conducting a singular underground activity for the Bolsheviks. It was she who introduced me to Trotsky. He was an arrogant, despotic person, devoid of any charm, but he was an eloquent and talented demagogic orator.

The book *My Life* was a complete panegyric of himself, but excellently written.

Sedov used to take and bring the proofs with the greatest punctuality. In the publishing company we called Sedov the *Dauphin*.

After completing the *Technische Hochschule*, Sedov went to Paris. There he developed appendicitis. He was operated on, and died in hospital. Rumour had it that he had died by the hand of the Cheka. Whether this was true or only talk, I cannot say, but my son [the reference is to me] maintains that the *Cheka* was involved, and had killed Sedov, the same as Trotsky himself later became a victim of a killer sent to him[142].

Chapter Twenty-One

Antiquarian Books and Ikons

Shklyaver frequently complained that although *Mosse's* paper and books had a market in Russia, it was forbidden to take out money in payment for these imports, while the expenditure on correspondents' fees (in Russia) that could come out of the above payments, was only small, so that the money was accumulating in Russia and losing its value. On account of this, *Mosse* intended to reduce operations in Russia, and his (Shklyaver's) position might become uncertain. And here we conceived an idea: Would not the Russians agree to supply books to *Mosse* for the already accumulated money and for future fees? If this could be arranged, then I would commit myself to Shklyaver to order Soviet publications exclusively through him, provided that *Mosse* would have me as their exclusive client. The ensuing correspondence between *Mosse* and the Soviet authorities ended in an agreement between them and *Mosse*, and I, in turn, concluded an agreement with *Mosse* in respect of the ordering and supplying of books.

Earlier, we also used to order antiquarian books, and books generally from Soviet Russia through *Mezhdunarodnaya Kniga*, but orders were fulfilled with great delays, and the prices for antiquarian books were entirely arbitrary, sometimes excessively and unjustifiably high, or they dropped. We did not know before actual delivery whether we would receive the books and at what price. Through the intermediary of *Mosse* the book trade took on a completely different character. We began to regularly receive new books and antiquarian books, which were at times very valuable. And the sale of Soviet books started to play an ever greater part in our activity, which was of great significance to us, since the books which were published by us did not either bring in any profit at all, or a minimal one. We developed the sale of antiquarian books quite successfully. I cannot say precisely how many complete series of *Starye Gody*, *Mir Iskusstva* and *Apollon* (high quality pre-revolutionary art magazines) passed through our hands, but in any case, many, many dozens. We also had very good connections with Paris and Prague. We also began to work with the Berenson Library in Italy[143], which bought up a huge number of antiquarian books, as did the Morgan Library in New York.

I remember there was one very large book, *Enamels and Cameos*, by Zvenigorodsky, in exclusively luxurious covers, with bookmarks made of brocade and a huge quantity of illustrations. The book was so large that it was hard to even lift it. The Morgan Library ordered one copy, but subsequently purchased all the copies that we could get hold of. The book was expensive, even according to today's prices. Rumour had it that the Morgan Library used this publication as a catalogue, and also that they supplied the whole collection of Zvenigorodsky to Hollywood, presumably to document Russian costumes and decorations for many films of coronations of Russian Tsars, etc.

We received an enquiry from the Morgan Library, as to whether we could supply them with ancient ikons. We tried, through the same firm of *Mosse*, to also order ikons among the antiquariat. This attempt proved to be successful, and we began to regularly receive ikons, often very valuable ones. The Morgan Library became a regular customer for ikons, and we also sent ikons to the Berenson Library in Italy and to many other connoisseurs of church art.

There was the following curious incident, Among our clients there was a German aristocrat, von Gitschow, who lived in his palace near Dresden. Through us he bought a huge number of Russian books, both antiquarian books as well as those on art. On one occasion, having somehow seen an ikon in our office, he became all excited. He said that he was longing to adorn a suitable room in his palace with ikons so as to establish a chapel. It turned out that his mistress, the actress Elsa Krüger was of Russian descent, and it was for her that the books and ikons were intended. Being an aristocrat did not interfere with von Gitschow being a tobacco manufacturer, and he did not only spoil his mistress with books and ikons, but produced cigarettes which he named after her, even with her portrait on the packet, and these were enjoyed over the whole of Germany.

Abram Kagan in his office, with ikons, Berlin 1930.

Chapter Twenty-two

A Change of Policy –
Books in German

It is true that Russians had settled all over the world, but since I lived in Germany, I had to concentrate on publishing books in German[144]. It had been my fault that I used to publish books only in Russian. As the demand for Russian books decreased, the problem of publishing books in German arose automatically.

I began in what would appear as a rather strange way: my first book in German was by Igor Grabar, *Die Frescomalerei der Dimitrij Kathedrale* (The Fresco Paintings of the Dimitry Cathedral), which I brought out together with the publishing company *Die Schmiede* (The Smithy). This was a firm, recently established by some rich young people of a fairly Left-wing trend, "Parlour-Communists", who however had no justification for their ideology, either by their way of life, or by their origin. For some time these gentlemen put me off publishing books in German. But there turned up in Berlin Pavel Nikolaevich Milyukov, who offered *Russlands Zusammenbruch* (Russia's Collapse) for publication in German. I entered into an agreement with the well-known German publishing company *Deutsche Verlagsanstalt*, which agreed to publish books of Russian authors in German, in association with me.

I noticed that there were very few books on social science and history published in German. I also noted the absence of a German translation of Klyuchevsky's *History of Russia*[145]. While Milyukov presented me his book in an already excellent translation, things were more difficult with Klyuchevsky, for apart from his own language, the translator had to know Russian thoroughly.

I turned to Karl Staehlin, who occupied the Chair of Russian History at the Berlin University. After some consideration, he agreed to translate, of course for a decent fee. Translating did not come easily to him. I received, with great delays, an insignificant part of the translation, and then he refused to continue due to lack of time. I could not understand his decision, because a translation of Klyuchevsky would have, by itself, advanced him as a specialist. But then I was very pleased at his refusal, for his translation was quite useless, and completely lost Klyuchevsky's beauty of style. I will quote the following example: Staehlin translated the word *tselovalnik* as "kisser", without any elucidation. The "kissing" referred to was the kissing of a cross as part of the oath of allegiance of a government servant.

I turned for advice to my old friend, the former Assistant Dean of the Petrograd University, F. Braun, who occupied the Chair of Russian History at the Leipzig University (in Petrograd this was not his field, which was that of Romanic Languages).

Braun agreed immediately, but only to edit Klyuchevsky. As for the translation, I had to entrust it to someone else. It was important for Braun to edit a classic Russian historian, for this would confirm his position at the university as Professor of Russian History, who, for the first time in Germany, brought out a classical work of Russian historiography by her classic historian.

I found a translator in Reinhold von Walter. Walter had an excellent knowledge of Russian, he was himself an expert in

Russian poetry and the translator of Blok. Walter happened to be in constrained material circumstances, and decided to get to work, completing chapter after chapter, volume after volume, and as parts of the translation were supplied, he immediately received his fee.

Braun turned out to be an excellent and very painstaking editor. The volumes began to be published in German, and I completed that project. Braun's work brought us even closer together; besides, his son who was an arts student, gave drawing lessons to my son. He was received like a relative in our home. I consider the publication of Klyuchevsky in German to be a major contribution to German science[146].

I would like to note a sad fact. After Hitler came to power, Walter, who had been so carried away with Russian literature, and who had been considered to be progressive, sent a letter to my publishing company claiming that he had been exploited, and demanded an additional fee. The situation was actually the reverse. He had received more than we had agreed upon for the translation, and he had expressed his gratitude for this on every occasion. It is interesting to note how deep the infection of Nazism could penetrate into the midst of cultured people.

The publication of books in German was just beginning to have great prospects, there was no need to search for readers. Klyuchevsky and Milyukov immediately provided a large clientele for us, but our publishing activity in Germany was cut short by the rise of Hitler.

Chapter Twenty-three

Berlin Postscript – Krymov, Pasternak, Nabokov

Vladimir Pimenovich Krymov was an extraordinarily interesting person[147]. I became fairly closely acquainted with him in Berlin, approximately two years after I had arrived there, having been exiled from Russia in 1922.

Krymov was a talented writer. His family belonged to the sect of Old-Believers. This was reflected in his books which were largely autobiographical. He also wrote about his extensive travels. One of the books about his travels, which I published, was *Barbados and Caracas*. I published altogether seven volumes of his writings. He used to subsidize his books by covering the cost of paper and printing, but I obviously paid him an author's fee. He was well known, his books were popular and he retrieved all the money (back to the last cent) that he had invested in his books which I published.

Before the Revolution, Krymov, together with Suvorin, was the publisher of the Petersburg journal *Novoye Vremya* (*New Times*). This journal was conservative in the full sense of the word, and even with some inclination towards Black-Hundredism. One of its contributors was Burenin, who excelled himself only in *pogromist* outpourings. Another contributor was Leshchikov, a character of the same order. But, on the other hand, the editors somehow managed to attract many persons from literary circles.

For example: Chekhov started his writing career by publishing in *Novoye Vremya* a whole series of stories under the pseudonym of "Anton Chekhonte".

Another contributor to the journal was a very talented person, Vasily Vasilievich Rozanov, whose book *Opavshiye Listya* (*Fallen Leaves*) I later re-published in two volumes, in Berlin. This was a limited edition for literature buffs. Rozanov was a philosopher, although it could not be said that he was generally accepted in society, but his propositions were often very interesting and attracted attention[148].

Krymov combined the publishing of *Novoye Vremya* with the editorship and publishing of his own journal, *Stolitza i Usadba* (*Capital and Country Estate*). Having graduated from one of the best agricultural academies, the *Petrovsko-Razumovskaya Academy* at Moscow, where he studied together with one of the Grand Dukes, through whom he acquired access to Court circles, Krymov was able to establish important connections. Being thus closely connected with the nobility, he described, for a certain fee, the aristocrats' country estates in his publication, but he described them in a comparatively objective fashion: he commented on their architectural qualities and on the works of art which the estates contained. The owners, generally, paid large sums for the publicity given to their property in a high-class magazine. Even though the journal was established for mercenary and prestige reasons, *Stolitza i Usadba* is of great historical interest to this day, and can be used for the study of the history of the Russian aristocracy and of Russian architecture. The journal achieved a wide circulation and, as a result, Krymov managed to amass a large fortune.

This was not the only benefit from Krymov's contacts at Court. Through one of the Grand Dukes he established connections with the Department of Munitions, and when the war broke out in 1914, Krymov arranged with Henry Ford to supply armoured vehicles, lorries etc. for the Russian Army. He was sent to New York in order to sign an agreement to this effect, which he did while at the same time arranging a special commission for himself (not more than five or ten per cent). Everything had been properly attended to. However when the October Revolution broke out, it became clear not only that Ford would receive no payment, but also neither would Krymov receive his commission. Krymov did not waste any time, he and his wife took the Trans-Siberian Express to the Pacific Ocean, then they went by ship to Japan, and from there by some circuitous route to Europe and eventually to Berlin, the whole trip taking some four to five months.

Then, after a few years, when I was already publishing his books, he suddenly disappeared. He went to America, presumably on a tour. When he came back, he told the following story. That being determined to obtain his commission from Ford, he had put the matter into the hands of an outstanding lawyer, and that he had instructed him to settle the matter amicably and not let it go to court. Eventually a settlement was arranged, and Krymov received one million two hundred thousand dollars! This was only part of what should have been his due, but he agreed to the settlement, for if the matter had gone to court, the case would have taken ten to fifteen years.

After he had received all that money from Henry Ford, he gave a huge party. Genya and I were there, Roman Gul was there, Boris Ivanovich Nikolaevsky was there, Alexey Tolstoy was there, Boris Pilnyak was there[149].

These were people of completely different convictions and different trends. For example: what would Nikolaevsky have in common with the editor of *Novoye Vremya*, a conservative, while Nikolaevsky was a Menshevik? Well that's how "broad-minded" Krymov was.

Krymov felt no conflict between his political attitudes and his business dealings. Actually he was politically uncommitted. He was not a person of rightist convictions, neither was he a liberal, but he hated Communism. Yet when he came to Berlin, he busied himself with some very strange affairs through his connection with the Soviet Trade Delegation. The Soviets purchased everything on credit and added 12% or 14% interest yearly to the amounts indicated on their cheques, which thus increased in value the longer the payment was witheld. What did Krymov do? He bought up those cheques, did not cash them anywhere, but received his 12% or 14% yearly, and thus acquired huge sums of money. The money came about by itself, small sums grew into huge ones. What an astute business procedure![150].

There was another example of Krymov's imaginative business sense. When inflation broke out in Germany, Krymov began to order huge numbers of copies of *New York Times*, and *The Times*, London. These publications comprised veritable volumes, especially on Sundays. I believe that he ordered 100 copies of each issue, and he did not acquire all these papers for reading, but to sell them for recycling! He made quite a business out of this, and in this way he made money, without anybody waking up to it, either in New York, or London. Krymov made money on everybody and out of everything!

Krymov had his own ideas about lending money. He liked to lend money. How did he explain why he liked doing this? "You know", he said, "the Berlin writers' fraternity is financially a very poor lot. If I lend any of them money, they are then somehow under an obligation to me. And once they have taken the money, they do not return it, but neither do they come back again for more. Thus I am rid of them, but I have fulfilled my obligations to those in need, and my conscience is completely clear on that score. Of course, there are limits to this". Well, that is the type of person he was!

One day, Krymov invited Genya and me to his home. During dinner, I was amazed by something very strange, for while he treated us to champagne, and the dinner was something quite remarkable, the plates and glasses were as ordinary as they could be. "You have noticed my crockery", Krymov said, "but you see, if you break a glass or a plate, I would not mind at all, but if the crockery was china, I would mind very much if you broke it!" To this I replied: "But why do you treat us then to expensive French champagne? Could you not treat us to some cheap German champagne or cheap German wine instead?" "No", he said, "French champagne has a very definite taste, and the important thing about a meal is the quality of the food and wine".

Genya and I used to see a lot of him after this dinner and visited him often. The meals that he provided were always sumptuous. He was a good host. Also, there was always a good company of visitors at his home, many writers etc. He never commented on material matters. He only spoke about his trips, the acquaintances which he had established, about the journal *Novoye Vremya*, its Chief Editor, Suvorin, and he spoke a lot about Chekhov, whom he had met frequently.

While he was quite a remarkable host, his hospitality was combined with unbelievable meanness. For example, when something had to be purchased, say meat or poultry for dinner, he would go shopping himself, and would bargain and buy whatever was cheapest. He used to buy not just one item but two or three, only so as to get a discount. When he bought wine, he did not buy just three or four bottles, but bought wine and champagne by the case, so as to get a discount. He used to buy perishable food, like fruit, also by the box, and much of the contents had to be thrown out later. Once he offered me a pear which was quite rotten, and he suggested that I should cut out the bad part and eat the rest.

Krymov was completely devoid of any anti-Semitic feelings. His first wife, whom he treated with the greatest respect, was Jewish. When she died, he again married a Jewess and prided himself that his second wife resembled very much his first, and was, so to speak, her continuation. He was not only a model husband, but he supported his wife's entire family, and when the Nazis came to power, he immediately, and at his own expense, arranged for his wife's family to settle in Majorca. As for himself, he bought a property not far from Paris. The property was huge. The house had many rooms, and there were many servants, etc. This acquisition seemed to be quite fantastic, hard to understand, and not normal, but knowing how he had become wealthy, he was quite capable of buying that property in France.

When I used to travel to Paris, he asked me to be his guest there. His wife used to pick me up in the car, and took me to their home, where I boarded with them. But there was the following incident. Once I forgot to take a blade with me for my razor and asked him to lend me one. He gave me a blade which was completely rusty. I said to him, "Do you want to kill me by causing me to cut myself and get blood-poisoning? Or do you want me to pay you for a new blade?" He apologized for forgetting that the blade was a used one, and to my offer of paying for a new blade he said, "No, this was my oversight".

The gardener who worked on the property complained to me about Krymov. "He is a decent person", he said, "but greedy, terribly greedy". "Now", the gardener said, "there are flowers growing here. But it is not enough for him that there are flowers here, he goes and sells them to the neighbours, as if he needs that for a living".

I could tell many more stories about Krymov, for example about keeping special crockery for "outsiders". When an "outsider" was given the use of a cup, that cup was then destroyed.

Krymov explained that as "old believers", they obeyed the Rule that there has to be absolute cleanliness, so there had to be special crockery for "outsiders".

Krymov was very particular about both his and his wife's clothing, but in a rather extravagant manner. He used to go to the most luxurious shops and order for his wife not just one dress, but ten dresses, fifteen dresses, twenty dresses, and the main consideration was to thereby obtain a discount. At his home he and his wife had an unbelievable store of all kinds of garments. His wife used to give away the superfluous stock later on. Well, such was his way.

Krymov was quite a remarkable person! Incidentally, he was almost blind. He wore spectacles with lenses like magnifying glasses, and finally he went completely blind. He died in France, and his wife went to live in Spain[151].

Chapter Twenty-four

Hitler's Rise to Power

The political situation was absurd: the Social Democrats revealed weakness and complete inconsistency. The *Zentrum* [a Catholic Party corresponding to today's Christian Democrats] headed by Brüning[152], tried not to provoke a disagreement with the Nazis. Personally, Brüning was beyond reproach, but he was too weak a person for such stormy times. An agreement between the Social Democrats and the *Zentrum*, who, collectively, were not at all reactionaries, could have forestalled a catastrophe, but both sides feared for the purity of their garments. The Communists exacerbated the crisis even more. It appeared that the battle was between the Nazis and the Communists. A coalition between the Social Democrats and the *Zentrum*[153] could have smashed both extremist wings to smithereens, had they taken strong measures, including the application of armed force[154]. The bulk of the German army was conservative, Deutsch National, but not Nazi, apart from very small exceptions. There had been examples of the application of armed force in the past. Thus the regime of Béla Kun had been overthrown with lightning speed in Hungary, the same as the Hitler Putsch in Munich, and earlier, immediately after the First World War, the Communist uprising in Bavaria. The country was sliding into political confusion, and the danger of the seizure of power by the Nazis was real[155]. Most people believed this, but somehow this thought receded into the background.

Petropolis was celebrating its 10th Jubilee in a suburban hall in Grunewald. One can say that all socially active Russian circles of Berlin had come together for the celebration. I.V. Gessen, Yakov Noevich and myself, were presiding. Writers, journalists, publishers, lawyers, doctors and social activists came together. Some two hundred people attended. I have preserved a photograph of this gathering. Towards the end of the evening we received the ominous news that the Reichstag was on fire. We parted under the impact of this news.

Petropolis Press celebrates its 10th Jubilee on the same night of the Reichstag fire.

Chapter Twenty-five

Under the Third Reich

In summer, my family and I usually went on vacation, either in Germany or abroad. In the German health resorts one did not feel the growth of anti-Semitism. There were, of course, hotels and guesthouses which, under different pretexts, and at times directly, did not accept Jewish guests. But this is how it has been from way back, and we were not surprised at that. For even now in the free United States one can meet up with such occurrences. For example, there are many such hotels in the Poconos. Some simply do not accept Jews, others emphasize, especially in their advertisements, that there are churches of different denominations nearby. This means that Jews are not admitted at all, or, if they are admitted, that this would be done unwillingly, and that it would be necessary to live surrounded by hostile glances. The same applies also to clubs, many of which do not admit Jews as members.

In Germany, once Jews were admitted to a hotel or guesthouse, they did not feel any special discriminating attitude towards them if they wished to mix with non-Jewish guests. And it remained like this until after Hitler had come to power.

We spent one summer in Hahnenklee, in the Harz Mountains. The Harz Mountains were the centre of conservatism. The proprietors of our guesthouse were *Deutschnationale*[156], an old father and a middle-aged daughter. One could not find fault with their hospitality. One fine day during lunch, two middle-aged people, husband and wife, came into the dining room. By appearance they were typical Germans, in knickerbockers, with rucksacks on their shoulders. The husband looked around, saw on the wall a portrait of Bismarck, and announced loudly for everyone to hear: "Here is our Bismarck, here we shall stay!" To our amazement, upon further acquaintance, the pair turned out to be patriotically minded Jews.

But, to return to the attitude of the Germans to the Jews at that time, neither in Berlin nor in the Harz Mountains, nor in Bavaria, where we lived in different places and among mainly (though not exclusively) a Christian population, did I ever hear even one single insulting word. The political change which occurred with the accession of Hitler into power was completely beyond comprehension.

The German Jews reckoned that they were as much Germans as those who were gentiles, and the majority of them believed that Nazism would be directed only against the *Ost-Juden* (Jews from the East)[157].

We lived in Berlin in a building which belonged to a Jew by the name of Weber. He was nicknamed "Spirit-Weber" because he was in charge of a department controlling the production of alcoholic beverages. He informed us that he intended to subdivide the building into smaller apartments, and asked us to move upon the expiry of the contract, which was due to happen very shortly. I refused, since there was a provision for the contract to be renewed automatically, except in the case of arrears, and I was certainly not in arrears. Following upon my refusal to move came a letter from Weber, saying that the times had now changed (a direct hint at Nazism), and the letter was signed *mit Deutschem Gruss* [with German greeting], i.e. as befitted a Nazi. One cannot generalize that incident, but it was characteristic.

I can remember another incident which took place in an aristocratic, cultured family. The well-known publisher Cassirer,

159

who collected paintings and indulged in sport, had arranged a reception in his villa in honour of Bunin, who happened to be in Berlin after receiving the Nobel Prize[158]. (I had sold to Cassirer the translation of Bunin's works into German.) Genya and I had been invited. At the dinner table, Cassirer asserted hotly that he did not intend to leave Germany, that he was a primordial German whose ancestors had already lived for centuries in Germany, that Germany was his native land, and that Hitler was a newcomer. This was the mood of the bulk of the German Jews, who also kept themselves apart from the Eastern Jews. Incidentally, Cassirer left Germany at the last moment, and thus saved himself.

The establishment of the Third Reich had an effect on my publishing company. The activity of the publishing company continued, although a *Reichsschriftkammer* (literally: State Chamber of Writing) had been established, into which all publishers had been included, or rather registered, and to which "non-Aryans" were not admitted. We did not even consider registering, and practiced the policy of the ostrich – perhaps we would not be noticed, perhaps the regime would change.

We tried to send as many books as possible abroad, actually to Paris. There we had connections with *Dom Knigi* (House of the Book), managed by Kaplan. Yakov Noevich and I thought of joining it. There was a large premium on the export of books, as on the export of goods generally. I think that the premium was one-third of the value of each exported article. It was only required to send copies of the accounts to a corresponding department, and a premium had to be paid before receiving payment for the goods. Certain sums were forwarded to us for the sake of appearance. We also sent small sums abroad. Together with this, we feverishly looked for possibilities to obtain a visa. In the end, nothing came of our plans in respect of Paris. Both books and money evaporated. Only Yakov Noevich obtained a visa, and set himself up with OZE (an organization for assisting refugees), whilst I remained in Berlin.

Life under Hitler turned into an uninterrupted strain on the nerves. I would like to mention one incident. From time to time, a young man, a German, used to visit the publishing company. He was interested in Russian poetry, especially in Alexander Blok. He asked for advice on literature. Through us he used to order Soviet editions of Blok and other poets. He was very dapper and polite. One day this young man came to our office, bringing with him a copy of the official Nazi daily, *Völkischer Beobachter*, which used to be published in Germany. In it there was a notice, black on white:

> ...what strange things can occur in the Reich. The publisher of the American paper *Foreward*, by the name of Kagan, had visited Moscow and had travelled quietly through Germany to New York, where he owns the Russian publishing company Petropolis. Where were the eyes of our police?

When I read this notice I was stupefied, one could not imagine a worse misfortune. This notice spelt a catastrophe with unforeseen consequences. I had been confused with the publisher of the largest American Jewish paper.

My first thought was to turn to my manager, Armin Oscarovich Kreutzburg, who was a member of the Nazi Party. But the abovementioned young man stunned me with the remark that he was employed by the *Gestapo*, and had come, not with the aim of causing me some unpleasantness, but to get me out of this misfortune. He would personally resolve the misunderstanding, and I should not stick my nose into anything. He said that there would be no retraction in the paper, for this would only exacerbate the situation, and that he would turn up in a few days time. He claimed that he had joined the *Gestapo* for certain reasons, that he was an opponent of the Nazis, and was happy to do me a good turn.

I did not sleep that night, nor on the following two. I considered the young man a provocateur. After three days he turned up again, and said that everything had been settled. The person who had placed the notice was unhappy himself, because he might get it in the neck for that mistake.

Now about Kreutzburg, the manager of Petropolis. Some of my staff told me that they had seen him wearing full Nazi uni-form, at the head of some detachment on a parade in the neighbourhood. I called him to my office in order to clarify this, and put the question to him directly as to whether this was true or not? There followed just as direct an answer, yes, he had joined the Party, and was carrying out certain duties. He explained the reasons. He had lived for many years in Russia, in Petersburg. He had worked there in a German book firm on the Morskaya (I also used to order German and English books from that firm), and after the outbreak of the October Revolution he, as a Ger-man, was repatriated and left for Berlin. He had worked in various firms and finally, took a job at *Kniga*, a Soviet establishment which was the official Soviet bookshop, where he had the advantage of knowing the Russian language well, while German was also needed for dealing with the public. It was there, at *Kniga*, that I made his acquaintance. He was unhappy at having to work with Bolsheviks, and when I offered him employment, he agreed willingly. He finally became the manager of my office. When Hitler came to power he joined the Party in the interest of self- preservation, because having worked at *Kniga* could be considered an unremovable stain: once you worked there you must be a Bolshevik. It was on his conscience that he had not informed me of this. He gave me his word of honour that he would be loyal to my family, and me and that I could count on him. He kept his word[159].

In the beginning of 1938 we quite suddenly received a notice to leave Germany within ten days[160].

When, to our great delight, we received a visa to Belgium through our friends, the Duprez, there arose an unpleasant problem. The Belgian Consul would confirm a visa only if the Chief of Police would certify in our passports a permit for a return to Germany. The Chief of Police refused to issue such a certification, but Kreutzburg went to the police with our passports, and he obtained this certification[161].

We surrendered our apartment. To be precise, we left it as it was, sending away whatever could be sent away to Belgium through a firm of removalists, leaving the furniture behind. Incidentally, I placed a certain sum of money among the things which we sent away (I sewed it into a pillow) but the money was missing upon arrival in Belgium.

We moved to a guesthouse. Genya fell ill, and I placed her in a hospital. Kreutzburg used to visit her, quite like a close relative, and brought flowers. Genya was still in hospital when Kreutzburg came with the news that I was about to be arrested, and that I had to leave immediately. I could delay for one or two days, but not longer. I took Genya out of hospital straight to the station. Irene was brought to the train by our acquaintance, Liza Wolkenstein, with whom Irene had stayed whilst Genya was hospitalized. Only on the following day did Kreutzburg report our departure, and upon the enquiry by the police, answered that he had only just then found out about it. He was told off for negligence over this. If he had not acted as he did, we would have been stopped on the way or at the border.

Tolya had left before our departure. His visa to England had been obtained by Yakov Frumkin and Natasha Tumarkina (later Natasha Frank, according to her husband's surname)[162].

PART THREE

THE SECOND EXILE
1938–1941

Chapter Twenty-six

Belgian Interlude;
Belgian Postscript – Nabokov Again

[A.S.K. 49–51 years old]

The journey to Brussels proceeded without incident. Nobody held us up on the way.

Our friends, the Duprez, met us at the station in Brussels and took us to a guesthouse into which they had booked us, situated in a quiet lane opposite the house in which the Prime Minister of Belgium, Spaak, lived.

Sonya and Christophe Duprez were extremely warm and kind to us. Christophe took Genya to the hospital on the following day to Professor Delayez, who found that her gall bladder was in such a condition that an operation was imperative and had to be done as soon as possible, a delay would be a threat to life. On the following day, Christophe booked her into the Red Cross Hospital, at which Delayez was the chief surgeon. He operated immediately. The gall bladder was already infected, and one could say that the operation was made at the last moment. Christophe, who was a heart specialist and a professor at the University of Brussels, was present during the operation and visited Genya several times during the following days, while Sonya did not leave the hospital at all, and spent the first few nights there. The Duprez took Irene to their home.

The operation was successful, and I was given a small bag full of the gallstones, which had been removed.

After a fortnight Genya was discharged. Sonya brought food and looked after us. I never expected such concern, it was beyond all measure. It is true that Sonya was Genya's friend from early childhood, and I too knew her from early years, but what they did for us was beyond price. Christophe became very attached to Irene, and André, Duprez's son, treated her as if she was his own sister. They offered me money. I was very touched. Since I had some small savings I declined their offer, but they made it with such goodwill, that if I really had been in need, I would have accepted it.

The Duprez had a wonderful home. The ground floor was taken up by Christophe's rooms, where he received patients. The top floor contained the family's living quarters, the intermediate floor was intended for visitors, and below there was a large room for gymnastics and table tennis. A glazed door from the dining room led to a good-sized garden. We visited them often, had lunch and dinner with them, and they called on us every day. They also found an apartment for us not far from them, in a building with all conveniences (146 Rue Antoine Bréart), a stone's throw from a park.

We had arrived with a temporary visa, and our position had to be legalized. Duprez introduced me to a lady lawyer, Mme Aimée Racine, Professor of Sociology at the University of Brussels. She arranged for the legalization of our position, and we received a permit for permanent residence and work in Belgium.

Sonya enrolled Irene at a school, and André took her there every morning, and later I took over that task. Not knowing the French language, Irene felt alien at school, and she was ashamed that she could only speak German. She was as if mute. I explained the situation to the teacher, who was most understanding. Irene proved to be very receptive, and she soon started to gabble in French and became a very good student.

It is interesting to note that in spite of exceptionally difficult conditions, not only was I not depressed, but I was not really worried as to how I would establish myself, how I would live, tied up as I was with my family, almost without means and acquaintances apart from the Duprez. They, of course, were a great moral support.

Once again I would like to remark what wonderful people they were. Christophe had an extensive practice, but he did not charge fees to those who were in need. However, he gave them the same attention as he did to his wealthy patients. Christophe and Sonya used to store up food, and on Sundays distribute it among the needy patients, while Christophe ordered medicines for which he paid himself. Of course, they lived comfortably, but the element of profit or love of money was completely absent.

I never had any doubts about being able to continue my publishing activity. It turned out that in Brussels there was a large Russian colony, and soon I became acquainted with many of its members. There was also a Russian club, the president of which was Alexander Moiseyevich Kulisher, who introduced me into it.

In Brussels there also happened to be a Russian printery, where they knew me and offered credit. There was a Belgian firm which imported Soviet books, and I could order these, and also antiquarian books, so that I could supply my foreign clients, as well as Belgian establishments and private persons.

I resumed correspondence with my authors, for example, with Nabokov, Khodasevich, Osorgin, Professor Vernadsky, Kaydanova and others. I made the acquaintance of Professor Ekk and his associates, and I established a connection with Antwerp. My reputation was good, and I was sure that I would find the necessary capital, or more correctly, obtain credit. After a short time, the carrying out of book orders began to bring in an income, and I could make ends meet.

To begin with, I published Kaydanova's book about popular education in Russia. I had already published the first volume of this work in Berlin. I received the manuscript of Khodasevich's *Memoirs*, a very interesting book. I also received from Professor Vernadsky his *Outline of Russian History*. Vernadsky had already moved to the United States, and had become Professor of History at Yale University. I began to publish one book after another[163].

I carried on a lively correspondence with Osorgin. His wife, Bakunina, had been working already for many years on a large work, *Encyclopedia of Russian Masonry*. The French Masons were interested in this work, and Professor Ekk was the connecting link. Bakunina could not find a publisher, and was very pleased when I accepted her book for publication. The work was extensive. The proofs travelled from Paris to Brussels and back. The typesetting (in French) was carried out in one of the best Belgian printeries. The book had a magnificent cover corresponding to the great significance of this work. Its publication was quite an event[164].

I became drawn into a milieu that was new to me. Acquaintances sprang up. I took a lively part in the Russian cultural circle. Professor Bem, a person close to me and with whom I corresponded, wrote about me to his disciple Landsman, who worked in the Belgian Ministry of Foreign Affairs, and we became acquainted. Landsman was a pure Fleming. His main interest was Russian literature. He had enrolled at the University of Prague, where he graduated. He had mastered the Russian language so well that he could speak it fluently and write to me in Russian. Genya and I became close friends with him and his charming wife. We visited each other, and they often took Irene to their small cottage on the outskirts of the town. I introduced them to the Duprez. Landsman used to travel to Moscow on ministerial business, and there he called on Sonya's sister to whom he passed on parcels and money.

I travelled all over Belgium. In Ghent I met up with childhood friends. We sometimes called on them and they called on us in Brussels. Life in Brussels proceeded fairly peacefully. Tolya visited us with his wife[165] on his way to Australia. We spent the summer at Niewport-sur-Mer where we stayed on full board at a Russian guesthouse. I travelled twice to Paris.

The events in Germany did not concern the Belgians greatly. It is interesting to note that we did not know about the existence of concentration camps[166]. Of course we knew about the persecution of the Jews, which, according to rumours, went as far as dispossession and enforced exile. There were rumours about disorders resulting in human casualties, Jewish of course, and the destruction of synagogues. Only in the beginning of 1940 was there talk about concentration camps. There were all kinds of rumours, but nobody believed these.

The majority of people were certain that the alliance of Britain, France and Russia would be the winner in the ripening conflict. All were firmly convinced that the Soviet Union would be on the side of Britain and France. There was some alarm after Chamberlain's trip and the betrayal of Czechoslovakia.

In the beginning of 1940 the Russian Club invited Mark Lvovich Slonim to give a lecture on the current situation. He produced a shattering impression on us. He pointed to the weakness of France, torn by party conflicts and the possibility of Hitler's victory over her. He pointed to the wavering position of the Soviet Union, talks with her were dragging on, and there was doubt whether she would join the Allies. Slonim's observations, of which I was sceptical, turned out to be prophetic.

I would like to point to a seemingly insignificant event. As mentioned earlier, I used to order Soviet publications through a Belgian firm. As I visited that firm one day, the manager, who apparently was a Communist, and with whom I used to talk about current events, stated directly to me, as if it was an accomplished fact, that Belgium, Holland and the northern countries, would be occupied by the German armies within a few days, and that France would be crushed within a short time; also that it was naive to consider Russia an ally, and that she would decide to break off relations with the Allies any day. The whole of Europe would be conquered by the Germans. I was overwhelmed by this forecast, but in the main that is just what happened. Soon the Second World War began[167].

Chapter Twenty-Seven

A Wartime Odyssey

[A.S.K. 51 years old]

In the beginning of May 1940 the German armies invaded the neutral countries, not encountering any effective resistance on the way, occupying one town after another, and coming down like an avalanche on Belgium and France.

I do not remember the exact date, but it was in the middle of May, when German planes began to bomb Brussels during the night. As we were in our underwear, we donned our dressing gowns and went down into the basement.

Next morning, when it was still dark, Christophe phoned and said that it was necessary to get on the way. We should take whatever was necessary, the same as he and Sonya, and should be ready for him to pick us up. There were three of us and two of them, since André had been called-up and was at the Front.

The Duprez' motorcar was spacious and comfortable. Sonya had taken a basket of food with her, the same as us, which was provident, since nothing could be obtained on the way. The car was filled with petrol, and an additional huge tank of petrol was also taken. The Duprez were ready in no time and came to pick us up. It was early morning, the weather was beautiful. The city was already choked up with motorcars. We moved at a snail's pace. Shells exploded around us all the time, but we did not notice any direct hits[168].

We took the course towards the French border. I distinctly remember that we, including Irene, kept cool and did not give way to nervousness.

After we had left the city and had come onto an excellent highway, a depressing picture revealed itself. Everything was choked with cars. Hand-carts and horse-carts as well as antediluvian carriages which had appeared from somewhere. One had the impression that the whole population of Belgium was leaving and moving West to France.

We crawled very slowly, only stopping to let Christophe have a rest. Late at night we were on a road leading through a forest, to which we had been directed by a squad of British soldiers. Having lost our way, we were moving cautiously along the forest. We were approaching some large home, apparently belonging to a big landowner. Here we were again stopped by British soldiers, and a young officer suggested that we should come inside. This turned out to be the Staff Headquarters. We were received in a more than friendly manner. We were given some strong tea with sandwiches. Some benches and couches were cleared for us, and it was suggested that we have a few hours sleep before proceeding on our way at sunrise. At night we would only wander around, be stopped by patrols, etc.

We were awakened at sunrise, were given precise road instructions and best wishes for success. Irene was showered with sweets. The British soldiers and officers were beautifully outfitted, disciplined and cleanly shaven, as if they were not at war.

Our directions had been given with mathematical precision, and after a few hours we came to the French border. We took our place in the queue of motorcars and carriages, and waited our turn. On one side of the border there stood Belgian soldiers and officers, on the other − French. In the centre there was a barrier, and a bridge could be seen beyond. The barrier was raised and lowered after the passage of each vehicle.

Our troubles started at the border. Belgian nationals were allowed through without exception, as well as those who had a visa into France. We had nothing apart from a residential permit, on which it was indicated that we were Russians. In spite of Christophe's eloquence we were not allowed through, but Irene, as a minor, was allowed to go with the Duprez. The officer in charge gave us his "officer's word of honour" that tomorrow morning everybody would be allowed through, and to apply to him personally if there were any misunderstandings. He also suggested that we should spend the night in a nearby village. We said goodbye to Irene and the Duprez, and took a few addresses in Bordeaux, for which they were heading in search of André's army unit which was supposed to be stationed there.

We were very depressed, as perhaps we would never see our little girl again. We went to the small village to seek accommodation for the night. We were received in a friendly way at the very first house at which we knocked. We were given a room with a bed and clean linen, and were also given some tasty black bread and butter, and as much milk as we wanted.

Here strange things started to happen. Late at night, voices were heard on the other side of the wall, a male and two female voices. They spoke German. We had a terrible thought: had the Germans arrived already, or did the voices belong to spies? Of course, we could not sleep any longer.

We decided to go to the border as soon as it was light. We opened the door of our room and saw a man and two women, apparently mother and daughter, and this is what they turned out to be. The daughter had a bandaged foot. They were also getting ready to leave, and their car stood beneath the window of the house. We introduced ourselves. Their name was Kaufmann, they were German Jews and they also intended to flee to France. We told them our story and asked them to take us with them. We indicated that, even if we crossed the border, our position would be one without a way out. The husband would not agree on any account to take us with them, but his wife and daughter began to plead with him and finally told him that if he did not take us, then they also would not go, and that he could go on his own. He had to agree, and we seated ourselves in the motorcar.

On the border the barrier was up. There was nobody there, but there was a guard on the bridge ahead. It was an opening bridge, and it was just about to be raised. Kaufmann gave full throttle without taking any notice of the shouting of the guard, and in a few minutes we found ourselves on the other side of the bridge, where the French guards did not stop us, and we drove on a marvellous road to Boulogne-sur-Mer.

Some five miles from Boulogne, Kaufmann stopped the car and delivered himself of a long speech. We were Jews of Russian descent, the Russians were on the same side as the Germans, whilst they were German Jews without any rights in France. If we were arrested, we would all suffer, and our connection would appear suspect. He had rescued us, we were now in France, it was not far from Boulogne, and we must part company. We had to agree with this, thanked him, and took our leave of the ladies. They even gave Genya a kiss.

We left the car and went on our way with our two small suitcases. It was a wonderful day. The wide road was planted with trees on both sides. Having gone some distance, we sat down under a tree in order to take a rest. A French patrol car went by, the officer alighted and approached us. He asked us politely where we were going. We answered: "To Boulogne". He did not enter into any further conversation and asked how he could help.

We explained our situation and thanked him for his enquiry. He left, and after a short time, the same patrol car returned, and again the officer approached us. He said that "Madame" was obviously tired, and he considered it his duty to deliver us to Boulogne. He stopped one of the numerous cars, which were all travelling in one direction, and ordered the driver to take us to Boulogne. On no account was the driver to take money from us (the car was a private one), and he should take us to wherever we wished, to either the police headquarters or to the station.

We thanked our unusual officer-saviour, and the car very rapidly took us to Boulogne, to the station, as we had asked the driver, who warmly took leave of us and wished us a happy journey.

I went up to the booking office. The booking clerk told me that one of the last trains was leaving for Paris in two hours. I had only Belgian money and U.S. dollars. The clerk said that she could not accept foreign money, and that I would have to go into town to change it. I left the station but a policeman told me that I could not get through to the town because the bridge had been raised. I returned to the booking clerk and told her of my bad luck and of what threatened to be in store for us. There was no need to beseech her for a long time, she agreed to take Belgian francs for the tickets. What is more, she offered to change a certain amount of money so that we would not be left without francs on the way. She effected the exchange at the rate current at that time, and not in the manner of a money lender. After shaking the booking clerk's hand we immediately boarded the train which was already standing half empty at the station.

So far we had been lucky.

There was no division into classes on the train. People boarded it wherever they happened to be. First there were hardly any passengers, but later, from the next stop on, there were so many that the eye could not take them all in. They were mainly soldiers and sailors, and not from any particular unit, but from different regiments. They were not on leave, but had lost contact with their units or were deserters. In our compartment there were only sailors. Genya had not quite recovered from her operation and was worn out from all that had happened during the last two days. The sailors kindly cleared a seat for us, and during the stops they went to fetch us boiling water[169].

The train moved at a snail's pace, not only stopping at every station, but anywhere on the line. First one could hear separate shots, later the noise strengthened, and the exchange of fire was so close that we could hear the bullets whistling, and everyone had to lie on the floor. As we approached Paris, the exchange of fire decreased until it eventually ceased altogether.

The thought that could not be pushed aside, as to what would happen to us upon arrival in Paris, worried us. Would we be allowed to get off the train? Would we be taken to the police? We had no documents at all to stay in France. Here again we were lucky: air-raid sirens wailed as we were approaching Paris, and as we stopped the gendarmes chased everybody out of the carriages. There was no way that documents could be checked. We waited at the station until the "all clear" was sounded. We immediately left the station and took the first taxi we could find. Our worry receded a little. We were in Paris, and we still had a breathing spell.

We drove to the Blokhs. They were about to leave Paris shortly, for the Germans were already close. We spent the night at Blokh's sister, Raya. She was about to leave at night, and her husband Misha had already left with their child. I called on the Lozinskys. Raya's apartment remained vacant.

In the morning I made tracks for the OZE, where Yakov Noevitch worked. There I met Frumkin and Dan[170] with Dan's wife, Lydia Osipovna. Their organization was also about to leave Paris. Frumkin and the others recommended that we should leave for Bordeaux without delay. Frumkin gave me a letter to an acquaintance who could assist us to find shelter, since

Bordeaux was already overcrowded. I had a lengthy conversation with Dan. He gave me a friendly letter to the Mayor of the City of Bordeaux, Marke, and to Professor Bonard at the local university.

Immediately after picking up our meagre belongings, we went to the station. We waited for a long time in a queue for tickets, and finally got onto the train, which was leaving for Bordeaux. The train was crowded to capacity.

We reached Bordeaux safely. There were crowds of people in all streets. It was unthinkable that we could find a room at a hotel. Here Frumkin's letter was of great help. We went to the address that he had indicated. The occupiers were people of modest means, husband and wife, still quite young. The apartment was tiny. They received us warmly, invited us to spend the night with them, and treated us to a modest dinner. They gave up their own bedroom for us, and slept on the couch in the dining room. But we were quite incapable of sleep: in all my life I have never encountered such a quantity of bedbugs and fleas!

In the morning I went to see Marke, the Mayor, but I was unlucky. He had been appointed a Minister, had left, and it was not known when he would return.

Then Genya and I made our way to the University to find out the address of Professor Bonard. His name was not in the telephone book, so that he would not be disturbed. The University, according to its rules, would not disclose his address, but somehow I succeeded in talking the clerk into doing so, and we obtained it.

In the morning, Genya and I set out to see the professor. A little old lady answered the bell, and said that her son (i.e. Bonard) had been appointed Minister for the Colonies, and was currently in Algiers. His wife, who turned out to be a doctor, had also left, for she had been "called up", and was at some military hospital.

We were desperate. On seeing our predicament, the old lady enquired as to our reason for calling on Bonard. I said that I had a letter to him from an acquaintance, containing a request to assist us. I handed her the letter, and asked that she open it, since it did not contain anything secret, but would only explain the request regarding assistance to us.

She invited us in and asked us to sit down. After reading the letter, she said that since her son and daughter-in-law were away, and it was not known when they would return, she was able to invite us to stay in their apartment. Bonard's mother lived in another part of the house with her daughter and son-in-law. She insisted that we should be their guests. We were overwhelmed by such a turn of events. After all the experiences, we found ourselves in a cosy environment among friendly and kind people. We stayed and boarded with them while we remained in Bordeaux.

Bonard's sister was Headmistress of the High School in Bordeaux, and when the Duprez brought Irene to us, she became enrolled there. Moreover, Bonard's sister used to take Irene with her and bring her back after studies. On weekends we went with them into the surrounding countryside. It was impossible to hint at any payment, and when once I brought a bottle of cognac for dinner, I was firmly chided, for this was taken as an insult, since we were thought of as being members of the family, and had to consider ourselves as such. If anyone had told us a story similar to ours, I would not have believed it. We were unbelievably fortunate.

As we had agreed, I informed the Duprez of our address, and they, as mentioned above, brought Irene to us. We had been very worried by uncertainty, but things turned out as best as possible. The Bonafous (Bonard's sister and her husband) loved Irene very much and spoilt her. Thus we lived for several weeks. Then the Duprez decided to return to Belgium. Christophe was a native of Belgium, a "pure Aryan" and a professor, and nobody would conceive that his wife was a Jewess. Then André Duprez turned up in Brussels. Fortunately, the Duprez survived the whole period of the occupation and, whilst in constant anxiety, remained unharmed.

But our quiet life was terminated by the approach of the Germans, and here our hospitable hosts came to our rescue. The husband of Bonafous' sister took us to a village near Cadillac, where the Council accommodated us in a vacated villa. Fortunately, as it turned out later, I was not registered with the Council, and, for the time being, we were not bothered. We lived there for about a week.

One morning, a messenger from the Council came to us and announced that we should call there. The Germans had arrived and were making a census of the population.

We immediately collected our modest luggage and made our way to the highway on the bus route between Cadillac and Bordeaux. We had decided that it was easier to hide in a large town. We plodded along the highway. Fortunately the bus arrived soon.

We found ourselves again in Bordeaux, and made our way straight to the Bonafous. To hide with them would be dangerous, and they suggested to us to leave for Toulouse, which was within the unoccupied zone. They took us to the station, purchased our tickets, and we settled down in the train bound for Toulouse.

On the border between the two zones, there had to be a check of the passengers. But the train did not stop, and the German soldiers did not manage to get as far as our carriage.

We got off safely in Toulouse. But at the exit one had to pass through a cordon of gendarmes. Again sheer luck came to our assistance. Irene had somehow become separated from us, we started to look for her, and in all the hassle the gendarmes let us through, seeing that we were trying to find our child. We found Irene among the crowd.

We went to the hotel opposite the station. There we met a large number of our acquaintances, amongst them: Nikolaevsky, the Abramoviches, Yugov [prominent Mensheviks] and others. But we could not stay at the hotel, for there were no rooms available, and we had no documents. It was necessary to think of finding shelter.

A group of the escapees from Belgium settled on the outskirts of the town. We were directed to a small street. There I saw a very plump elderly woman standing in front of one of the houses. Noticing that we were going from house to house, she asked us for whom were we actually looking? When I told her that we were looking for temporary accommodation, she said that if we would not spurn an annexe adjoining her house, she would gladly give us shelter. Having found out that we were refugees from Belgium, she melted completely.

There was no furniture in the annexe, apart from a wardrobe and a couple of chairs. There was a washbasin and a toilet off the corridor connecting the annexe with the house. A door gave access to the garden in which there were seats and all kinds of fruit trees. The woman offered us some mattresses and bed linen, and we bedded down straight on the floor.

Our hosts, the abovementioned woman and her husband, an old man, were very good to us. We bought food in a small shop nearby, and our hosts brought us boiling water for making tea. We frequently shared our meal with them. There was an abundance of berries and fruit in the garden, and our hosts brought plenty of these to us, if we did not pick them ourselves.

We spent several weeks there, and this is where we lived when we were visited by Yakov Noevich, who had left Paris together with the OZE staff. He offered to take Irene and enrol her in one of the OZE children's homes. We declined, since we did not want to part with our child.

In the morning I went into town to look up some acquaintances and to ascertain the situation. I found out that Rabbi Dr Eisenstadt, who was a friend of my father's in St Petersburg and a friend of our family, was in Toulouse. I went to see him. He was very happy to see me and told me that I could count on him to get me out of my difficult situation. It turned out that he, together with Vladimir Abramovich Goldenberg (we used to be friends with the Goldenbergs in Berlin), were assisting refugees upon instructions from the aid organization JOINT.

A Jewish committee, *Société des Juifs en France*, also assisting refugees, was operating in Toulouse. It was composed of representatives of all Jewish parties, and prepared lists of refugees by which Dr Eisenstadt and Goldenberg were guided when distributing assistance.

Dr Eisenstadt did not intend to remain in Toulouse. He expected a United States visa. He asked me if I would like to take his place after he had left? Of course, I agreed on the spot, and it came about that I began to work with Goldenberg before Eisenstadt's departure. I was co-opted into the Committee. The circle of my acquaintances increased every day.

I asked Dr Eisenstadt to establish contact with my relatives who were already in New York, and to apply for a visa for my family and myself. On the day before his departure Dr Eisenstadt left me a small sum of money, as he had been requested by my relatives.

Among my acquaintances, there happened to be Cassorla, the Rabbi of Toulouse. He was a member of the Aid Committee for Foreign Students, which had representatives of different religions, Catholic and Protestant, and, among their number, the Archbishop of Toulouse, who later rendered me a great service. A representative of the Jewish community by the sonorous name of Picart, was also a member of the Committee. Cassorla, who was of Spanish descent, was an exceptionally good person, who had worked hard for his congregation, in which activity he was assisted by Eisenstadt and Goldenberg and later by myself. Cassorla achieved the legalization of my position, and I received a *carte d'identité*. I worked hand in hand with Goldenberg, and our friendly relations were strengthened.

We moved into town, Irene enrolled at the school, and life somehow got onto an even keel. I hoped all the time to obtain a visa to the United States.

Goldenberg and I worked in complete harmony, if one leaves out of account that Goldenberg, who was usually cool and had good manners, used to fly into a rage at the slightest cause. One reason for this was that among the refugees whom we had to assist, there were quite a few people who, when applying for assistance, invented stories about the composition of their families, the degree of their need, etc. Goldenberg used to get beside himself over this. To be sure, in such circumstances it was difficult to accuse people. For example, one rabbi tried to get assistance from us, concealing that he had been receiving aid from another source (it was actually from the same JOINT). The writer "Y"[171], whose books I had published, used to receive assistance from us as a Jew, and from a Christian committee as a non-Jew! Of course this was bad, but then, after all, he was not a rich man.

Goldenberg used to work in Berlin at the French Legation, and had already received French citizenship there, having changed his name to Dormont[172], which of course, he did not use in Berlin. Whilst in France he used it only when dealing with the authorities. Goldenberg was a good person, but was a stickler for formality, and when the Jews were being registered, he foolishly also registered himself as such, although nobody induced him to do so. Besides, his French name and citizenship would have protected him from all suspicion. I, of course, did not register. When the general arrests of all Jews began, which occurred after my departure, Goldenberg and his wife were also arrested and sent to a concentration camp where he perished, but his wife survived.

In the *Société des Juifs en France* we were kept busy not only by compiling lists of refugees, but we often met to discuss the situation as it had arisen. People who worked in the *Résistance*, both Jews and pure-blooded Frenchmen, also called on us. We were kept informed on all that was going on.

To all appearances we lived normally, went visiting, Irene went to school, had girlfriends. She even received a *Certificat de Mérite* for her progress, signed by Pétain, Hitler's puppet, presiding over "Unoccupied" France. There are such jokes!

The position of foreigners was by no means a secure one. Many started to leave, especially the Mensheviks. I began a determined correspondence regarding a visa to the United States. Nikolaevsky made strenuous moves on our behalf in New York, but as yet had no positive news to convey. Our relatives, who were now in New York, were also slow. A lady of our acquaintance, Z. Kuchuk, who, when working for me in Berlin, was brought into contact with a photographic news-agency, and who, through that agency, managed to get to the United States, declined to send an affidavit, although she was very much under obligation to me.

I have already mentioned that I had friendly relations with Professor Vernadsky whose books I had been publishing in Brussels. He had moved from Prague to the United States, where he became a professor at Yale University. I wrote to him, asking him for an affidavit. At the same time, I wrote to Countess Sofya Vladimirovna Panina, who had not as yet left Prague. She answered that I had acted correctly by writing to Vernadsky, and that she was also writing to him about me. Both of them made my hopes rise.

One of my good acquaintances, Goldstein, a Menshevik, had left for the United States with his family, and passed his apartment in Avenue Bonnefois on to us. I was very pleased that I finally had my own corner, but my satisfaction turned out, or rather could have turned out tragically for me in connection with the German occupation, for on one not so fine day, French police came to the house where we lived, and asked the porter whether there were any Russians living there? The porter pointed to me, and I was arrested. Genya and Irene were left free.

Here I would like to mention one incident which occurred before I was arrested. Since at that time it was impossible to get to Spain or Portugal, even if one had a visa, and since these countries demanded a passport for the visa, I had to undertake something in this respect. In Toulouse there was a Polish Consulate which was full of bribe-takers. Through an intermediary I obtained a genuine, not a false, Polish passport, although I had had no connection with Poland at all. Such passports were signed by the Consul, numbered, and entered into the books. In short, all as was required. When they came to take me into the camp, I went to the toilet and tore up this passport into bits and dropped these into the bowl. I busied myself there for a long time, for the tough paper was caught up in the toilet and could not be flushed down. The gendarmes started to lose patience and knocked on the door. All I needed was to be charged for concealing my nationality!

I was taken to the camp of Récébédou, situated in immediate proximity to Toulouse. I was placed in a separate building together with all the others who had been arrested. Almost everyone there turned out to be an acquaintance. Goldenberg with Genya came to visit me, and I asked Goldenberg to inform Rabbi Cassorla and the Bishop of Toulouse about my arrest. In the camp they held mainly Spanish prisoners who had fled to

France during the Spanish Civil War. While the gendarmes were polite to us, they were beastly to the Spaniards and beat them for any sort of reason. The Spaniards were very badly fed, one could say they were on the verge of starvation. We could see from the windows of our barrack how the Spaniards were sauntering singly over the field in search of food scraps. They carefully collected cigarette butts and hid them in their clothing. We had enough food for ourselves due to the food parcels we used to receive, and we managed, not without difficulties, to pass on the surplus, as well as the camp rations which we had not touched, to the unfortunate Spaniards.

I would like to remark regarding the life in the Recebedou camp, that we, the people of Russian descent, were not subjected to any measures of coercion. We could receive parcels which were not checked, could move freely in allocated places, and the French gendarmes generally did not harass us. But what poisoned the existence was that there were no separate toilets, that one had to go to a common latrine which was a real cesspool. One would not even consider to sit down, and the stench was incredible. People often defecated outside the latrine, especially when it became dark, so as not to be noticed by the gendarmes. The latrine was a source of infection, for the population of the camp was numerous, and many suffered from dysentery. The latrine was a nightmare for everybody.

I was released after a short time, thanks to the efforts of the Bishop who vouched for me. Incidentally, the policeman who took me back to Toulouse got talking to me, and having found out that I intended to go to the United States, asked me seriously to help him also to emigrate.

Professor Vernadsky kept his promise. A short while after my release from the camp I received a letter from him, in which he stated that he had asked one of his pupils by the name of Bromberg, who was a member of the *Eurasian* group, to sponsor me. Vernadsky had already sponsored a number of persons and feared that he could only spoil things by applying for yet another.

Several days after receiving the letter from Vernadsky, I actually received quite an extraordinary letter from Bromberg, whom I did not know at all, in which he wrote that he would be happy to give me an affidavit and undertake all measures in order to speed up all formalities, and that this was negligible compared with what I had done for him. I had made the dream of his life come true! I was so overwhelmed by this letter that, in the beginning, I thought he was confusing me with somebody else. Then I remembered that many years ago I had published Bromberg's book, *Europe and Eurasia*, upon the recommendation of my Prague friend, Pyotr Petrovich Savitsky. Savitsky attended to the proofs and the editing, but I never had any correspondence with Bromberg.

I immediately conveyed to Bromberg my boundless thanks, and wrote that I did not know how I had earned his attitude towards me, but that he was really saving my family and me. The reply was not late in coming, and it really turned out that my favour had consisted in publishing his book, which he previously had unsuccessfully tried to bring out, and that he was at my disposal for the rest of his life! And soon after this I received news from the U.S. Consul in Marseille, that an affidavit had arrived for me, and that I should come to Marseille to receive the visa.

Our preparations did not take long. I took my leave from acquaintances and friends, especially from Goldenberg. I saw him several more times in Marseille, which he visited in connection with the affairs of our Jewish Committee.

In Marseille I was taken up with the affairs of *Société des Juifs en France* and calls to government departments in connection with receiving the visas. Birth certificates, which we did not possess, were required. Our case was far from singular. Fortunately, in Marseille, there was still a pre-revolutionary Russian Consulate, and there we received our birth certificates[173].

It turned out that without passports we could not obtain transit visas through Spain or Portugal, but had to travel via Casablanca. This involved travelling by ship from Port Vendres to Oran, and from there by train to Casablanca.

We set out to the U.S. Consulate to obtain the visas. Here an unpleasant surprise awaited us. We had a *sauf conduit* (travel safe conduct) for a relatively short period. The Consul stated that he could not issue a visa on such a document. What if we were delayed on the way, and the document would expire? I tried to convince the Consul that this was our risk; that it was important to obtain the visas; that misunderstandings could be cleared up on the way, for the visas issued to us would be permanent; that after a certain time we would become U.S. citizens, and that he, as a Consul, would have to display to us, as future U.S. citizens, the most favourable attitude, and not place us under threat of falling into Nazi hands. None of my entreaties helped, and the Consul stated that he could not issue visas on our *sauf conduit* papers, unless we extended these. This meant sending the papers for extension to the Police Department in Vichy, which was by then already in the Occupied Zone, and the documents would not be extended there.

Next morning, in despair, I went to the Police Department. The porter obviously thought that I had come from the U.S. Consulate and not on my own private business, and let me pass. The square in front of the Department was crowded with people waiting for the doors to open, and if I had not been admitted into the building there and then, I could not have got in there on that day.

I made my way to the Secretariat. The Secretary turned out to be a young and beautiful woman. I told her frankly what had happened at the Consul. At first she also said that my papers must go to Vichy, but we got to talking, and she said that she would "try something". She took the *sauf conduit* papers, and asked me not to leave but to wait in her office. Then, in my presence, she saw a few more applicants and left, having locked the door behind her. I waited for about an hour until she came back.

"You were lucky", she said. It turned out that she had put my papers among a large heap of others, marking them *Valable jusqu'à l'arrivée aux Etats Unis* (valid until arrival in United States), and the Sub-Prefect signed them without reading. I thanked her warmly, saying that she had saved us from a great misfortune. She asked me to call on her after I had seen the U.S. Consul, and gave me a pass so that I would be allowed into the building.

Next day, I called at the U.S. Consulate. Although I maintained that I had already been at the Consul on the previous day, and had brought what he had requested, we were again made to wait in the queue. After having waited for several hours, we were finally admitted to the Consul. When he saw the signatures on our papers, he could not believe his eyes. "How did you achieve that?", he asked. "Quite simply", I answered. "There are still humane people who adopt an attitude which is actually the one which you, and not the Chief of Police, should have taken". He became embarrassed by my pointed remark, and only replied that he was an official and had to stick to the letter of the law.

Then Genya and Irene were placed at two separate tables and were questioned separately, while I remained with the Consul. All this amounted to an attempt to catch us out by revealing some contradictions. I told Genya to say that she could not speak French, while Irene was still a little girl and simply could not give any evidence, since she did not know anything.

It turned out that the fare had to be paid by us, and that our guarantor had to be prepared to assume responsibility for our maintenance. Our visas were issued, but as yet not given to us. There were still to be various inoculations against smallpox, etc to be undergone.

We went to the U.S. doctor, that is, the doctor at the Consulate. He looked the three of us over and asked if we had ever been inoculated? We answered in the affirmative, and he asked us to pull up our sleeves. This was the end of the "inoculations". The doctor then presented us with a bill, which we had to pay on the spot, our first encounter with corruption. On the ship, the ship's doctor discovered that no inoculations had been carried out by the Consulate's doctor, and then we were all duly inoculated by him.

The inoculation certificate of the Consulate's doctor remained at the Consulate attached to our file. I must say that the attitude towards us and to other clients was rude and unfriendly. And this was the attitude displayed to future citizens of the United States, where, once we had arrived, we found the attitude to us to be the very opposite to that displayed by the Consul.

Early in the morning of the next day, I took some flowers to the Secretary at the Police Department. I was immediately allowed in with my pass. After much entreating the Secretary accepted the flowers, saying that she only wanted to help, and she was very pleased that everything had gone well for me at the Consulate.

We remained in Marseille while making daily enquiries about the ship. Every day that I went to the *Société des Juifs en France*, we looked at the surroundings which, by the way, were very attractive, and visited friends who were leaving one by one.

Finally it was ascertained that we had berths on the Portuguese ship *Serpapinto*, which was to sail from Casablanca.

We went in a whole group by train to Port Vendres. We left in the morning and arrived at night. In Port Vendres there was a single hotel, and all rooms had been taken. We could have just as well spent the night in the street. The hotel porter came to our rescue. He was on night shift and offered his room until the morning. Thus we slept without getting undressed. We boarded the ship early next morning, and there we washed and tidied ourselves up.

The crossing was quiet and we arrived at Oran, where we boarded the train for Casablanca. We were escorted by gendarmes like prisoners.

In Casablanca we were all crowded into a bus and were taken to a tropical park. There, we stayed in some shelter which was open from all sides. The Park was wonderful, but not to live in. The food, some mishmash with groats, was prepared in a large cauldron by Berbers. They were half naked, and their perspiration poured in streams into the cauldron. It was quite impossible to eat such food.

We were guarded by the gendarmes, and not allowed out of the camp, or rather, out of the park. But for a small bribe one could obtain a pass into the town, where, we managed to get all that was necessary for food, in exchange for clothing. The Berbers particularly liked men's shirts.

The town, that is the European section, was exceptionally beautiful. It was all white (it fully earned its name: Casablanca), with its graceful buildings, mosques with minarets, clean tidy streets, and a mass of greenery. But the native quarter was a slum, where there was incredible filth, excreta in the streets and an unbearable stench.

There was also a Jewish quarter. The Jews could in no way be distinguished from the Berbers by their exterior appearance.

They were just as filthy and talked in the native language. The wealthy ones, and there were quite a few of them, lived in the European quarter. There was also a synagogue there, while there were prayer houses in the native quarter.

We returned unwillingly to the park. God only knows why such a wonderful park had to be turned into a latrine. Of course, there were no toilets. Water for washing was brought in clay jars. And yet all around us there was such beauty!

Finally our ship, the *Serpapinto*, arrived. We were to board it the next day, but unfortunately Genya became sick: vomiting and diarrhoea, apparently it was food poisoning. She had a high fever, but carried herself well. We could not afford to miss the ship, and one could not imagine how we would have fared in such a case. Genya pulled herself together, took my arm firmly, and the three of us made our way to the ship. Genya and Irene were accommodated in one cabin, whilst I, together with some German Jew, was in another. We travelled tourist class, for one had to take what one was given. Generally, the cabins were acceptable, they were bright and had portholes.

The ship was not due to sail until the next day. Genya was given tea and rusks, and she soon recovered. Finally, after all our experiences, we were able to settle down. The rocking of the ship did not affect me in the least, and during the whole trip, which lasted almost three weeks, I did not miss a single meal, but poor Genya and Irene were completely emaciated from seasickness. The ship moved very slowly, and if it were not for Genya's and Irene's seasickness, the voyage would have been a good rest[174].

The ship was only of 9,000 tons displacement, and this is why it rocked so much. Once during the night it stopped, and remained stationary for a long time. Next morning we learned that we had been stopped by a German submarine. Its crew had come on board, but left after lengthy deliberations with the captain. Our ship was Portuguese, and had no British military personnel on it. The passengers were spared all anxiety since the whole incident occurred during the night.

We arrived at the Bermuda Islands after twelve days of sailing, but we could admire the islands only from the ship, since we émigrés were, for some unknown reason, not allowed on shore. Only the children were allowed to do so in the care of a British nurse. Irene, like all the other children, was very happy. The children were given many sweets and presents[175].

While it had been unbearably hot during the stop in Bermuda, it was, in spite of the tropical heat, quite bearable on the ship while we were at sea. The ventilation worked well. The food on the ship was plain, but healthy and plentiful. There was an abundance of white bread, which soon became boring. There were also plenty of oranges.

In Bermuda the ship was boarded by British officers and sailors, and they only left when the ship was about to sail. Everybody was impressed by how remarkably the British were attired, everything was made to measure from good quality material, and I would like to say, extremely elegantly, in contrast with the attire of U.S. military personnel (as we were later to observe), on whom all clothes looked second hand. We were also amazed at the politeness and friendliness of the British, quite different from what I had imagined them to be.

Immediately after our departure from Bermuda, the question of inoculations arose, and, as I remarked earlier, it turned out that the certificate of the medical officer at the U.S. Consulate at Marseille was not worth a cent. The inoculations were carried out by the ship's doctor, as required, and without cost.

The trip from Bermuda to New York took place without any particular incidents.

PART FOUR

IN THE NEW WORLD

1941–1983

Chapter Twenty-Eight

Zip Fasteners in New York

On arrival in New York, all immigrants had their temperature taken. Everyone had a thermometer inserted into his or her mouth, and each one who believed that he or she had a raised temperature, tried to manipulate the thermometer, since a raised temperature threatened quarantine on Ellis Island, which was not all fun.

The US citizens disembarked first, then the First class passengers, and finally we immigrants. A representative of HIAS (Hebrew Sheltering and Immigrant Aid Society) boarded the ship with a list of all of us, which he had already received from Marseille.

We descended to the wharf together with the others and looked among the crowd of welcomers for Bromberg, who had promised to meet us. This presented some problem, since I had never met him before. Among the crowd of people, who came to meet the ship, I noticed Professor Zaitsev, whom we knew from Berlin. He noticed me, we approached and greeted each other warmly, and with Zaitsev there was Bromberg, who had asked Zaitsev to accompany him to the wharf, since he did not know me.

Bromberg turned out to be a very nice person. Very tactfully, he offered financial help, and also suggested that we rent a room in a hotel. Although I had very little money I, of course, declined all financial assistance, and I also declined to stay at a hotel, preferring to stay on with HIAS, as this had already been offered to me on the ship by a representative of that organization.

Bromberg was employed as an engineer by the New York Municipality. We became friends, and he visited us often, almost daily. He was familiar with Russian affairs, and, all the time, he came up with projects of various matters, which he intended to be published.

HIAS received us very well. We were not made to wait, and those who were to stay there, were allocated to their rooms and informed that at such and such hour there would be lunch in the common dining room. We tidied ourselves up and descended to the general lobby, where we were expected by the already unfailing Bromberg and by Rabbi Eisenstadt. We were very touched by the presence of the latter. He was very kind, especially to Genya. He gave us the phone number of our relations, who had asked us to phone them upon arrival.

We lunched in the common dining room together with Eisenstadt. The dining arrangements were set up in such a way that none of us felt embarrassed, for there were no queue numbers and no requirement to produce any kind of documents. The food was very satisfying. HIAS must be credited for acting on humane principles in their way of assisting refugees.

We phoned the relations, and were invited to dinner for the next day.

On the following morning we again went to the HIAS office. I was asked about my intentions regarding work, and was directed to their labour exchange. There I filled in an endless questionnaire, like a curriculum vitae. A young girl read what I had written and announced in an authoritative way that I could not dream of setting myself up in the work in which I specialized, but that in some publishing company they needed a man in the dispatch section. I thanked her sarcastically but politely, and decided then and there that I would not remain in the keep of HIAS, and that come what may, I would move. But where?

On that day, we dined with our relations who received us hospitably. They were already well established. They asked about our plans. Of course, I did not mention our need for assistance since I still had a few dollars in my pocket.

In Paris I had bought a large, a very large, bottle of Guerlain perfume. This was a minor matter, but somehow I remembered that an acquaintance of ours from Berlin, Yelena Isaakovna Joffe, had earlier come to New York, and that one of her relatives worked at *Macy's*. Through her *Macy's* bought the perfume for the sum of $100. In those days this was a lot of money.

Eisenstadt said that his friend, Mrs Luria, the sister of the well known Jewish writer Ginsberg, was living with her daughter on 115th Street near Riverside Drive, and that there were vacant rooms there. We rented two of these and moved in immediately. Many Russian *émigrés* lived there at one stage.

Irene was enrolled at the public school on 109th Street. In those days it was peaceful to live where we were, and one could also come home safely late at night. In the evening one could safely sit on Riverside Drive whilst escaping from the heat, even right near the water[176].

In the beginning, masses of people came streaming to visit us, both old acquaintances and those acquired locally. Bromberg called almost daily, and still kept on offering financial assistance.

I started commuting to the office of Aron Yefimovich (my great-uncle, the cousin of my father) on 50th Street, in the General Motors Building, to work as his secretary. Aron Yefimovich was a gifted man, and was always engrossed in various projects, but he was a stubborn and difficult person, although good by nature. I used to accompany him to his home for lunch. He was already blind, and I wrote down various projects for him, visited the Public Library for data on world oil production etc. Often I went to his home at night in connection with the above projects. He did not pay very generously, and I was very worried about the uncertainty of the position. When Aron Yefimovich started a zip-fastener factory, I preferred to start work there as an ordinary worker, and to work six days a week, eight to nine hours a day. Besides, from time to time, Aron Yefimovich involved me with his projects.

Zinaida Abramovna, Aron Yefimovich's wife, recommended Genya to the *Dembo Salon*, on Central Park South. Our earnings were sufficient for us, and we could live, even though not extravagantly, but in any case satisfactorily. Later we rented two rooms on West 137th Street, in the apartment of the above-mentioned Mrs Y.I. Joffe, but we did not live there for long. We were driven out by bedbugs!

We were by now tired of furnished rooms, and we rented quite a reasonable apartment in a decent building not far away on 113th Street. This was a very quiet and clean street, inhabited mostly by students and Russians. The apartment had six rooms, space to spare, an elevator and services. It had been recently repaired, and the rent was $50 per month, with two months for free. The owner, who for some reason was kindly disposed to me, asked me to recommend tenants. It was through me that the writers Gul and Vishnyak settled there.

Opposite our building there was another, which was entirely inhabited by *émigrés* from Russia.

We purchased our furniture for a pittance from the Salvation Army, but it was quite decent. We still have a china cabinet, which I converted into a bookcase, and which Irene likes very much.

I became terribly sick of zip-fasteners. Of course, Aron Yefimovich knew that I occupied myself with this only temporarily.

In New York there lived Zylia Kuchuk[177], who was the co-owner of a photographic agency. I had some experience in photography, actually I was a good amateur photographer, and I offered her my services. I worked in the dark room for a very short time. I worked well, but too slowly "Allah be with her!"[178].

I established contact with Tolya in Australia, and several times he sent me $10. I asked him to immediately stop doing so, but I shall never forget his gesture.

Chapter Twenty-Nine

Publisher Again!

One day I was visited by George Gourvitch, whose book *Rousseau and the Declaration of Rights*, I had published long ago in Russia. At that time this was his thesis, the publication of which was very important to him, and the fact that I had made this possible, established good relations between us. Now, after having been a Professor of Sociology at the Sorbonne University, having escaped from Hitler and finding himself in the United States, he was imbued with the idea of publishing an English quarterly, *Journal of Sociology*. For this he had received a small grant from some foundation.

I found out from Gourvitch that a certain Rivkin, who had come originally from Russia, had arrived from Sweden, had started a publishing company in New York, and wanted to begin publishing Gourvitch's journal. But Gourvitch did not trust him, and suggested that I should see Rivkin. Perhaps I could arrange things with him, and then the publication of the journal could be started.

I remembered that a certain Rivkin, a publisher from Stockholm, had called on me in Berlin, and that I had sold him the copyright to publish certain writers in Sweden. The contract had been signed according to all rules, but in spite of a fee having been repeatedly mentioned, I did not receive a single cent or an answer. I had not thought to ask for an advance payment.

I located Rivkin, and he actually turned out to be the person who had purchased the Swedish copyrights from me. This was not at all to my liking, but one had to start somewhere.

The publishing company was situated on 13th Street between 7th and 8th Avenues. It consisted of one large room which contained the lot: Rivkin, the employees, the dispatch, two young ladies and the actual books. Rivkin's brother dropped in frequently. Rivkin's wife, a very beautiful Swede, seemed to be devoted to her husband.

As I soon found out, the so-called publishing company was based on hot air. Upon someone's advice, one of the young women had lent Rivkin some money which, by the time I came onto the scene, had already evaporated. The other young woman, the wife of a dentist, had left her husband and lived with Rivkin's brother. She also had lost money which she had lent to Rivkin. Where the money went is unknown, for only three books had been published of which one, *Psychoanalysis Today*, had been purchased from a publisher who had liquidated his business. There was no program. The dispatch and the bookkeeping, if it could be thus called, were in the hands of a barely adolescent girl.

I was to receive a very modest salary. To begin with, things had to be put in order. I knew that without a radical purge the publishing company was doomed.

One of my drawcards was the journal offered by Gourvitch. Apart from this journal I had a number of other drawcards in my hands, since Gourvitch, who also published the journal *Legal and Political Sociology*, was not happy with *Philosophical Library*, his current publishers, and he was ready to hand over the publication to me.

I also had a connection of long standing with the European Headquarters of the YMCA through P.F. Anderson. I had applied to him in the beginning, whilst looking for a job. He did not think that this was a good solution for me. The YMCA publishing company was purely Christian and I could have no hope of advancement. He suggested that instead of taking a job, I should publish the Russian Classics in Russian: Pushkin, Gogol, Tolstoy, Turgenev, Chekhov, Leskov, Lermontov, which were to be distributed by the Red Cross to Russian prisoners of war[179]. Anderson promised to give me an order for a large number of copies of each title, and also an advance payment on account of such order. We came to an agreement regarding the price and I was able to start fulfilling the order.

I received a share in Rivkin's publishing company, but the business still had to be radically reorganised. Rivkin was a chronic alcoholic and was invariably useless by mid-day. By some miracle, he got rid of the two women who had invested money in the business (I believe they lost everything), and he allocated some books to his brother for leaving the company. Thus I remained alone with Rivkin, but this did not solve the problem, for he used to spend all the cash on drink and was incapable of systematic work.

I had an acquaintance, Sheiner, who had money, and who was prepared to invest in the publishing business. We made an arrangement with Rivkin regarding a certain sum. We signed a formal contract, and my new partner paid the arranged sum to Rivkin.

Next morning, when we came to the premises, we found the door to the office broken down, and on the floor there was an unimaginable mess: correspondence, accounts and books had been thrown about. We called the police, and at the investigation the neighbours pointed to Rivkin. He was brought in together with his wife. He called his lawyer, and we called our lawyer, my friend Bolotovsky. Rivkin admitted that he had been very depressed, got drunk and did all this in a drunken state. Neither Sheiner nor I wanted to press charges (for what could we have claimed from him?), and so we let him go.

I speeded up the publication of the Russian classics and took over Gourvitch's journal, which he and my friend M.Y. Lazerson edited. Gourvitch introduced me to Professor Boris Mirkine–Guetsevitch, with whom I was earlier slightly acquainted. The latter offered me the publishing of the journal *République Française*, which was subsidised by the owner of the well-known *Wildenstein Gallery*. Offers for us to publish books came from everywhere. I published Gourvitch's second book: *Bill of Rights*. I also published a book on Czechoslovakia and one on Poland, then a book by my friend Frenkley, *Stones of France, Stones of Glory*, in French and in English, and two books dealing with concentration camps: *Ashes and Fire* by Jacob Pat, and *I was a Doctor at Auschwitz* by Gisella Perl. I took on the publishing of the book *Proust and Painting* by Maurice Chernowitz, and also a series of smaller publications.

Chapter Thirty

Psychoanalysis

The publishing company, which was given the name *International Universities Press*[180], still lacked an identity and a definite purposeful program. It was necessary to contain the sphere of one's activity within a definite framework. In order to follow the road of the big publishing companies and publish books on a varied and massive scale, it would have been necessary to have the resources of those big companies, the possibility of circulating shares on the Stock Exchange and of issuing additional shares in case of the need for new resources. These we did not possess. We were already experiencing difficulties in financing our company.

It was then that I decided to concentrate on a field which had just emerged in the United States, and which corresponded to my personal inclination: psychoanalytic literature. My idea turned out to be correct. In my further activity I concentrated on literature on psychoanalysis and only rarely digressed. However, I published books on other subjects arising out of purely personal connections with authors, or in respect of subjects that attracted me. *Psychoanalysis Today*, with the many authors whose articles were placed therein, rendered me a great service. I began to have dealings with these authors and a number of others who later established the backbone of my company.

Already after a short time, having published a series of books at short intervals, I became convinced that I could not continue work with my partner, a person from a purely business milieu who, while an honest and decent person, interfered practically in everything without having sufficient qualifications. Besides, with the expansion of the business, new funds were required. But every time when money was needed I had arguments with him. He was not disinclined to leave the business, and I had to start thinking of a way out of this situation.

As is customary, my bookkeeper kept books under the supervision of a certified accountant who was working with many firms. This was Paul Safro. I communicated my ideas to him about the possibility of Sheiner leaving the business, and asked for his advice. Safro, who was acquainted with all the particulars of the business from a financial point of view, even in minor matters, stated straight away that he wished to be my partner, that he would not interfere in the conduct of the business, not having any experience in it, that he trusted me without limit and would put all required means at my disposal.

Sheiner left, and his place was taken by Paul Safro. Obviously we had to return to Sheiner his entire investment. In form of a guarantee he received the whole of the published books and the proceeds from them, with a deduction of the authors' fees and the proceeds from the books already sold, until the whole sum would be covered. In time we paid the whole of this debt.

The partnership with Safro turned out to be a success. All shares were divided equally between the two of us. He did not interfere in the business of publishing, did not draw any salary except for his work in supervising the accounting and the interest on the invested capital and bonuses. He was an ideal partner, there were no more worries about money. He insisted all the time on an increase of my salary, but I was modest in my requirements. We were both interested in the success of the business.

As the financial situation improved, I covered my indebtedness to him. I could not even dream of a more ideal partner. After many, many years, when the children began to take an active part in the business, and after the indebtedness was fully covered, we paid him a certain sum, all papers were taken over by us, and we parted as friends. This had been an "ideal marriage". During all my long life I never had such a friendly collaboration[181].

If I occupied myself[182] principally with the publication of books in the Russian language: poetry, literature, history, philosophy, while in emigration, in Germany as well as in Belgium, then this was a labour which was tending to be beyond my strength, for it was necessary to struggle for the very existence of the publishing company, while at the same time to create satisfactory material conditions for my family. These two objectives could not be tackled together.

However, I am unrepentant over my publishing activity in the field of Russian literature. I am proud of it. I have made my contribution and would have continued to work along the same lines in the United States, if there had been even the slightest possibility to penetrate into those areas that interested me. But here in the United States the conditions of working in the Russian field were completely different. The output in this field concentrated mainly on political issues and also conflicted with my world outlook. Besides, the publications were funded mainly by bequests from various establishments.

Because to simply re-publish Russian books would not be a paying proposition, I decided to change over to the publication of books in English. As soon as the company had established itself more or less firmly by the publication of various books about which I have spoken before, I turned towards that field which had interested me for a very, very long time, namely books on psychoanalysis.

Sometime in the past[183], in Germany, I had published the Russian translation of Jung's book *Psychological Types*[184]. Since then the urge to publish books in this field, which interested me more and more, did not leave me. When I arrived in the United States, I made contact with Dr Milstein (thanks to his sister), and with the Eisslers, as well as with Mrs Eissler's brother, with whom I had already become acquainted in Berlin. These people received me very cordially, and thanks to them, I entered, properly speaking, the circle of the psychoanalysts. Mrs Eissler introduced me to Freud's daughter, Anna, and I became a constant publisher of Freudian literature.

As in every share-holding company, it issued "common stock" and "preferred stock" shares. (Those who held "preferred stock" had no voting rights, and therefore could not interfere in the running of the company). I involved a whole array of psychoanalysts as shareholders and as holders of "preferred stock". These included Oberndorf, Lorand, Meerloo, Heimann, Tarachow and others. I limited their investment to not more nor less than $1,000. This, of course, did not establish a financial base for the publishing company, but it linked this circle to the company[185].

My publishing company has actually played a very great part in the evolution of psychoanalysis, and no one can deny this.

I began by publishing *The Yearbook of Psychoanalysis*. This was a collection of articles which had already been published before.

The Yearbook of Psychoanalysis was not a journal but a series of hard-cover anthologies. The publication of *The Yearbook* which was launched in 1944, continued for some ten years. By that time the volume of psychoanalytic papers had become overwhelming, and in 1952 the *Annual Survey of Psychoanalysis* edited by John Frosch et al., was initiated, but *The Yearbook of Psychoanalysis* was not discontinued until 1954. At that time the

Annual Survey of Psychoanalysis had also become increasingly unwieldy, and it too was finally abandoned in 1971.

I was yearning to create something new in this field, and something that would be more organically linked to this field. What I had in mind was the creation of an official journal for the American Psychoanalytic Association[186].

I began negotiations with Dr John Frosch regarding the publication of such a journal. In New York there already existed a semi-official journal, *Psychoanalytic Quarterly*, to which prominent psychoanalysts contributed, but I endeavoured to prove to Frosch, and he agreed with this, that it was necessary for the American Psychoanalytic Association to create its own journal expressing the views of the Association independently from the *Psychoanalytic Quarterly*. This was a difficult task in view of the existence of the other publication. I was supported in my endeavour by the President of the Association, Hendrick, and also by Kaufman. The others, however, were rather cool towards my proposition. But when the matter came up for decision, I nevertheless succeeded in overcoming all difficulties and, in principle, achieving a decision, to publish the *Journal*. And when Frosch and I eventually organized its publication, this proved to be completely within the capacity of the Association and the scope of its tasks.

The American Psychoanalytic Association comprised the great majority of the psychoanalysts who were known in the professional literature, and when the first issue of the *Journal* appeared, the question of the need for the establishment of such a publication was fully vindicated.

Thanks to the *Journal*, I gained the opportunity to involve practically all psychoanalysts, and in this manner, to ascertain exactly the nature that the publication should have[187].

A whole series of problems arose in the course of my dealings with the Association, arising from the following circumstance: the Institute of Psychoanalysis, which was connected with the Association, made it obligatory for every psychoanalyst who wished to obtain from the Association the right to practice, to undertake a three year course. The Institute published anthologies of its work and of the discussions, which, so to speak, were dealing with the internal work of the Association. Now these anthologies did not bring in any income, in fact, they were even causing financial losses. Nevertheless I undertook their publication, and in this manner rendered a great service to the Association. I continued to publish one anthology after another[188].

Here in the United States there was another organization which was close in its aims to psychoanalysis, the Group Psychotherapy Association. I was closely acquainted with A. Slavson, who was at the head of this group. One day Slavson suggested that I publish a journal for his group. I said that his group was still a very small one, that they had only two hundred members, while a journal, in order to make ends meet, would have to have at least two thousand subscribers. One negotiation followed another. Slavson guaranteed the subscription of two hundred copies on behalf of the Group Therapy Association (that is, from its members). As for the remaining subscribers – I would have to find them myself. I had only three hundred subscribers to begin with. But later the demand for the journal began to grow, and it achieved a distribution exceeding that of the psychoanalytic journal which I was publishing[189].

I was also closely connected to the psychoanalyst and philosopher D. Rapaport. He came up with the idea of publishing a series entitled *Psychological Issues*. But it was not until after Rapaport's death that I brought his idea to fruition. At present 40 issues have already been published[190].

These three publications: the *Journal of the American Psychoanalytic Association*, the *International Journal of Group Psychotherapy* and the series *Psychological Issues*, formed the cornerstone of my publishing company.

Apart from the above, I should mention another major undertaking in this field, the publication of the series *Psychoanalytic Study of the Child*. I published 25 volumes of this series, which achieved a very extensive distribution and established a firm basis for the publication. Unforeseen circumstances, resulting from the re-organization of my publishing company, led to the loss of this particular undertaking, which was taken over by the *Yale University Press*. To this day I am very sorry about this loss. Also, apart from the above, I began publishing the *Journal of the Academy of Child Psychiatry*. I continued doing so for some five years until that organization got onto its feet and started publishing its journal on its own.

The first two issues of *The Psychoanalytic Study of the Child* after the defection from IUP were published by a subsidiary of the *New York Times*. The *Journal of the Academy of Child Psychiatry* also went to *Quadrangle Press* and eventually to *Yale University Press*.

I would also like to mention that the *Journal of the American Psychoanalytic Association* brought out separate issues on different scientific topics, with contributions by Brenner, Arlow, Jacobson, Hartmann and others. These were all important publications, and I published all of them.

Besides, I would like to mention another series of collections of articles which I published in connection with the yearly lectures devoted to Freud. These publications (there were more than 16) were well received. They dealt with subjects which, until these days, have not lost their topicality. All these collections were published by me, and only by me.

Then I must not fail to point out that I published the materials pertaining to the very birth of Psychoanalysis, that is, to the formation of the Vienna Psychological Society, namely the

Minutes of that Society, comprising four volumes, right from its inception, as edited by Herman Nunberg and Ernst Federn.

Further, right from the beginning, the question of publishing an Index of Psychoanalytic Literature had been debated for a long time within the American Psychoanalytic Association. A committee was established for that purpose. It existed for a number of years. One meeting followed another, but they led to absolutely no results. Then I suggested that I would undertake that task. I asked only for one thing: that the Index should be published under the sponsorship of the Association. When I proposed this to Hartmann, he said: "You know, this is a very complicated affair, I do not recommend it in any shape or form; this is an utterly impossible job... you will not be able to complete the task, and our committee will then not be able to do anything about it at all". I replied to him: "...in my life I did not take many risks, but I would like to take this one on and make a success of it"[191]. At first, five volumes were published, then another five, and then another four. The same Hartmann who had tried to dissuade me from undertaking that task, and who was, so to speak, the father... the leader of Psychoanalysis in the United States, wrote the Foreword, in which he praised the project. He praised it up to heaven!

I would like to mention[192] the classical work written (in German) by Eugen Bleuler, which has been in existence for many years in Europe. It was the basic work for the study of Freud's psychiatry. Bleuler's work comprised his writings on the subjects of *dementia praecox*, *schizophrenia* and *anorexia nervosa*. I published Bleuler's *Dementia Praecox or the Group of Schizophrenias* in English translation, as well as a synopsis of this book, and they were a huge success. I consider this to have been an important contribution to science.

I also had a connection with the Paul Schilder Society. Paul Schilder was a scientist well known for his achievements in the study of *neurasthenia* and psychiatric illnesses generally. My friend David Rapaport played an important part in the Paul Schilder Society. One day, Rapaport said to me: "You know, I have been trying for a long time to publish the works of Schilder which I consider very important. I shall introduce you to his wife".

Schilder's wife was Loretta Bender. She was in charge of a very large psychiatric hospital. Her fate was very tragic, namely the unusual death of Paul Schilder. He was one of the chief physicians in the same hospital. One day, when he was expected to arrive, she stood at the window and saw him crossing the street, and before her very eyes he was run over by a car, and thus the life of this significant scientist came to an end.

I published a number of Schilder's books which had already been published before, but had been sold out, and then I decided to publish also his other works. I had a very good working relationship with Loretta Bender, and until the present [1977] my company continues to publish Schilder's unpublished works, and I believe that we shall bring this endeavour to a successful completion. Comments in the press have been very favourable.

Thus, in the field of the growth of psychoanalysis in the United States, possibly no other publishing company played such an important part as mine, and it continues to maintain its reputation in this field.

Today, my publishing company, apart from some minor departures, which however are also tied up one way or another with psychoanalysis, philosophy and some other related fields, continues to operate in the same direction[193]. Irene is in charge of the editing department. She will continue in this capacity, and as long as I am alive she will continue to take part in the management[194].

Well this, apart from the books which I published one after another without any interruption, represents substantially my activity in this field.

Chapter Thirty-One

Politics in Exile

When I arrived in New York I found many different organizations here[195] [i.e. organizations of refugees from Europe]. In spite of the fact that my position was still a very shaky one and I had to think about the next day, I soon participated in most of these.

Our former organization, the Sociéte des Juifs en France, which had been founded in Toulouse, and which existed in the major cities of France not yet occupied by the Germans, existed also in New York. At the head of that organization were the well-known sculptor, Aronson, and Rabbi Dr Eisenstadt. Then there were also Dr Ginsburg, Wolsky, Shapiro, Tereika and others. Of course I took part in that organization as a matter of priority and became its secretary.

Since the organization actually maintained contacts with France through underground channels, we used to receive news about the struggle of the French against the Germans, and about the plight of the Jews who had remained behind. Our activity consisted mainly in arranging for the transport of as many people as possible to the United States. That activity was rather monotonous, but then the monotony was broken by us receiving news of the formation of Jewish partisan detachments in the South of France, which had linked up with patriotic Frenchmen and were conducting a successful struggle against the Germans. But then many negative sides to the fighting were revealed: the detachments indiscriminately killed Germans wherever they met them, they raped women. When I raised the question: "Are we any better than the enemy?" and argued that the information received could not be left without response, and that we must in some way express our attitude towards actions which were practically the same as those of our enemies, my intervention caused some embarrassment. Some pointed out that vengeance was quite legitimate, but I stated that vengeance was not worthy of Jewish people, and that we must in every way condemn the above actions. A discussion ensued which dragged on for a long time. Anyhow, to whom could we have sent our protest? What could we have done? And thus the question remained hanging in the air[196].

Also completely unexplainable arrests of Jewish writers (for example Ehrlich) and of artists (such as Mikhoels) began to take place in the Soviet Union. Then news started coming through to us that these people had been liquidated. I declared that it was necessary to make a protest; that it was necessary to carry a resolution to this effect within our own ranks, but also that such a resolution should be put to the notice of the press, pointing out that such affairs were scandalizing our Society. Aronson, who was the president of the organization, stated that we did not know all the facts that we could not interfere in this. I insisted on my point of view: "Listen! These are the very people whom we are supposed to represent. Ehrlich, for example was the president of the Bund, and all of us knew him at some time or other. We knew he is not capable of the mean action of which he is accused, etc..." Finally we carried a resolution expressing our protest, which was published in *The New York Times*, and the Jewish paper *Forward*, so as to give it, in this manner, full publicity. In the end, Aronson, who was inclined towards the Left (he was not a proper Communist, but just an "Armchair-Communist") resigned over all this. He was at first replaced by Rabbi Eisenstadt and later by Dr Ginsburg.

I mentioned that there were many organizations in New York when I arrived here. There was, among others, the *Horizon Club*, which consisted mainly of wealthy Jews. They were all active in some way or other, but I utterly disliked the social composition of this club. In spite of the fact that I was invited to take part in it, I declined to do so.

There were also societies of friends of Russian culture. The president of one of those was a very pleasant, friendly person by the name of Novitsky. Regular lectures by writers and poets were arranged, and generally, discussions on questions of literature and poetry took place. I participated fairly actively in all these activities.

Coming back to the organization, the *Sociéte des Juifs en France*, its work was very effective. Apart from helping refugees etc., by sending food parcels to those trapped in Europe, it conducted excellent work in searching for relatives and for people who had managed to escape to the United States. Through this organization I received the advice about the whereabouts of my father and the address of my son, so that I could enter into correspondence with them. To my surprise, I began receiving letters from both of them. Later, my father found himself again in Riga, and in this manner the communication was firmly established.

In New York there existed an organization called the Literary Fund. I was introduced to it by Mrs Zetlin, with whom I had been acquainted for a long time and knew well, and by her husband who was one of my authors. I started to take part in that organization and became a member of its management. As its secretary I carried out some fairly responsible work. I was re-elected several times, but once, during the elections to the management, Y.S. Zenzinov, a long-time active member of the organization was blackballed, and I left in protest. I was asked to remain, but I insisted on making a principled stand although I had received the same number of votes as the head of the management. I stated that if a person after such a fruitful, ten-year-long activity could be blackballed, then it meant that something was not right with the organization. After this, Zenzinov and I conceived the idea of forming the *Nadezhda* (Hope) Society, which in fact was to pursue the same aims as the Literary Fund. We arranged cultural evenings, we provided relief by sending food parcels to whomsoever we could. The *Nadezhda* Society existed for quite a long time. Then Zenzinov died, others also died or retired from activity, and somehow that society ceased to exist.

Well, there were other organizations formed by people who had escaped from Europe, but I did not take part in their activities since these were identical with those of the Literary Fund and the *Nadezhda* Society. Neither did I take part in an infinite number of "fellow-countrymen's associations" which had sprung up, but I had dealings with a Jewish Labour organization which generously supported activists arriving from Europe, and as I have mentioned, I even published a book *Ashes and Fire* by the secretary of that organization, J. Pat, dealing with concentration camps.

This, then, is how my activity was gradually taken up, apart from my becoming, as it were, familiar with American life and American conditions. I was able to devote great efforts towards all this until my time and energy were completely taken up by my publishing activity. I gradually retired from all those organizations. Of course I still took part in them as a member, but did not any longer play the part which I used to in the beginning.

I must still mention another organization in which I took an active part. This was the group of the Mensheviks to which I used to belong in Russia. Raphail Abramovich and Boris

Nikolaevsky with whom I was very close, were members of that group, which published the journal *Sotsialistichesky Vestnik* (*Socialist Courier*), and organized regular meetings and lectures on various questions. But this group too began to fall apart, due to the surfacing of different trends in it. Dallin, Gurevich and Aronson took the point of view that somehow we should find a common platform so as to co-ordinate the work of the organization with what was going on in Soviet Russia. This was one orientation. The other orientation was that of the so-called Vlasovite movement[197].

Some considered Vlasov to be the same Black Hundreder as all the other Black Hundreders and did not excuse his behaviour in any way. Among those who thought so were Nikolaevsky, Abramovich and I. But, at the same time, there was a strong emphasis on the circumstance that, after all, the Vlasov people were patriots that they fought not as traitors, but for the liberation of Russia from the Bolsheviks. The factional conflict was not resolved. There were three groups: the group in which I took part against the Vlasov people, the group of Dallin, Dan and Gurevich, which insisted on the unmasking of the Bolsheviks, and an intermediate group. All these factions shook up and upset the whole organization, and the meetings became more and more fraught with arguments. There were those who opposed such a drift, but they did not always take part, or were leaving the organization. It was against this background that *Sotsialistichesky Vestnik* ceased to exist. At first Nikolaevsky left, then the others, leaving only Abramovich on the Editorial Committee. And thus *Sotsialistichesky Vestnik*, which was founded in Berlin in 1921, and which had existed for so many years, ceased its existence forever[198].

Chapter Thirty-two

The Last Entry

Whilst in the mountains in the summer of last year [1982], I met Sedykh, a person close to me, who mentioned that I had got into print. There was an article about me in some Russian newspaper. I was amazed, since I had not heard anything about this, and had not commissioned anyone to write an article. Sedykh kindly agreed to obtain a copy of that article for me.

In terms of the origins of that article this is really what happened. I had attended an evening of the *Literaturny Fond* [Literary Fund], at which I had been hospitably received. When leaving at the end of the evening, I was met by Tulchinsky, who introduced himself as the photographer of *Sevodnya* [*Today*], a paper that I used to read. He asked for permission to take my photograph. I agreed, and he took a photograph of me in one of the rooms. Since Tulchinsky intended to take more photographs, in particular, of Nadya Rosenberg, Sedykh, who happened to be near us, said that this was not the place for taking photographs, after which the photographing ceased.

Several days later, Tulchinsky phoned informing me that he had the photographs, and asked if he could come over? He arrived with a friend and brought four copies of the photograph. I was given two of these, and he and his friend kept the other two.

A lively discussion ensued between us regarding my publishing activity. Generally, the conversation shifted from one subject to another.

After a few days Tulchinsky phoned me that he had been commissioned to write an article about me, and asked for a meeting for that purpose. We arranged a date, but Tulchinsky did not turn up. After a few days he phoned again with another request for a meeting. Again I appointed a day, and once again he did not come. He kept on phoning, but I did not grant him any more appointments, and in order to disengage myself, I said that I had given all particulars to the Institute of Slavonic Studies at Columbia University. This is how we finished up.

Then, as I indicated above, Sedykh told me about the article, which he was then kind enough to send to me. A few days later, Tulchinsky also sent me a copy of the article. Apparently he had heard about my conversation with Sedykh, who worked for the paper *Russkoye Slovo* [*Russian Word*], and apologised for the delay.

Earlier, I had found out about a disagreement between Sedykh and Tulchinsky, but I knew nothing of the article about me.

The actual situation was that I did not ask, and was not asked, to supply material for this article, not to mention to give my approval to it. I saw the article for the first time when it was sent to me, and its very tone, and the amazing number of errors and distortions, spoke for themselves[199].

Names were mercilessly jumbled: instead of Karsavin – Krasavin, instead of Lossky, the famous Russian philosopher – Lassky. Annenkov was never Petrovich. Instead of Antony Yosifovich Bukovetsky (who recommended the Agricultural Institute to me, where he was a Professor of Political Economy), there is indicated – Bogolepov. Even the ship on which we travelled from Petrograd was not the *Kreussen* but the *Preussen*[200].

When speaking about the founding of Petropolis, he added that all the production part was entrusted to me, and that I had already published Freud's book *The Psychology of Dreams*.

Nothing like it! I never published that book. As for becoming a member of the management of Petropolis: I was already the head of a number of major publishing companies, and was so overloaded with work that I did not immediately agree to enter into yet another company[201].

And as for Freud, this must have been derived from Tulchinsky's question as to what exactly had attracted me to Freud? I had pointed to "dreams", and that I seriously occupied myself with the problems of psychiatry and psychoanalysis in America where my publishing company held an honourable position in this field. Among other things, I had published a full collection of writings by Anna Freud, the *Journal of the American Psychoanalytic Association* and other publications.

Speaking of Nabokov, I have indicated previously that I had known him already in Petrograd, and that I had accommodated his butler in my publishing company *Naooka i Shkola*, where he was employed in packing and dispatching books. This could not be related to Berlin, where the Nabokovs-Sirins lived in very constrained circumstances, and where there was no possibility of assisting[202].

Abram, 88 years old in Manhattan.

EPILOGUE

Abram Saulovich generally enjoyed good health. Anatol could not remember his father ever being ill. Abram prided himself on never having had a headache. Then at the age of 94 he caught a chill that turned into pneumonia. But the condition he always feared, and from which he thought he would seek to escape by terminating his own life, mercifully did not last too long. He died of congestive heart failure on 5 December 1983, and was laid to rest next to Genya who preceded him twelve years earlier in 1971.

At the 35th Congress of the International Psychoanalytical Association, which met in Montreal in July 1987, a Certificate of Distinguished Service to Psychoanalysis was awarded posthumously to Abram Saulovich. Abram's daughter, Irene Guttman, received it on his behalf. The text was as follows:

> This certificate acknowledges distinguished service to the science and profession of psychoanalysis, to its position, its promotion and its dissemination internationally. The International Psychoanalytical Association awards it with deep appreciation.

Psychoanalysis was only one of the fields in which Abram Saulovich had given distinguished service during his long and active life. More considerable was his role as publisher in the field of Russian literature, philosophy and historiography, from Akhmatova, Gumilyov and Mandelstam, to Berdyaev, Zamyatin, Klyuchevsky and Trotsky.

The words of Pushkin resonate with Abram's abilities:

> I write the letter, but I will give the letter to you
> little people, because you have some special skill
> in knowing where to deliver it.

Abram Saulovich certainly had that special skill. His name may not appear in many history books, but his endeavours as a publisher of literature, philosophy and science are sufficient justification to put on record his life as a significant contributor to human culture.

Anatol and his wife, Dawn, Sydney 1998.

Appendices

(i) An obituary by Charles Brenner, MD (1913–2008), leading US psychiatrist and champion of Freud. Excerpted with permission from the *Journal of the American Psychoanalytic Association* Volume 44, number 4, 1996, 1015–6:

Tribute to Abram S. Kagan

When the *Bulletin* became the *Journal of the American Psychoanalytic Association* it was a matter of course that its publisher should continue to be International Universities Press, the publishing house founded and headed by Dr Abram Kagan. IUP was far and away the premier publisher of psychoanalytic literature in the United States and Dr Kagan was eager for the new journal to be a success as were its founders. The great majority of IUP's titles during the time Dr Kagan headed it with his daughter, Irene Guttman, were in the field of psychoanalysis. IUP continues to be a leader in the field to this day.

Dr Kagan was born in czarist Russia to a wealthy family in a society that discriminated against him because he was a Jew. (The English cognate of Kagan is Cohen; there is no "h" in Russian.) He nevertheless received a full university education through a combination of innate intelligence, indomitable courage, and patient toil.

As a young man he established himself in St Petersburg where he was a member of the Socialist intelligentsia. It was there that he began his career as a publisher, mostly of scientific works, though he also published the works of writers and poets of the time. During the few months of the Kerensky government in 1917, after the Czar had been deposed and before the Bolsheviks under Lenin took over, he was actively engaged in politics as a member of the ruling Socialist (Menshevik) party. After several turbulent years he and a number of other intellectuals were expelled from the new Soviet Union and he made his way to Berlin with his wife and young son. Though without funds of his own, he was able, with the help of some relatives in Germany, to get on his feet financially and to become, in time, a publisher of books translated into Russian from other languages, mostly German. These works were distributed in the Soviet Union, freely though technically illegally. It startled and amused Dr Kagan when, after he had become established in Berlin, the son of Trotsky, the man who exiled him, came to him and asked him to publish Trotsky's autobiography. Dr Kagan accepted the book for publication and had it circulated in the Soviet Union at a time when Trotsky himself was either already an exile or about to become one.

His departure from St Petersburg was the first of Dr Kagan's escapes from violent death. He was in fact arrested before being deported and not a few of his associates were summarily shot during his final years in Petrograd, as it was then called.

The rise of Hitler to power in Germany forced Dr Kagan to decamp again, this time to Belgium and France. It was only after the fall of France that he, his wife, and his daughter left their new home once again, this time for the United States, via Casablanca. For those of us who have been spared such experiences it is hard to appreciate the courage, the determination, the ingenuity, and the fortunate hairbreadth escapes that were necessary to survive. Like so many others of the relatively few who did survive, Dr Kagan deserves our utmost admiration.

In New York Dr Kagan had to start from scratch for the third time. It was here, for the first time that chance threw in his way the opportunity to publish books in the field of psychoanalysis and it was in New York that his career as a publisher of psychoanalytic books and journals began.

He chose the name of his new publishing house in imitation of the Parisian firm, Presses Universitaires. The name reflects the nature of his devotion to his work. Making money was never his chief aim. He wanted above all to publish works that would enrich the culture of the society in which he lived and that would bring credit to his firm and to himself. He was a scholar whose intellectual and cultural interests took precedence over business interests even though he gave careful and wise attention to the latter. He was a charming and interesting social companion, one with whom it was always a pleasure to talk. It was fortunate for psychoanalysis as well as for Dr Kagan the last forty years of his life were, in such contrast to the first fifty, peaceful and productive.

(ii) An obituary for Anatol Kagan by Hall Greenland, with permission:

A comrade to the end:
Anatol Kagan – architect, activist

By the time he arrived in Australia 70 years ago, Anatol Kagan had been deported from the Soviet republic and fled his temporary place of refuge, Nazi Germany. Full of hope, he immersed himself in the life of his new country, especially politics. To the extent that there were messages of condolence from three Labor prime ministers at his funeral following his death, aged 95, at the Montefiore Nursing Home in Hunters Hill, Sydney.

Kagan settled in Melbourne in 1939 and joined the Labor Party after World War II; he also recruited his own Trotskyist group before moving to Sydney in 1955 with his third wife, Dawn. In Sydney, he met Jim McClelland – later a Whitlam minister but then a Marxist revolutionary – who put him in touch with the Balmain Trotskyists, where he met such figures as Nick Origlass, Issy Wyner, Laurie Short, and Gil and Edna Roper.

While in Melbourne, his company, Anatol Kagan and Associates, designed the wonderful Mount Scopus College. State and media archives still perpetuate the myth that Dr Ernest Fooks was the designer, but he was involved with the administration of the project.

Born in St Petersburg, Kagan was a child of the Russian Revolution. He could remember being hurried home by his nanny as angry workers chased police down the street, with shots ringing out from snipers on the rooftops. It was 1917 and his family lived close to Znamenskaya Square, where the February Revolution began.

He recalled, too, the nightly fireworks displays after the Bolsheviks liberated the tsar's arsenal of sky-rockets, and the ragged ranks of workers and soldiers marching through the streets with their tattered banners and red flags.

By the age of eight, he was visiting his father, Abram Saulovich, in prison. Kagan senior was a prominent Menshevik, an academic and publisher, and one of the 120 liberal and left-wing intellectuals expelled on Lenin's orders from the Soviet Union in 1922. To illustrate the different fate of dissidents under Lenin and Stalin, Kagan would point out that his family was given first-class tickets on a liner that took them to Germany.

The family settled in Berlin, where his father resumed his life as a publisher, and counted such titans as Carl Jung, Yevgeny Zamyatin, Anna Akhmatova, Vladimir Nabokov and, eventually, Leon Trotsky, among his authors. As a 17-year-old, Kagan read the printer's proofs of Trotsky's *History of the Russian Revolution* and was dazzled and converted.

As a Jew, holder of a Soviet passport and by then a Trotskyist, they were dangerous times for Kagan after Hitler came to power in 1933. An architecture student at Berlin University, he was part of a small Trotskyist group that met secretly in nearby woods and left anti-Nazi leaflets on buses and trams.

After their leader, another Soviet refugee, Oscar Grossman, was arrested in 1934 and sentenced to two years in jail, the group fell apart. When Grossman was released, Stalin's police sent him to a gulag, where he disappeared.

In March 1938, Kagan's family, caught between two brutal regimes, were tipped off that the Gestapo intended to arrest and deport them back to the Soviet Union. If Nazi Germany was a dangerous place, Stalin's Russia was, at that point, even more so. The family quickly fled, the son making his way to London, before continuing on to Melbourne. He had received his degree in architecture from Berlin University in 1936, complete with Nazi swastika emblazoned on the certificate.

As a Soviet refugee from Nazi Germany, he had to register with police in Melbourne as a political alien. The policeman interviewing him asked about the scar on his chin: "I suppose the Gestapo gave you that?" Kagan replied: "No, my chest expander broke and hit me on the chin".

When he moved to Sydney, he joined the Government Architect's office. It was the 1950s; he entered the competition to design the city's proposed new Opera House, and was long listed. As a follower of the Bauhaus style, however, he was never entirely happy with the result of that competition. It was an unhappiness made worse by the fact that Jørn Utzon, the Danish architect selected to build the multi-function facility at Bennelong Point, on Sydney Harbour, had not complied with the entry conditions. "And those sails", Kagan would argue, "were just four inches (10 centimetres) thick in Utzon's winning design... if it had been built as designed, it would have blown away in the first stiff breeze". Yet, for all that, he led the walk-out from the Government Architect's office when Utzon was sacked.

Meanwhile, he became actively involved in the Labor Party and for the next 40 years carried out all those mundane and necessary duties a party loyalist undertakes. In 1995, the Party made him a life member, and when the end came, there were messages of condolence from Prime Minister Kevin Rudd, and two of his Labor predecessors, Paul Keating and Bob Hawke. It has to be added, however, that for some of that 40 years, Kagan had simultaneously been a member of the Greens, while still driven by the faith of his youth.

Kagan never gave up on his dream of a better world. Right to the end this gentle Marxist democrat attended his Labor Party branch meetings armed with resolutions or his latest letter to the prime minister about the need for genuine action to tackle the climate crisis.

He is survived by his wife, Dawn, children Peter, Natalie, Stefanie and Catherine, and numerous grandchildren. (Hall Greenland was then editor of *The Week*. He met Anatol Kagan in 1964 and was a comrade of his in the Fourth International, the ALP and the Greens.)

NOTES

1 The name "Kagan" is rather popular among Russian Jews. It would correspond to the German "Cohen". It appears also in Russian as "Kogan", and non-Jews almost invariably would spell "Kagan" as "Kogan". The name could indicate descent from one of the supposedly surviving tribes of Israel, the *Kohanim* or priests. But is may also be derived from the same root as the name "Khan", as in "Ghengis Khan", meaning "Lord" among the Mongol tribes who invaded the South of Russia in the third century AD and established their empire there. Anyhow to what extent does a surname really indicate the actual descent of a person? Surnames are also of relatively recent origin. In times gone by people were generally known by their first name followed by their profession, or family status, or some other characteristic. A surname could have been assumed by its bearer some time in the past, or imposed by the authorities for registration purposes.

2 Not only did my grandmother give birth to my father at Lyady, but also she remained there for the greater part of the years following that event. This was due to the fact that my grandfather, Saul Natanovich, was in the oil business, which took him on continuous business trips so that he was seldom at home.

3 Abram Saulovich Kagan's parents had their permanent residence in St Petersburg, and officially this city was considered his place of birth. In those days, it was unusual for a woman to give birth in a hospital. This occurred generally only in those cases where the mother-to-be had nowhere to go to be taken care of. It was the custom for the pregnant daughter to return to the home of her parents to give birth there, and the midwife took the place of the doctor. And thus Abram Saulovich's mother went to stay with her parents at Lyady.

4 Irrespective of the ethnic origin of the Jewish population, the Jews in Russia were considered a "nation", and this was given significance in Russia in the past, as well as it is at present. In fact, as far as I know, the Soviet Union was the only country in the civilized world in which a person's "nationality", but meaning his or her ethnic descent, was recorded in official documents. Thus, the word "Jew" could figure in a passport in the same way as "Ukrainian".

5 Saul Natanovich, was also politically concerned. He was a member of the *Kadet* Party. This was the popular name for the "Constitutional Democrats". Later also called "Party of the Peoples' Freedom".

Depending on the situation, it was a liberal party with conservative leanings, or a conservative party with liberal leanings. It stood in favour of a constitutional monarchy, and eventually, after the Revolution, for a republic. It was the party of the progressive landowners, middle classes and bourgeois intelligentsia. Its leader at the time of the 1917 Revolution was Milyukov, a professor of history. Later, during the Berlin exile, Abram Saulovich will publish Milyukov's book *Russia's Collapse*. But this will happen thirty years later.

6 Saul Natanovich was in the oil business. Originally he was in charge of oil stores, which belonged to the Mantashevs, who were among the biggest oil-well operators in Russia. Their oil stores were situated in Vitebsk, in the Northwestern part of Russia (today the Belorussian Republic). Later, Saul Natanovich, bought up all these stores and merged them with those of the company *Petrol*, a family business headed by his uncle.

7 Abram's family stayed in Lyady in the summer months.

8 The Shneerson who had given shelter to Abram Saulovich's family possessed an extensive library which, in Soviet times, found its way into the Lenin Library in Moscow. As various religious bodies began to emerge following Glasnost, so did the Hasidic sect. The latter-day Hasids argued that the books in Shneerson's library were intended for religious purposes and should therefore be returned to this purpose. In 1991 they submitted a case to this effect to arbitration. The arbitrator ruled that Shneerson's books should indeed be removed from the Lenin Library and be returned to their original purpose, provided that they were not taken out of the country. This decision established a potentially revolutionary precedent, for according to it; any article destined originally for a religious purpose could be removed from a museum or library and returned to its original use. Thus thousands of icons could disappear from museum walls.

9 Hasidism was a mystical religious movement among East European Jews. It laid emphasis on the emotional communion with God by means of "religious joy": a combination of prayer, music and dance. Hasidism was founded in the eighteenth century by Israel Baal-Shem-Tov (the name meaning in Hebrew Master of the Good Name), who believed that the Judaism of that period was too rigid and lacked humanism. He counter posed to the concept of God as the stern judge who meted out punishment for transgressions, that of the God of mercy and love.

10 What is generally referred to as "high school" in English-speaking countries, was called, at that time in Russia, a Gimnaziya. It provided primary schooling (one primary class) from the age of eight years, and secondary schooling (eight secondary classes, the last two classes corresponding to the first two years of college in the USA), enabling the student to enter a university.

11 There was a quota system for Jews, who were admitted in only limited numbers. If there were more applicants than available admissions, those who achieved the highest results in the entrance examinations were admitted, provided their number did not exceed the quota. If the quota was exceeded, the applicants had to cast lots. Ironically, the result of the intended exclusion of Jews from availing themselves of higher education, was that the prospective Jewish students studied hard to achieve the very best results in order to be included in the quota. They often began their schooling at a higher level of excellence in the entrance examinations than the ethnic Russian contestants, and then kept up a high standard of scholastic work. Unfortunately, the resulting jealousy that was aroused among non-Jews provided a fertile soil for anti-Semitism.

12 In 1900 a liberally minded aristocrat, Prince Vyacheslav Tenishev, provided a grant for the establishment of a gimnaziya in St Petersburg, which was to become the only one of its kind in Russia, for, above all, the Tenishev Gimnaziya, thus called after the Prince, did not discriminate against Jews. The number of scions of the well-to-do Jewish middle class who were taught at that gimnaziya, was far in excess of the quota limiting the enrolment of Jewish students throughout Russia. But when young Abram Saulovich was about to commence his education, the establishment of the Tenishev Gimnaziya, which would have provided him with ideal opportunities, was still three years away. Since my grandparents still resided in Vitebsk, due to my grandfather's business involvements, his son had to apply for enrolment in the gimnaziya in Vitebsk where only one vacancy was available. Six candidates competed for this single vacancy. Three candidates, including Abram Saulovich, passed their examination with exactly the same top marks. The successful candidate had to be determined by casting lots, and Abram Saulovich was not the lucky one.

13 The boy developed a high fever. Can shock produce fever? In any case, the boy's reaction to his failure to become enrolled at a Gimnaziya was far in excess of what could be expected in the case of one of his age, but this reaction may shed light on a certain aspect of his personality. In his life Abram Saulovich suffered many setbacks, but he always managed to overcome them by sheer determination, acting rationally and deliberately. It was only towards the last years of his life that he became overpowered by adverse circumstances. Until then, such a reaction as was triggered off by the news that he had not managed to be included in the enrolment quota, was not repeated until the end of his life. It took the boy a whole week to recover from the shock. His parents tried to console him in all sorts of ways. They, and especially Saul Natanovich, insisted that attempts to enrol their son at a gimnaziya should be deferred until such time that the family would return to its permanent residence in St Petersburg. Since Saul Natanovich was a "Merchant of

the First Guild", the family had the right to reside in St Petersburg to where it eventually moved. But in the meantime the boy was to study at home.

14　The problem of the boy's schooling caused the first disagreement between his parents witnessed by him. His father spoke of sending him to a boarding school in Germany or England, while his mother argued that her son was still too young to be sent abroad, and wanted him to stay at home. The boy, who was rather attached to home, for this included spending considerable time in Lyady, took his mother's side. In any case, for the time being, his schooling was to take place at home in Vitebsk.

15　One could be puzzled by what criterion a boy, at the age of eight, considered Mme Osoline's husband, an officer in the Russian Army, as "brilliant", and how he could assess the command of French of that gentleman as "perfect", having just started to learn that language himself. Anyhow, he made good progress in French with the "very imposing" Mme Osoline, who was a "real" French woman (whatever he had in mind by this qualification).

16　The lessons in German and French gave the boy a good grounding in both languages, which stood him in good stead in his adult life in exile in Germany and later in Belgium. His knowledge of English could not compare with the above two languages, for he was over fifty years old before he had to give English sufficient attention to be able to carry on with his publishing activities in the United States.

17　Saul Natanovich had an uncle in Warsaw, who found a gimnaziya in Pultusk, a small town nearby, where there could be vacancies for Jewish pupils. The uncle obtained information on the actual enrolment at that school. Most students were Poles and Catholics, one hundred and sixty of them. There were a few Russians who were of Russian Orthodox faith, the sons of officials and teachers, and then there were fifteen Jewish students, a relatively high percentage, considering the usual limitations. Poland, before the 1917 Revolution, was part of the Russian Empire, and to study there was not considered "going abroad". Yet to study in Pultusk meant leaving home. However there was no other option, and thus the thirteen years old boy went on his way, in the care of one of his father's employees. He had to sit for an examination to gain entry to the fourth grade. He did very well. He now had to be fitted out with yet another new uniform, and he took great pride in wearing it. He found it hard to part with home, and fretted for a long time.

18　In his first year at the *Pultusk Gimnaziya*.

19　The manner in which Abram Saulovich dealt with the incident at the time it happened, and especially subsequent to it, characterized his reaction to finding himself in a hostile environment: not to squeal, not to turn the other cheek, not to escape but to overcome – as indeed was the case in Pultusk.

20 The boy spent the long annual holidays with his parents, first in Vitebsk and then in St Petersburg. During the shorter holidays he was generally invited to the homes of his school friends.

21 Beginning with 1903, the revolutionary ferment that eventually culminated in the events of 1905, was quickening throughout the Empire of the Tsar. In Poland that ferment took the form, among other things, of a struggle for national independence. After Abram Saulovich had spent only two years at the Gimnaziya, a students' strike broke out. The Polish students demanded independence for Poland and equal rights in respect of languages. They went on strike in support of their demands. The Russian students, several Germans and a few of the Poles, who were children of small merchants and who feared repressions against their parents, were prepared to finish schooling and did not join the strike. The Polish students were given an ultimatum to terminate the strike, or be expelled without the right to enrol at any other school. However they continued the strike, and for this they were expelled. Abram Saulovich, against whose nature it was to be a strikebreaker, declared his solidarity with the Polish students, and he too was expelled, with a so-called "wolf's passport" denying him the right to enrol at any other gimnaziya. He was not even given a certificate in respect of the course, which he had completed, even though he had achieved top marks in all subjects.

22 In those days there was as yet no technology by means of which an expulsion from the Pultusk Gimnaziya would have been communicated to all the schools of the Russian Empire. It was a matter of picking a place as far away from Poland as possible, and the Ukrainian city of Novgorod-Seversk in the Chernigov Province where Abram Saulovich did not know a soul, was apparently far enough, although he was not sure why precisely he had picked that godforsaken place and not some other, just as remote.

23 The train travelled to Novgorod-Serversk, Ukraine.

24 Some of the events of 1905 are as follows: January – Port Arthur fell to the Japanese; "Bloody Sunday" occurred when thousands of St Petersburg workers were fired on by soldiers of the Guards Regiments. February – strikes spread throughout Russia and Grand Duke Sergey (Governor-General of Moscow and leader of the reactionary party at the Court) assassinated by a Social Revolutionary. March – peasant disturbances spread throughout Russia. May – bulk of the Russian fleet destroyed by the Japanese at Tsushima. June – the first Soviet organised in the course of a strike in Ivanovo-Voznesensk, armed uprising in Lodz during which two thousand people killed, barricades raised in Warsaw and in Odessa, in the course of a general strike and mutiny on the cruiser *Potemkin*. July – a Soviet organised in Kostroma. August – Tsar agreed to allow the establishment of a parliament, the *Duma,* but

without representation from workers, and with an inadequate representation from peasants. September – the Russo-Japanese war brought to an end by the Treaty of Portsmouth in New Hampshire, USA, with President Theodore Roosevelt acting as intermediary; Russia lost four hundred thousand, killed and wounded, lost most of her navy and had to cede the best part of Sakhalin to Japan. October – railway strikes and general strikes in St Petersburg, Moscow, Kursk, Saratov and several small places; elections held for the St Petersburg Soviet of Workers Deputies; The St Petersburg Soviet challenged the authority of the Tsar by assuming the functions of a national government. November – the Soviet decreed the eight-hour day, and proclaimed the freedom of the press. December – the Soviet issued a manifesto urging the withholding of tax payments, and warning foreign governments that, after a successful revolution, the loans granted to the Tsarist government would not be repaid; a wave of pogroms swept the country, instigated by the reactionary forces with the connivance of the Tsarist government, whose minister, General Trepov, was standing behind the Black Hundreds, members of the Union of the Russian People, the Russian precursors of the Fascists and Nazis and their latter-day successors. The aim of the pogrom organizers was to divert popular anger into the anit-Semitic channel by exploiting anti-Jewish feeling among sections of the population, and, at the same time, to intimidate progressive elements such as intellectuals and socialists; Tsarist government arrested the entire Petersburg Soviet; in Moscow a general strike broke out, leading to an armed uprising which spread to other places; the Tsarist government eventually gained the upper hand and the revolutionary movement was temporarily crushed. Abram wasn't involved in any of these events as he was only sixteen at the time.

25 The Bund (Yiddish for Union) was founded in 1897 as the Union of Lithuanian, Polish and Russian Jewish Workers. The Bund joined the RSDLP in 1903. Among the Russian Social Democrats of that time, the Bund took up the Menshevik position. However, its Socialism was not merely Menshevism propounded in Yiddish. It was also suffused with much of the Jewish nationalism displayed by those who professed Socialism in the Zionist camp (who formed the party known as Poale Zion, which later operated in Palestine). This characteristic of the Bund which likened it to Zionism led Trotsky to call the Bundists "Zionists who are afraid to become seasick". Abram Saulovich's Bundism arose from the Jewish milieu in which he moved at that time but was devoid of any Jewish nationalism whatsoever. The process of his self-education took him to wider fields.

26 Had Abram Saulovich known that this part of his *Memoirs* were to be published, he would possibly have expressed himself more modestly in respect of something of which he was rightfully proud.

238

27 Even though Abram Saulovich considered A.M. Skabichevsky (1838–1910) "utterly boring", this was the author of a quite informative work: *Literaturnyie Vospominaniya* (*Literary Reminiscences*).

28 V.G. Belinsky (1811–1848) was the most outstanding literary critic of the three. His analyses of the works of many great Russian writers have preserved their validity to the present day. He exerted a considerable influence on the writers of his time. He contributed to the journal *Otechestvennye Zapiski* (*Annals of the Fatherland*) and later to *Sovremennik* (*The Contemporary*), in which he propounded democratic and revolutionary ideas and applied principles of materialist philosophy to aesthetics. He was an opponent of reactionary trends and a sponsor of the "natural school" in literature. He attracted the unfavourable attention of the Tsarist Okhranka (The Secret Political Police Department), but his early death from consumption at the age of only thirty-seven, saved him from incarceration.

29 D.I. Pisarev (1840–1868) was not only a literary critic, but also a pamphleteer, a philosopher of the materialist school, and politically – a revolutionary democrat. He had been incarcerated in the Peter-Paul Fortress for one of his pamphlets. If he had not accidentally drowned at the age of twenty-eight, he could, no doubt, have evolved into a more sophisticated writer, than one who, according to Abram Saulovich, was "very primitive".

30 N.G. Chernyshevsky (1828–1889) was a philosopher, economist, writer and literary critic. Like Pisarev and Belinsky, he was politically a revolutionary democrat, and like Belinsky, he was a contributor to the journal *Sovremennik* (*The Contemporary*). He was arrested in 1862 and incarcerated in the Peter-Paul Fortress. There, while in solitary confinement during the years 1862 and 1863, he wrote, in only four months, his novel *What Is To Be Done?* – mentioned by Abram Saulovich. After two years of incarceration, he was exiled to Siberia. Of particular significance was Chernyshevsky's attitude on the role which art should play in society. Chernyshevsky argued that art should be realistic, that it should reflect life that it should explain it and pass judgement on the negative aspects of life. It is ironical that Abram Saulovich, who was to become a Menshevik in his political orientation, came to Marxism through his reading of Chernyshevsky the same way as did Lenin, the leader of the Bolsheviks. Lenin is quoted to have stated to the publicist and professional revolutionary Vaclav Vorovsky:

> Before I came to know the works of Marx, Engels and Plekhanov, only Chernyshevsky wielded a dominating influence over me, and it all began with *What Is To Be Done...* It was through Chernyshevsky that I first became acquainted with philosophical Materialism. He was the first to point out

to me the role of Hegel in the development of philosophical thought, and from him came the idea and the concept of the dialectical method – after which it was much easier for me to assimilate the dialectic of Marx.

31 The first volume was translated and published in Russia in 1872. This was the first translation of that work into a foreign language. The Introduction was written by Peter Struve, a Marxist who later turned Monarchist!

32 This is the first mention of me in Abram Saulovich's *Memoirs.* "Tolya" is the Russian diminutive for Anatol.

33 As Abram Saulovich mentions, Jewish youngsters were at that time joining the revolutionary movement. This was not surprising considering the miserable conditions of existence of the bulk of the Jewish masses in the empire of the Tsar. And this accounted for the relatively large proportion of Jews among Russian revolutionists. Jewish youth was breaking with the tradition of accepting the constraints of ghetto existence and of the designation of the Jews as the "Chosen People", according to which tradition it was also considered un-Jewish to resist the violence of the pogroms, interpreted as a punishment meted out by God for supposed sins. But the Jewish youth, which had espoused the cause of Socialism, followed the Marxist proposition that "social existence determines social consciousness", and believed that phenomena like anti-Semitism were the result of specific social relations, and that a social revolution would remove the soil spawning that evil phenomenon. Incidentally, the word "revolutionary" – meaning a radical social change – must not necessarily be taken in the violent sense, even though democrats and revolutionaries alike sang an anthem to the melody of the Marseillaise with the words: "Let us break with the old world, let us shake its dust from our feet". In fact, the Bund, with its Menshevik orientation, was opposed to revolutionary violence, although it accepted the need for self-defence as exemplified by the issue of a revolver to Abram Saulovich when a pogrom seemed imminent.

34 Bathing once a week was considered hygienically adequate in those days

35 Who was Lobachevsky? During the fifties, more people outside Russia heard of Lobachevsky from a satirical song by Tom Lehrer than had known him before. One of the memorable words of Lehrer's lyrics was "plagiarise". But this was hardly a fair characterisation of Nikolay Ivanovich Lobachevsky (1793–1856) who was a pioneer of mathematics, and who developed a system of non-Euclidean geometry, known today as hyperbolic geometry. According to Stephen Toulmin. Lobachevsky had been dead for almost half a century when Abram Saulovich began his studies at Kazan University, and it was at about the same time that the system developed by Lobachevsky had gained

importance as Albert Einstein set out to base theoretical physics on a non-Euclidean system of geometry.

36 Abram Saulovich found that attendance at lectures at the Faculty of Pure Mathematics was not compulsory. The students were not given any written exercises. All that was required was to be enrolled and then sit for the examinations.

37 In order to properly appreciate the above prices, it is necessary to know what financial means Abram Saulovich had at his disposal, and how this compared with wages, rents and other costs of living during that period. In response to my enquiry, he could not give me any figures in respect of wages generally since he did not move in working class circles, but at least he gave me some figures which could give an indication of the situation at that time. The salesman employed by my grandfather was paid 35 roubles (US\$17.50) per month. The bookkeeper received 50 roubles (US\$25.00) per month. Students generally, had to spend 25 roubles (US\$12.50) per month on their living. Abram Saulovich used to receive from his father 25–35 roubles (US\$12.50–17.50) per month, but in addition to this he also had his own source of income – he used to give lessons.

At one time he was coaching a gimnaziya student, the son of wealthy parents. He was paid 1 rouble (US 50 cents) per lesson, six times per week, 24–26 roubles (US\$12–13) per month, and he could actually subsist on this alone, for this was what the average student spent in one month.

The mother of the student he was coaching was rather anxious to become conversant with all the latest best-sellers. However, she could not go to the trouble of reading them, and thus she organized a group with four similarly minded ladies, and engaged Abram Saulovich to give them a weekly summary of the latest books. He was an avid and fast reader, and it was not a problem for him to appease the voracious but lazy literary appetite of the ladies, for which the group paid him 15 roubles (US\$7.50) per week. These lessons alone brought in more than twice as much as the allowance that his father used to send him. Thus he became quite wealthy, for these lessons went on for quite some time. He claims that towards the end of that stint, he attempted to raise the level of literary appreciation of the ladies and to induce them to do their own reading, but in this he was only partly successful.

He also gave lessons to fellow students, among whom there were those who studied mathematics in order to graduate as gimnaziya teachers. In addition, he used to coach his fellow-students for the examinations. This did not really tax his time, for he used those lessons to also prepare himself.

With all that income, he did not even want to avail himself of the allowance that his father used to send him. He spent about 10 roubles (US\$5.00) per month on food, and about the same on rent.

38 Upon reaching the age of eighteen, Abram Saulovich applied again to the Ministry of Education to be transferred to the St Petersburg University. He had passed all the required examinations in "The Theory of Probability", "The Theory of Numbers" and "Differential and Integral Calculus". He felt that he had attained all that was possible to attain at Kazan. He was granted a transfer to the Physico-Mathematical Faculty at the St Petersburg University. This also meant that he could henceforth live with his family. However he still wished to be admitted to the Faculty of Law. With this in view he called on Professor Grimm, who, at the time when Abram Saulovich had just obtained his Matriculation Certificate, had suggested to him to apply for admission to the St Petersburg University. Difficulties to gain admission had to be overcome, but since he already had been admitted to another faculty at St Petersburg, he was successful in his application.

39 Thus Abram Saulovich felt like a fish in water. Since, as in Kazan, there was no obligation to attend lectures and workshops, he made use of that circumstance to choose lectures at other faculties. Thus he used to attend the lectures at the Philological Faculty given by Maxim Kovalevsky. As for Lossky, it would seem that he was a rather poor lecturer, but Abram Saulovich was interested in the subject, and he attended Lossky's lectures regularly.

40 Statistics was a subject which, while obligatory, was mainly of interest to those students who, after graduation, intended to work for insurance companies, or to take on a job with the Government or with a Zemstvo (Land Council, a representative body elected by limited franchise). Generally, the students did not display any keenness about this subject as such, and there were very few progressive people among them. The chief lecturer was Professor Kaufman. He had written a textbook on statistics, however the bulk of the students did not use the book. Instead, they used a synopsis on that subject, and they did not even go to Kaufman's lectures until Professor Grimm gave the instruction that groups of five students should take turns in attending the lectures. The students obliged out of respect. Abram Saulovich felt that he knew sufficient about statistics, but kept up his studies in that subject. He wanted to gain the highest possible mark in at least the majority of subjects, so as to obtain a Diploma of the First Degree, which would qualify him for a position at the St Petersburg University, something he always longed for. Of course there was a quota system for Jewish applicants for such positions.

41 This conversation happened between Anatol and Abram. That is, it doesn't appear in the memoir.

42 Abram Saulovich was, as ever, an assiduous reader. But now he was reading again, as part of his university studies, those books which he had avidly read as a youngster as part of his political education: Beltov's

(Plekhanov's) *About the Monistic View of History*, Bogdanov's *Political Economy*, and, of course, *Capital* by Karl Marx.

43 Abram Saulovich worked only a short time as such an assistant to the solicitor who acted for the oil company Petrol, which was owned by our relatives in Knyasevka, near Saratov. Such activity did not attract him particularly, and he kept on seeking an academic appointment. Bukovetsky had offered him such an opportunity.

44 This was the thesis which Abram Saulovich set out to write on his return from Knyazevka. He went in search of accommodation where he thought that he would not be disturbed in writing the thesis. Having caught sight of a newspaper advertisement to the effect that a room was being let by a student, he rented that room. The student turned out to be Andrey Yakovlevich Levinson, two years his senior. Levinson, who was to become an outstanding authority on classical ballet, was then still a student with a voracious taste for diverse subjects. These included philosophy, psychology, philology, ancient and modern languages and the history of art. He later became a professor of French literature at the St Petersburg University, and when he emigrated to Paris, he taught Russian literature at the Sorbonne. But his main fame was that of a writer on ballet. In his writings he opposed the innovations of his great contemporary Diaghilev in favour of the purity of classical choreography, which he felt was threatened by spectacular stage-craft and dramatic music which Diaghilev introduced into his productions. Thus, for example, Levinson considered Stravinsky's music as barbaric.

Levinson's fame as a champion of classical ballet was still to come. In the meantime, his lifestyle as a student made a rather negative impression on Abram Saulovich, who abhorred any kind of untidiness. Levinson, was already married and had a child. Abram Saulovich thought that Levinson's wife was rather plain and also a bad housekeeper. The place was filthy and evil-smelling, but the room which he had rented was clean. According to him Levinson went out every night to the theatre or the ballet, but the search for aesthetic satisfaction apparently did not extend to his home life.

45 On 1 August 1914 the First World War broke out. In the preceding years, and especially in the first half of 1914, there was a mounting wave of strikes, which, more and more, took on a political character. In Russia there were clashes with the police and other evidence of increasing discontent, but this process was brought to a halt by the outbreak of the war.

46 In the years before the war Socialists throughout the world had generally opposed militarism and armaments. But the outbreak of the war led to a crisis of the socialist movement. Social Democratic Parties lined up behind their respective governments, although these parties were members of the same Second (Socialist) International. Social Democrats,

who were committed to the same Socialist Objective, now faced each other as enemies. The Social Democratic deputies in the German Reichstag voted in support of the war loans, with the honourable exception of Karl Liebknecht, the one who later, together with Rosa Luxemburg, founded the German Communist Party. The Russian Social Democratic Workers Party split into two groups: the "Defencists", comprising mostly the Mensheviks, and the "Defeatists", who were generally identical with the Bolsheviks. These designations indicated their position for or against participation in the war. The principal leader of the "Defencists" was Plekhanov, originally called the "Father of Russian Marxism". The most prominent "Defeatists" were Lenin, Trotsky and Zinoviev, who considered the war to be an imperialist war of the big powers for a resubdivision of the world, and from which the masses had nothing to gain. But some Mensheviks were also "Defeatists". Chief among them was Martov, a theoretician and a leading Menshevik He took an internationalist position, even though he opposed Lenin. Abram Saulovich, as a Menshevik, did not spell out specifically his support for Martov's position, but he certainly did not share Plekhanov's patriotism.

47 In his capacity as Science Secretary, Abram Saulovich was involved in the checking of the theses submitted by the students, and had access to the printing of these theses. It was this circumstance which made him interested in the whole business of publishing. He took a hand in the publishing process himself.

48 Abram Saulovich disagreed with Lenin politically, but what offended him especially, was the manner in which Lenin presented his arguments.

49 Abram Saulovich acquired Vestnik Yevropy and continued to publish it for some time, for he had already actively entered the publishing field shortly before the revolutionary year of 1917. He conducted this and other forays into publishing while simultaneously lecturing and otherwise assiduously working at the Agricultural Institute. The Revolution intervened before publishing became the main venue of his activity.

50 My parents and I still lived in Khersonskaya Street at the outbreak of the Revolution. Abram Saulovich does not indicate any dates, but 8 March 1917 has remained indelibly in my memory. On that day I was taken for a walk by my nanny in front of our block of apartments, when a policeman came running for his life along the footpath, with a crowd of people hot in pursuit. This was, of course, an unusual sight, and it could have happened only on that particular day which has gone down in history as the start of the February Revolution (according to the old Russian calendar which was thirteen days behind that used in the rest of the world). There were shots fired from the garret of a nearby building, where other police were supposed to be sheltering, and we

took cover under the arch over the entrance of our block of apartments. That event makes it possible for me to determine my first childhood memory with precision: I was three years and five months old.

51 1917 was the year of two revolutions which have gone into history as the "February" and the "October" Revolutions.

52 This was essentially the view taken by Abram Saulovich, which governed his activity in the Petrograd Soviet. When working in the Military-Industrial Committee before the Revolution, he had met Boris Osipovich Bogdanov, a leading Menshevik. On the very first day of the February Revolution, Bogdanov left the Committee to take part in the organization of the Soviet of Workers and Soldiers Deputies, which was being established in the Tauride Palace, the seat of the Duma.

53 The rider of the Pale Steed of the Book of Revelation was Death.

54 It stands to reason that Abram Saulovich, a Menshevik, who imagined that the evolution of Russia towards Socialism would proceed along the road of parliamentary democracy, could only feel antagonistic to characters like Moiseyenko and Savinkov, who had espoused acts of individual terror against those in power. While the Social Revolutionaries considered such acts as effective methods of bringing about revolutionary change, such methods were rejected as unsuitable by the Bolsheviks, who believed in the action of the masses to bring about the change. The Bolsheviks also argued that the individual terrorist, of necessity preparing his act in secrecy, would alienate himself from the popular masses.

Far from being "insignificant", and much more than just a "cutthroat" (as characterized by Abram Saulovich) Savinkov was a very gifted man. He was, among his various qualities, a talented writer. Abram Saulovich mentioned his popular book *The Pale Steed*. In his writings, Savinkov propounded a philosophy expressive of his spiritual turmoil. He was, of course, outstanding as a terrorist, and was launched on that career by no less a person than the infamous Azef, an agent of the secret police who, in the beginning of the twentieth century, had wormed his way into the headquarters of the Party of the Social Revolutionaries located in Geneva. Azef, in fact, acted as one of the leaders of that party. (Incidentally, Abram Saulovich later published a book on Azef: *Istoriya Odnovo Predatelya* (*History of a Traitor*) by Nikolaevsky).

In the period of the decline of the revolutionary movement following the defeat of the 1905 Revolution, Savinkov quarrelled with the leadership of the Social Revolutionary Party and left it in 1907. He again devoted himself to writing. It was during this time that The *Pale Steed* was published. Its theme was repentance over blood spilled in futile revolutionary struggle.

55 Lev Borisovich Kamenev (1883–1936) had been attracted to Marxism as a student in Tiflis. He had met Lenin in Paris in 1902, and had

become a committed Bolshevik. He was elected to the Central Committee of the Bolsheviks in April 1917.

56 Olga Davidovna Kameneva was not only Trotsky's sister, but also the wife of another prominent Bolshevik, and thus, according to Abram Saulovich, it was "natural" that the Bolsheviks would be in the know of everything going on in the Administration.

57 Abram Saulovich does not explain how she was "removed".

58 Characteristic of the axiomatic acceptance of Capitalism as a "completely unavoidable" historical stage for Russia, was the statement made by Plekhanov – that "father of Russian Marxism" – at the State Conference in Moscow (see note 46) when he addressed the "Left" delegates at that abortive gathering:

> ...Russia is now in the process of capitalist revolution, and it is absolutely inappropriate for the working class to seize power, full political power... Once you subscribe to this point of view, once you understand the entire political and theoretical depth of these words, you must, in accordance with this, define your attitude towards the commercial-industrial class. There can be no bourgeois revolution in which the bourgeoisie does not take part. There can be no Capitalism in which there are no capitalists... And if both the proletariat and the bourgeoisie do not want to damage their interests, both classes must look for ways to achieve economic and political accord.

59 Here Abram Saulovich's narrative is at variance with historical fact: Trotsky was arrested after the uprising, and was held in the Kresty prison. He was not released until the Kornilov uprising. Kornilov was actually the one to play the part of the "General on the White Steed". His failure to crush the Revolution led to the subsequent October uprising and the victory of the Bolsheviks.

60 We must have stayed in Khersonskaya Street till the summer, or according to the revolutionary calendar, until the July days, for at that time we stayed at Oylilo in Finland, and when we returned it was to my parents' second apartment.

61 Mishelina also restored my regard for womanhood, which had been all but destroyed by a sadistic female whom my parents had engaged after we had to take leave of my first nanny – the one who was, as Abram Saulovich wrote, "as is described in old novels". He writes about her successor:

We hired another nanny who accompanied us to the summer resort of Oylilo in Finland. The people in the neighbouring summer cottage told us that she used to punish the child for no reason whatsoever. We immediately dismissed her.

I must have been putting up with all the ill-treatment without, as would seem natural, reporting it to my parents, but keeping my problem to myself. In retrospect, I have become aware of what must have been a lack of communication between me and my parents, arising from their busy life. At that time I hardly ever saw Abram Saulovich, who was busy with all his publishing, teaching, as well as political activities. He was distant and severe. In contrast with him, my mother was very affectionate, but then I did not see much of her either, for she was a teacher at a primary school situated in the outskirts of Petrograd, and her job necessitated lengthy journeys by public transport, which at that time was in a disastrously poor condition. Thus the "mothering" was delegated to other women and accepted by me as natural. In this context Mishelina established my concept of the ideal woman.

62 In addition, my parents engaged a governess, an elderly Swiss lady, who talked to me exclusively in French, so that when I was five years old I could speak French fluently, and could read and write in that language before I could do so in Russian. Mishelina, for her part, taught me German. Incidentally, engaging a governess in those days was not unusual for a middle class family, since many of those ladies who had been previously engaged in educating the progeny of the nobility and the wealthy, were thrown on the labour market following the flight of their former employers. Thus Mishelina and Madame Richard substituted for my mother, who occasionally came to play with me, as one plays with a toddler.

We could not have stayed very long in Spasskaya Street, for I can still remember some very definite features of the building where we had our third apartment, in Zhukovskaya Street, namely the front stairs, a part of the building which I would not have been able to see after the October Revolution, because those stairs were no longer accessible. Apartment buildings in the aristocratic and bourgeois districts of St Petersburg had front stairs referred to as the "parade" stairs, and service stairs referred to as "black" stairs. The front stairs were closed after the Revolution, "to put the gentry into its place", and make them use the "black" stairs. I can remember the white marble steps, the red carpet and the brass balustrade of the front stairs to our Zhukovskaya Street apartment, which means that we must have moved there before the October Revolution.

The apartment in Zhukovskaya Street was actually that of my paternal grandfather, Saul Natanovich. As mentioned earlier, he had the right, as a "Merchant of the First Guild", to reside in St Petersburg in the days of the Tsar, and eventually he moved there permanently from Vitebsk. I well remember my grandfather who lived with us in Zhukovskaya

Street, but my paternal grandmother had already died when I was too young to remember her.

63 Since Liber had no cause for hiding until after the October Revolution, the apartment referred to must have been that in Zhukovskaya Street.

The building in which we had our apartment was situated on the corner of a street called Ertelev Pereulok (Ertelev Lane) before the Revolution. It was named thus after a previous landowner. In 1923 it was re-named Ulitsa Chekhova (Chekhov Street) after the great Russian writer Anton Chekhov (1860–1904). Actually Chekhov did not live in St Petersburg, he was a Muscovite, but his publisher, A.S. Suvorin, had his premises and dwelling in Ertelev Pereulok, separated by one building from the corner building which contained our apartment. Suvorin was also the publisher of the paper *Novoye Vremya* (*New Time*). His partner was the writer Vladimir Krymov, whose works Abram Saulovich was to publish in the years to come. Krymov left Petrograd after the victory of the October Revolution, and Abram Saulovich was to meet him a few years later in his Berlin exile.

64 Zaslavsky's case was characteristic of those who had opposed the Revolution, but who, after its victory, exploited it for their own ends. It was from among these elements that Stalin established his cadres. It could be suggested that had Zaslavsky lived to see the rise of Yeltsin, Zaslavsky, like certain erstwhile prominent Communists, would have become a champion for the introduction of capitalism into Russia. But not all those who went over into the Bolshevik camp after the Revolution were characters like Zaslavsky.

65 Since the wealth of the rich was considered to be the result of exploiting or "robbing" the people, it was now considered legitimate to reclaim or "rob" that wealth.

66 This was in persuance of measures to resettle people from the slums into the dwellings of the bourgeoisie.

67 After the October Revolution Abram Saulovich concentrated more and more on his publishing activity. It must be kept in mind that the major part of that activity proceeded while the country was in the throes of the Civil War (1918–1921).

68 This three-storey building (36 Liteyny Prospect) was erected at the end of the eighteenth century and has maintained its architectural features. Today it houses the Nekrasov Museum, and Basseynaya Street has been renamed Nekrasov Street.

The building had been acquired in the 1840s by the publisher A.A. Krayevsky, who was the editor of the progressive periodical *Otechestvennye Zapiski* (Annals of the Fatherland). His successors owned the building until the Revolution.

It was in this building that Nikolay Alexeyevich Nekrasov (1821–1877), one of Russia's greatest poets and writers, lived for twenty years

(1857–1877). But there were also other famous people who lived there at various times.

The surgeon N.I. Pirogov lived there before Nekrasov, and the great literary critic, revolutionary democrat, philosopher and poet N.A. Dobrolyubov lived there for two years in a small apartment during Nekrasov's time.

It was here that Nekrasov edited another progressive periodical: *Sovremennik* (*The Contemporary*), which had been founded by Pushkin, and when that periodical was stopped by the Tsarist Government, Nekrasov became the editor of *Otechestvennye Zapiski*, mentioned above.

Nekrasov's apartment became the venue for literary discussions and a meeting place of people who had espoused the revolutionary democratic cause, and where heated debates took place on the destiny of Russia. Constant visitors to Nekrasov's apartment included many famous writers: Turgenev, Tolstoy, Goncharov, Dostoevsky, the playwright Ostrovsky, and many others.

Today there are four memorial tablets affixed to the facade of the building, recalling that Pirogov, Nekrasov, Dobrolyubov and N.N. Figner had lived there, the last mentioned was a famous Russian tenor. But the building had still another famous tenant, for, after the death of Nekrasov, his apartment was occupied by the scientist P.N. Yablochkov, the inventor of the "electric candle", which he had patented in Paris in 1876, and which preceded Edison's development of the incandescent lamp. Yablochkov's apartment was the first in St Petersburg to be lit by electricity. During experiments, people used to congregate on Liteyny Prospect to watch the peculiar light emanating from the brightly lit windows, from which the curtains had been purposely pulled aside.

The last owner of the building before the Revolution was a Mrs Nagel. She was Nekrasov's granddaughter, and since the building, up to the Revolution, belonged to Krayevsky's heirs, it is likely, although I do not possess any documentary evidence, that there was a marriage link between the heirs of Nekrasov and Krayevsky.

When *Naooka i Shkola* rented the former Nekrasov apartment, it was not only of financial benefit to Mrs Nagel, but it also prevented the premises from being taken over during the revolutionary upheaval.

Nekrasov's office, with the writer's bookcases, writing desk, couch, chairs etc., was the room, used by Abram Saulovich as his office. He shared it with Kotlyarevsky and Karsavin. But since his partners were teaching during the day and therefore were absent most of the time, Abram Saulovich was practically the sole user of the room. When he was forced to leave Russia, he passed on the furniture to the Pushkin House, which was attached to the Academy of Sciences, and when, by a resolution of the Council of Ministers of the USSR of 7 December 1946, Nekrasov's apartment was turned into a museum, the furniture was returned to its original location. In this manner the physical environment of *Naooka i Shkola* was also restored, at least as far as Abram Saulovich's office was concerned.

69 The last catalogue of *Naooka i Shkola*, published in 1922, contained some thirty-five titles of books published, or still in print between 1918 and 1922, ie. until *Naooka i Shkola* ceased to exist with the expulsion of Abram Saulovich from Russia. Of the books published, more than half had already been sold out by 1922. Particularly successful was the series of *Introductions* into various topics: into Philosophy by Lossky and Radlov, into Gnoseology by Alekseyev, into Logic by Povarnin, into Aesthetics by Lapshin, into History by Karsavin, and into Archeology by Zhebelyov.

The first books published in 1918, i.e. the first year after the Revolution, (and sold out by 1922), were Vernadsky's *Novikov*, Lossky's *Logic* and Vulfius' *Europe in the New Age*. One of the first books published in 1919 was Karsavin's *Saligia, or a rather brief meditation, helpful to the soul, on God, the World, Man, Evil and the Seven Deadly Sins*. A copy of that book containing a dedication to Abram Saulovich is preserved in the Bakhmeteff Archive. Reflecting the post-revolutionary period, the publishers are listed as Labor Cooperative (Troodovaya Artel) of Professors and Educationalists *Nauka i Shkola*.

As mentioned above, in the beginning of his activity Abram Saulovich published, among others, the book about Novikov by Georgy Vladimirovich Vernadsky. Later he cooperated with him when Vernadsky lived in Prague, and later still in America. It was thanks to Vernadsky that Abram Saulovich had the possibility of coming to the United States.

70 Kotlyarevsky was the author of *Nashe Nedavneye Proshloye* (*Our Recent Past*) and *Devyatnadtsatyy Vek* (*Nineteenth Century*) published by *Naooka i Shkola*. Other books on history included S.A. Zhebelyov's *Ancient Greece and Ancient Rome*, O.A. Dobiash-Rozhdestvensky`s *The Middle Ages*, G.D. Gourvitch`s *Rousseau and the Declaration of Rights*, I.I. Kareyev`s *The French Revolution and the Napoleonic Period* and, by the same author *The Nineteenth Century*, also A.G. Vulfius's *Europe in the New Age and Problems of the Spiritual Development of Western Europe*, and V.V. Bartold's *The Moslem World*. There was finally the *Outline of Ancient Russian Literature* by the academician V.M. Istrin.

71 William James (1842–1910), the brother of novelist Henry James, shares with Willhelm Wundt (1832–1920), the acknowledgement of being the fathers of modern psychology. The term "psychology" was coined by the Protestant reformer Philip Melanchton (1497–1560) who defined thus "the study of the soul". Both James and Wundt graduated in medicine in their respective parts of the world, and later became professors of physiology before they turned to psychology. Wundt spoke of "physiological psychology" to distinguish it from the psychology which belonged to the field of philosophy and was referred to as "mental philosophy". James, who in 1875 had set up the first psychology

laboratory in the United States, laid down his propositions in his two-volume work *Principles of Psychology* which appeared in 1890.

72 For these were the times of the Civil War.

73 It is significant that at that time, the publication of non-Marxist literature was not interfered with – contrary to what could be assumed to be the case in this period of Revolution, Civil War and its aftermath. In later years, under Stalinism, such publications would be completely impossible.

74 Among other publications were works by Lossky, whose authority in the academic field of that time was very great, as well as works by Karsavin. The works referred to were Lossky's *Vvedenye v Filosofiyu* (*Introduction into Philosophy*), *Osnovnye Voprosy Gnoseologuii* (*Basic questions of Gnoseology*), *Sbornik Zadach po Loguike* (*Collection of Articles on Problems of Logic*) and *Loguika* (*Logic*). The work by Karsavin was *Vvedenye v Istoriyu* (*Introduction into History*).

Of the scientific works, *Naooka i Shkola* published the translation of Einstein's *Theory of Relativity*, edited by A.P. Kudriavtsev. Later *Naooka i Shkola* published the translation of the book by E. Cassirer on Einstein's theory.

When Abram Saulovich became closely acquainted with Y. Perelman, the author of popular scientific books, *Naooka i Shkola* published, in huge quantities, Perelman's *Zanimatelnaya Fisika* (*Entertaining Physics*) and *Zanimatelnaya Matematika* (*Entertaining Mathematics*).

In the field of economics *Naooka i Shkola* published *Osnovy Finansovoi Naooki* (*Foundations of Financial Science*) by I.M. Kulisher, who had been Abram Saulovich's teacher.

A book that was of interest in the field of philosophy was I.I. Lapshin's *The Philosophy of Invention and the Invention in Philosophy*.

75 Incidentally, Beyer, et alia, list as "foundation members" of the Petropolis Publishing Company, apart from Abram Saulovich, Blokh and Lozinsky, also Alexander Mikhailovich Rosener and the professors Lev Platonovich Karsavin and Dmitri Konstantinovich Petrov.

76 I regret that I am unable to present a catalogue of publications by Petropolis. However, I ascertained that, apart from the already mentioned Akhmatova's *Anno Domini MCMXXI*, Gumilyov's *Ognennyi Stolp and Kostyor*, and Mandelstam's *Tristia*. *Petropolis* published between 1921 and 1922: Georgi Ivanov's *Sady* (*Gardens*), Fyodor Slogoub's *Svirel* (*Flute*), Mikhail Kuzmin's *Nezdeshniye Vechera* (*Supernatural Evenings*) and *Vtornik Meri* (*Mary's Tuesday*), *A Play for Live and Wooden Dolls*.

Among the books in the A.S. Kagan collection of the Bakhmeteff Archive there is also the translatiton by Adrian Piotrovsky of *The Elegies of Theognis of Megara,* published by *Petropolis* in 1922.

77 In the above interview, beside indicating the supposed time of Raissa's visit, Abram Saulovich also gives a more specific explanation of the

object originally pursued by the *Petropolis* cooperative, namely, the buying up of antiquarian and other valuable books, at the time when the political situation had created a market for such books on which to base a business venture.

Furthermore, Abram Saulovich indicated the order in which the first books published by the new company appeared, also that *Petropolis* had published Akhmatova and Gumilyov both before and after the October Revolution. Going by such testimony, there should be no doubt as to precisely when the *Petropolis* Publishing Company was established – namely 1917.

However there is factual and implied evidence to the effect that the publishing company was launched not in 1917 but in 1920. Thus Thomas R. Beyer et al., specify the year 1917 as that in which Blokh's and Lozinsky's enterprise, the *Kooperativny Knizhny Sklad* (Cooperative Book Store) Petropolis was established, i.e. the year of the Revolution, which had caused many of the wealthier citizens who possessed libraries or valuable antiquarian books, to leave Petrograd and to liquidate their libraries, while others utilized this situation to acquire books, and it was this situation which provided the basis for Blokh's and Lozinsky's business venture. As for the establishment of *Chastnoye Izdatelstvo* (Private Publishing Company) Petropolis, Thomas R. Beyer et. al. specify the summer of 1920. That this is chronologically correct can be supported by the fact that the first book published by Petropolis (according to Abram Saulovich) was Anna Akhmatova's *Anno Domini*. The full title of the book was *Anno Domini MCMXXI.* (With such a title, it could hardly have been published in 1917. It was followed by Gumilyov's *Ognennyi Stolp* published, according to the title page, in the same year, i.e. 1921. Thus both Akhmatova and Gumilyov were not published "before and after", but definitely after the October Revolution.

From the earlier quoted extract from Abram Saulovich's *Memoirs* there is also some implied evidence that Raissa Noevna's visit occurred not in 1917 but in 1920. It was then that Abram Saulovich had established for himself quite a reputation as a publisher, and also as one who had taken over the management of other companies, while 1917 was the year when his main activity was connected with the "Other Towns Department" of the Soviet. Significant is also his remark placed in brackets: "at that time I was managing the best printing establishment in Russia". This establishment was that of Golike & Vilborg, which had been nationalized, and this obviously occurred after the October Revolution, when it had become the "15th State Printery".

Thus it is safe to say that Raissa visited Abram Saulovich in the winter of 1920 and that Petropolis became a publishing company in the summer of the same year. At the age of ninety-two, Abram Saulovich can be forgiven if his memory which had served him so well practically everywhere before, had slipped a little.

78 Only the confusion created by the revolutionary situation can explain why Golike & Vilborg, being nationalized, was not completely taken over by the new administration, and why Abram Saulovich was able to take charge of it after it had been passed on to him by Glasberg. But by taking charge of Golike & Vilborg, he also assured its further functioning, although ironically, the "luxury" publications forthcoming from this foremost high quality printing establishment, were quite out of keeping with the stern times. The following incident related by Abram Saulovich represents, no doubt, the climax of such publishing activity:

79 An *ex libris* is a label bearing the owner's name, crest or some design, intended to be pasted into a book to indicate the owner. In English dictionaries it is generally listed under "book plate".

80 The book was published in a limited edition of only 500 copies. The cover and the decorative features throughout the book were by Mitrokhin. Incidentally, the place of publication was indicated as "Petersburg", although in 1922, the year of publication, the city was called "Petrograd". As mentioned earlier, its original German-sounding name of "St Petersburg" was changed to the Russian "Petrograd" at the outbreak of the First World War.

The book contained numerous illustrations of *ex libris*, some in colour. It listed 652 names of artists engaged in their design, including such well known artists as Altman, Annenkov, Bakst, Alexander Benoit, Bilibin, Dobuzhinsky, Fomin, Golovin, Konashevich, Kupreyanov, Kustodiev, Lanseré, Lukomsky, Mitrokhin, Ostroumova-Lebedeva, Petrov-Vodkin, Somov, Sudeykin, Vasnetsov, Vidberg, Voinov and Vrubel.

Yonov's *ex libris* was designed by Vidberg. It showed a semi-nude male figure holding in his outstretched arms an open book, defying the black-cloaked figure of Death slinking away with a broken scythe. No doubt Yonov should have been flattered by that symbolism which presented him as a champion of enlightenment. One of Abram Saulovich's *ex libris* by Voinov, showed an eagle holding in its claws a snake forming an oval surround to the inscription in the centre. Another of his *ex libris*, designed by Kupreyanov in a style tending towards Cubism, showed a figure seated at a table reading a book. A third, listed but not illustrated, was by Mitrokhin, who also designed my *ex libris* which included a beetle, a butterfly, a flower and a bird.

Due to Yonov's assistance, Petropolis was also able to publish a book of portraits by Russian artists. Abram Saulovich mentions that a portrait of Yonov was included in a book of portraits by Annenkov.

Annenkov was kept very busy in those days. He had drawn, among others, portraits of Lenin and Trotsky, as well as portraits of practically all the writers and poets living in Petrograd at that time.

81 These were grim times: civil war, economic disruption and famine. It was not the time to publish books on art and poetry, some of which

seemed to be quite out of keeping with the stresses and problems of that period. But Petropolis was not the only enterprise favoured then by being able to publish high quality editions. Mention must be made of Alkonost, and other private idealistic endeavours which sprang up at that time, filling the cultural gap created by the closing down of the major publishing companies, and before the new power had succeeded in taking up publishing as a monopoly.

I can recall Abram Saulovich telling me that Alkonost was one of the publishing companies with which Petropolis had "a friendly relationship". This must not be construed as a business relationship in the modern pecuniary sense. It was rather a partnership formed not for commercial gain (there was hardly any in those days), but for the purpose of bringing out specific works of high artistic and literary value, with the maintenance of a high level of typographic art. All this for a limited public, often based on subscription, during a period not conducive to such pursuits.

Alkonost was established by Samuil Mironovich Alyansky in 1918. Alyansky was then only twenty-seven years old, and Abram Saulovich twenty-nine. Alyansky was an admirer of the poet Alexander Blok, and his production of Blok's Twelve, in 1918, was quite a masterpiece, in which the rather short poem forms a harmonious whole with the illustrations by Annenkov.

This poem, which was to become one of the landmarks of Russian literature of the revolutionary years, was published in an edition of only three hundred copies, twenty-five of which had the illustrations hand coloured by Annenkov.

The poem, written in spare and incisive rhymes, some in the nature of political slogans and replete with visionary symbolism, traces the progress of twelve Red Guards through the dark night of a hurricane-lashed Petrograd, past the debris of the old order, swept away by the storm of the Revolution. The Red Guards are imbued with fervour for their heroic mission to change the world. But, for all their revolutionary histrionics, they are frail humans. Yet ahead of them, but hidden by night and blizzard, and carrying a red banner – strides Christ.

82 In years to come, Abram Saulovich will publish works by authors of various political attitudes, including attitudes completely opposite to his own. But this was not yet the case in the first years of Petropolis.

83 By the way, the Derzhavin mentioned above is, of course, not Professor Derzhavin whose *Grammar* was withdrawn from further publication by *Naooka i Shkola*. The Derzhavin whose monograph Abram Saulovich published is the poet Gavrila Romanovich Derzhavin (1743–1816) who devoted much of his poetry to singing the praise of the "Palmyra of the North", i.e. St Petersburg, while other poems by him had been inspired by the works of art in St Petersburg's museums, and by the palaces and parks of Tsarskoye Selo.

84 As for Pushkin's *Gavriiliada*, a poem dealing with the intervention of the Archangel Gabriel against the Devil in the defence of the Virgin Mary, it should be noted that, as a rule it was not included among the collections of Pushkin's works, because of what had been seen to be pornography and blasphemy. The manuscript of *Gavriiliada* had been preserved in the Academy of Sciences, where the distinguished scholar, Tomashevsky, had made a study of it. There have been numerous printed editions of the poem produced by anonymous publishers for purely mercenary reasons, seeking to exploit its supposed pornographic content. Abram Saulovich had made the acquaintance of Tomashevsky, and it was with the latter's cooperation that he was able to publish the book as a work of art worthy of Pushkin. The book was produced by *Golike & Vilborg*. It was put together exceptionally handsomely, with illustrations and tail pieces, and printed on high quality paper. The year was 1920, and it was quite remarkable that a book of such quality could have been produced at that time. But such books could be brought out only in limited editions − 1,500 numbered copies, and then possibly another 1,500.

85 A copy of Iretsky's *Graviury* (*Engravings*) is in the Bakhmeteff Archive, as well as a copy of Karsavin's *Noctes Petropolitanae*. Only one thousand copies of the last mentioned book were published. The one in the Archive is No.3.

86 It may be queried how such purchases could have been effected in those days, when the Soviet currency was almost worthless. Transactions were often carried out in foreign currency (speculation in such currency was rife, and attracted the special attention of the Cheka). Barter also played an important role. I do not know, however, how the purchases of the above albums were effected.

87 The *gymnaziya* had a reputation for its high educational standard. It was co-educational, and its pupils were generally the progeny of the "liberal" intelligentsia, but also included scions of prominent social and political activists. At the time that the young Shostakovich and Lossky attended the gymnaziya, they rubbed shoulders with the sons of Trotsky, Kamenev and Kerensky. After 1918 the gymnaziya was nationalized, and, according to Lossky: "... became, in all probability, the *Soviet School of Labor No.108*". [95]. When my parents enrolled me at that school's kindergarten, Maria Shidlovskaya, its former director, was still in charge, but gone were the distinctive uniforms comprising blue and white striped "sailor's" tops and sand coloured overalls, described by Lossky. Gone too was Shostakovich, as were the sons of Trotsky, Kamenev and Kerensky. Some ten years later, my path would cross, in a rather odd way, with that of Trotsky's son − Leon Sedov.

88 Before the Revolution, there existed in St Petersburg a so-called Free Economic Society, a body which was barely tolerated under the Tsarist

regime. It provided the venue for the meeting of economists and persons connected with related disciplines and who held progressive views. The Society continued its existence in the years immediately after the Revolution. Abram Saulovich used to attend its meetings, and on one occasion he made the acquaintance of a certain Lutokhin. The latter worked at *Glavbum*, the department in charge of paper supplies. Abram Saulovich and Lutokhin conceived the idea of publishing a journal devoted to current problems of economics. An editorial committee was formed which included Ozerov, a Moscow Professor of Economics. Lutokhin was to be the chief editor. The paper came from *Glavbum*. Several issues of the journal, appropriately called *Ekonomist*, were published, and were a great success among the public to which it was directed. But in one of the issues, Professor Ozerov published an article dealing with the effects of the Revolution on the Russian economy. The article was quite outspoken in its condemnation of the Soviet power. Considering the times, the article could have had the gravest consequences for the author and those involved in the publication. Surprisingly, the censorship passed it, but Abram Saulovich considered the publication of the article to be "a great impudence, a play with dynamite". He insisted, that in future the contents of the articles should be assessed by the editorial committee and not be left only to Lutokhin. This led to some arguments resulting in the editorial committee falling apart. Several more issues of Ekonomist were published before it ceased to exist.

Also before the Revolution there existed in St Petersburg the publishing company *Pravo* (*Justice*), at the head of which stood Yossif Vladimirovich Gessen. *Pravo* used to publish a rather authoritative journal by the same name, and Abram Saulovich used to subscribe to it when he was still a student. The editorial committee of this journal consisted mainly of members of the Constitutional Democratic Party. After the Revolution, the journal became politically unacceptable, and its publication ceased. In 1919 Gessen went abroad and left the management of *Pravo* to a close relative, Yakov Matveyevich Gessen, who decided to convert *Pravo* into a cooperative, but he and his wife were the only partners. Then Yakov Matveyevich offered Abram Saulovich a partnership in the company, which he accepted. An economist, Professor Victor Morisovich Shtein also joined the cooperative. Under the editorship of the latter, *Pravo* launched a new journal called *Ekonomicheskoye Vozrozhdenie* (*Economic Revival*), which replaced the defunct *Ekonomist*. *Ekonomicheskoye Vozrozhdenie* was not, of course, a Bolshevik journal. Its articles did not support the economic measures of the Soviet power, but they were cautiously formulated, containing purely factual information without comments, assuming that the reader could draw his own conclusions. *Pravo* also published a series of books, some of which Abram Saulovich translated, and others which he edited. Among these were: Bogolepov's *The Economy after the War*, and Angell's *Treaty of Versailles*.

89 Perhaps the attempts at the raising of the cultural level of the nation after the Revolution had something to do with this, but these were still the times of the aftermath of the Civil War, when the reconstruction period had hardly started.

90 It was also at the beginning of the twenties that the Russian book market began to be flooded with Russian books published abroad, especially in Berlin. There were innumerable books, including the classics, for example those published by firms such as Ladyzhnikov, established by *émigrés*, as well as by German firms such as *Walter de Gruyter* and *Göschen*. The last-mentioned firm produced a vast library of cheap paperback editions of the classics, mainly for use in schools.

Abram Saulovich considered that the establishment of cooperative publishing companies in Russia could stem the influx of Russian books published abroad.

91 To simply entrust to the postal services a memorandum directed to the Council of Peoples Commissars in Moscow, appeared impractable, due to the possibility of interception by the Censors, or unreliability of postal services at that time. Abram Saulovich therefore decided to take the memorandum personally to Moscow. To be able to do so, he sought the assistance of the Commissar of Justice, I.N. Steinberg, who resided in Petrograd at that time.

Steinberg, a lawyer by profession, was a Left Social Revolutionary, but combined his radicalism with being a religious Jew, who used to pray every day, and who refused to write on Saturdays, since Saturday was the day of rest determined by God. Steinberg was one of the seven Social Revolutionary delegates to the October 1917 Soviet Congress, who, after some deliberations, had joined the Council of People's Commissars.

Abram Saulovich was friendly with Steinberg, although he did not share the latter's combination of Socialism with religious devotion, but while not exactly in sympathy with the Left Social Revolutionaries, he still considered them allies in the quest for justice. But disappointment awaited him: Steinberg refused to be party to a proposal to denationalize the printing establishments, and thus he declined to cooperate in the proposed plan. Abram Saulovich then decided to "go it alone" without Steinberg's permission or blessing. As an additional safeguard, he decided to obtain a letter from the Academy of Agriculture to the effect that he was travelling to Moscow on business.

92 He was supposed to have died from typhus was the official explanation, but he died somewhat too soon after his arrest to have succumbed to that disease. Since he was an aristocrat and an officer, he belonged to

that group of people from among whom hostages were taken in those days, in response to actions by counter-revolutionary elements, so that Vera's husband no doubt must have fallen victim to one of these ugly aspects of the Civil War.

93 This journey took place after the one described in the previous chapter.

94 The Blokhs left a little while later without any trouble, taking Petropolis with them to Berlin.

95 It was Yenukidze's compassionate nature that was one of the principal causes of his downfall, for Abram Saulovich was not the only one on whom Yenukidze's compassionate nature had made an impression. It was this characteristic which was particularly noted by Alexander Orlov, a former NKVD general, who defected to the USA in 1938, after almost twenty years of service in the Soviet security organs. Orlov had been a participant in the operations of these organs and an observer of the events which characterized Stalin's obsession to rid himself of anyone who he felt could not be made fully subservient to him. In 1953, shortly after Stalin's death, Orlov recorded his experiences and observations in a book and in a series of articles in *Life* magazine, under the title *The Secret History of Stalin's Crimes*.

Orlov wrote that Stalin, in his obsession, did away with more revolutionaries than all the Tsars put together. But it was the execution of Yenukidze which Orlov found the most staggering event of a long series of "liquidations" ordered by Stalin.

When Abram Saulovich went to seek Yenukidze's assistance in the two cases mentioned in his *Memoirs*, Yenukidze held the post of Chairman of the Central Executive Committee of the Supreme Soviet. This was still an important position at that time, but very soon the real seat of power shifted to the Politbureau of the Communist Party. According to Orlov, in 1926 Stalin had offered Yenukidze a position on that all-powerful body which was already dominated by him, but Yenukidze declined, which was not due to lack of ambition on his part, but to his realization that one had to be both cruel and unprincipled to join that body.

But already while he was occupying the post of Chairman of the Central Executive Committee of the Supreme Soviet, Yenukidze had changed from a revolutionary to a bureaucrat. He had now become a member of the new social elite. Yet although he was quite content to enjoy the fruits of power, he did not lose his compassionate nature. Orlov writes that Yenukidze loved to come to the assistance of people, who at the moment of an everyday misfortune, thought to turn to him. Thus, almost every plea for the extenuation of a sentence, if it had been addressed to Yenukidze, was granted by the Central Executive Committee. He helped the wives of those arrested. He actually assisted many of them with food, and directed physicians to them when their children were sick.

96 Abram wouldn't have been surprised by this arrest given others had been arrested before him. Yury Petrovich Novitsky who was a member of the management of *Naooka i Shkola* and who was arrested and shot in connection with the "Case of the Churchmen". By implication, the "Case of the Churchmen", which led to Novitsky facing the firing squad, was linked to the case known as the "Conspiracy of the Three Ambassadors", and to the alleged connection between Patriarch Tikhon and Bruce Lockhart, the head of the British Mission in Moscow who unsuccessfully plotted to overthrow the Soviet Government. Bruce Lockhart, together with a British Intelligence agent Sidney Reilly and the Consuls General of the United States and France, organized a conspiracy to seize the Bolshevik leaders during a session of the Council of Peoples Commissars in the Kremlin, and to shoot Lenin during that operation. In the second half of 1921, parts of Russia, and especially the Volga region, were ravaged by the worst famine, the combined result of a crop failure and the disruption by the Civil War. More than twenty-three million people were starving. The Soviet Government set up the "Committee for Helping the Hungry", and in February 1922, the All-Russia Central Executive Committee carried a resolution to confiscate Church valuables which were to be sold to buy grain for famine relief.

The context in which this measure was taken was that of the aftermath of a most savage civil war, in which the Church was seen as part of the old regime. Many churches were looted and destroyed. But the Church still held on to enormous wealth, and the Soviet authorities requested that it should give up some of this wealth to buy food for the starving millions.

Resistance to the confiscation of church valuables due to claims that the Church was already raising money from collections from among its congregations, led to some fifteen hundred violent clashes during the spring of 1922. Those supposed to be responsible for the disturbances were put on trial: this was the "Case of the Churchmen". Trials were held in Petrograd and in Moscow. The Court in Petrograd passed the death sentence on two high dignitaries of the Church: Metropolitan Veniamin and Archimandrite Sergei, as well as on two professors who were supposed to be implicated: Kovsharov and Abram Saulovich's partner – Novitsky.

In addition to the shock of losing his partner, Abram Saulovich was particularly shocked by the execution of Nikolay Stepanovich Gumilyov. The poet Nikolay Gumilyov was three years Abram Saulovich's senior. The case of Gumilyov, who was shot for his alleged participation in the so-called "Tagantsev Counter-revolutionary Conspiracy", was an example of the perversion of justice as it was administered in those years by the Cheka.

From an examination of the documents it becomes clear that Gumilyov was condemned to death on the basis of flimsy, inconsistent and unproven charges, and that the passing of the verdict was illegal, even in the terms of the Rules applying to the Cheka procedures in those years.

With his partner, Novitsky, and now his personal friend Gumilyov, whose works he had published, both shot as counter-revolutionaries, Abram Saulovich had cause for great concern about what could be in store for him. One year went by in such suspense, and then Abram Saulovich underwent his own experience with the Cheka.

97 Abram Saulovich was rather short.

98 A few years after presiding over the "case" of Abram Saulovich and the other academics, Agranov was appointed to a special section of the GPU (previously the Cheka) organized to combat the activities of the opposition within the Communist Party. Eventually the extermination of all real or assumed opposition to the "General Line" of the Party – to secure Stalin's dictatorship – became one of the main functions of the GPU, which later became the NKVD, the Peoples Commissariat of Internal Affairs. These operations culminated in the infamous Moscow Show Trials, in which Lenin's comrades-in-arms and other opposi-tionists were accused of treason, terrorism and other equally absurd crimes. Many thousands of those who had taken an active part in the October Revolution and in the establishment of the Soviet Power during the first post-revolutionary years, were "liquidated" in the course of the NKVD operations, and it was at that time that Agranov advanced into the top echelons of the security organs. In 1933–1934 the NKVD was reorganized, assuring Stalin of an even firmer grip on that instru-ment of coercion. Genrikh Yagoda was put at its head, and Agranov, who was a personal friend of Stalin, became Yagoda's deputy. But ultimately Stalin's obsession to remove his real and potential rivals, turned against his most faithful underlings who had carried out his criminal instructions. They, in turn, had to be eliminated by new security cadres, whose memory was not burdened by complicity in the earlier "liquidations", so that Stalin could rid himself of embarrassing and unwanted witnesses. And thus Yagoda was arrested in April 1937, and the NKVD underwent a purge involving the execution of some 3000 officers. And this was when Agranov himself was "liquidated".

99 In particular, Abram Saulovich was accused of being closely acquainted with General Yudenich, and of taking part in the attack on Tsarskoye Selo during Yudenich's advance on Petrograd in the summer of 1919. He was also charged with an attempt to save the Tsar. Apparently all the others were accused of exactly the same crimes.

100 Nikolay Ivanovich Bukharin (1888–1938) indeed played an important part at that time. He had joined the Bolshevik faction of the Russian

Social Democratic Workers Party at the age of eighteen, and was active as a student organizer. During the years following the crushing of the 1905 Revolution, he went abroad, spending some time in the United States. He returned to Moscow after the February Revolution and played an active part in the preparation of the October Revolution. He was elected to the Central Committee of the Russian Social Democratic Workers Party at its Sixth Congress, held in August 1917. The Congress was all Bolshevik in composition, and took the course towards a new revolution as it came about in November (but is known as the "October Revolution", according to the old Russian calendar). In the period immediately following the Revolution, Bukharin took a position on the extreme Left of the Party.

Abram Saulovich, who throughout the revolutionary year of 1917 was an official of the Soviet in Petrograd, held the Menshevik view that the establishment of Socialism was inconceivable in a backward country with a predominantly peasant population such as Russia, and that therefore the Bolshevik course towards the seizure of power by the Soviets was adventurism.

By contrast, the Bolsheviks viewed the revolution in Russia in the international context. They did not identify the victory of the revolution in Russia with the establishment of Socialism in that backward country, but saw it as a prelude to the world revolution.

In spite of their political differences the two men remained friends, and thus it came about that Bukharin, who occupied a key position in the Party, came to his friend's assistance by giving to his friend's wife that letter in which he vouchsafed for him.

As for Zinoviev, the addressee of Bukharin's letter, in 1922 he occupied a position which was just as exalted as that occupied by Bukharin.

Gregory Yevseyevich Zinoviev (1883–1936) was then the Chairman of the Petrograd Soviet. Like Bukharin, Zinoviev had joined the Russian Social Democratic Workers Party at the age of eighteen. In the 1890's he helped to organize the first economic strikes in Russia. He fled abroad to avoid arrest and did not return to Russia until April 1917, together with Lenin. He had met Lenin in 1903 and became his closest assistant and co-editor of all of Lenin's publications. In 1907 he became a member of the Bolshevik Central Committee. Although he had been a staunch supporter of Lenin, he, as Trotsky put it, "silently stepped aside" from Lenin when the latter published his *April Theses*, outlining the steps to be taken which were to culminate in the October Revolution. Again, he and Kamenev declared themselves in opposition to Lenin's proposal for revolutionary action to be implemented in the October Revolution. Nevertheless, Zinoviev remained in the Bolshevik leadership. He became Chairman of the Petrograd Soviet and head of the Komintern, the Third Communist International organized in 1919 to coordinate the activity of the newly formed Communist Parties throughout the world, and to replace the Second International which had fallen apart with the outbreak of the First World War, when the various Social Democratic parties came out in support of their respective governments.

101 Any leniency by the authorities towards a person subject to expulsion, but who was slow in leaving the country, would seem to be quite out of place considering that, according to the legal code of that time, execution by firing squad was the measure to be applied if expulsion from Soviet Russia could not be effected. Yet Zamyatin was not under any pressure to leave after being released from jail. He left Russia on his own accord and settled in Berlin, where Abram Saulovich was to publish two of his books: Muiy ("We") and *How the Lad Erasmus was Healed*. (This was its title as translated literally from Russian.)

102 Alexander Nikolaevich Ostrovsky (1823–1886) wrote almost fifty plays ranging from comedies to tragedies. While his work included fantasies and historical plays, he was mainly a dramatist of the realist school who was particularly outstanding for his critical portrayal of the Russian middle classes (eg. *A Family Affair* and *Poverty is no Crime*). His greatest work was *The Storm* devoted to the cause against intolerance and hypocrisy.

103 A third person to be expelled and then allowed to remain, was a certain Shtein. Abram Saulovich does not know why there was a remission of the punishment in Shtein's case. He lost contact with him, and does not know what happened to him subsequently. Shtein's case would seem irrelevant in the context of this biography, except for the fact that it indicates a lack of consistency on the part of the authorities in their attitude towards those originally charged with "treason". Yet this lack of consistency had a decisive bearing on the lives of those thus involved. Perhaps Abram Saulovich could have remained in Petrograd after all, and I would have chosen a different title for this biography, which would have been altogether different, as would have been my own life. But this is speculation.

104 This autograph album, which is in my possession, contains poems by Gumilyov, Kuzmin, Georgy Ivanov and the poetess Berberova, as well as a watercolour by Mitrokhin.

105 A book published by *Petropolis* and illustrated by Annenkov.

106 The actual words published were "I am dreaming of returning to my beloved motherland". A.K.

107 By the middle of 1921 a million people had left Russia. Some went East to Harbin and Shanghai. Some crossed the Atlantic to the United States. But the overwhelming majority of the *émigrés* remained in Europe and settled in the various capital cities, primarily in Berlin and Paris, but also, though in smaller numbers, in Prague, Riga and Sofia.

One of the main reasons for the *émigrés* choosing Germany was economic, for while Germany had been defeated in the First World War, and while its economy had been crippled and was in need of rebuilding, life in Germany at that time was cheaper than elsewhere, while prices were rising in France, causing a movement of *émigrés* from Paris to Berlin. Germany was also the only country which had recognized Soviet Russia. Soviet citizens could enter Germany relatively easily, and Russians who had left their homeland could still return if they so desired, although few took that opportunity.

By the end of 1921, Berlin had become the indubitable centre of Russian emigration. Estimates varied, but between a quarter and a half million Russians had made Berlin their home. Berlin had acquired the nickname "Russia's Second Capital".

The post-revolutionary exodus from Russia included the bulk of the intelligentsia, which naturally comprised the most cultured, as well as the most vocal section of the émigrés. As for the majority of the other social groups who had emigrated, it differed from the population of its homeland in being literate in its overwhelming majority. Thus centres of émigré life became centres of Russian émigré culture and, in the early twenties Berlin, where the bulk of the émigrés had settled, if only temporarily, was unique. Berlin had become Russia's cultural centre outside Russia..

The stormy growth of Berlin as a centre of émigré culture and its impact in this respect, stretched over three years: from the end of 1920 to 1923. Then the vitality of the cultural activity began to decline, as the economic situation in Germany worsened with inflation becoming virulent. Berlin ceded its cultural pre-eminence to Paris, and also to Prague. The decline continued even though, beginning with 1924, the German economy became stabilized, but was then shattered by the great depression from 1929 on. The decline of émigré culture accelerated after the Nazis had come to power in 1933, and whatever was still left of it was snuffed out in 1938, one year before the outbreak of the Second World War.

Abram Saulovich intended to commence his publishing activity in Berlin at the very peak of the upswing of émigré culture there. He was to continue that activity there until his expulsion from Germany in 1938.

108   I was rather mystified by the circumstance that the further reading of the *Memoirs* did not reveal any information regarding the possible participation of Kotlyarevsky in creating a new publishing company in Berlin. And what had become of Kotlyarevsky after he had been driven off by David Yefimovich to that other relative of ours? I knew from other sources that Kotlyarevsky held the position of Director of the *Pushkin House* in Petrograd until his death in 1925. This meant not only that he must have returned to his homeland, while the exiles had started

a new life abroad, but that he had also been able to retain his position at the head of one of the foremost cultural institutions of Soviet Russia.

Kotlyarevsky did not participate in actually establishing the proposed publishing company. But he left all his books, which included all those previously published by Stasyulevich, and those still to be produced, at Abram Saulovich's disposal. Kotlyarevsky also gave the name to the publishing company: *Obelisk*, and his works were the first to be published there.

109 Thus the inflation that ruined millions of people in Germany, helped us in a perverse way. The project of establishing a publishing company, which had been discussed with Kotlyarevsky, Karsavin and others on board the *Preussen* finally came to fruition. But while both Kotlyarevsky and Karsavin, together with Abram Saulovich, were the foundation members of the new firm, and while Kotlyarevsky gave the venture its name, *Obelisk*, neither he nor Karsavin could take part in its actual management, since neither of them stayed in Berlin, and had to leave in pursuance of their separate commitments. Since it was a matter of physically establishing the publishing company, Abram Saulovich entered into partnership with his great-uncle David Yefimovich for that purpose. David Yefimovich was not only the "intellectual" among the Berlin relations, he was also the one who could financially underwrite the project. *Obelisk* was established on 11 December 1922.

110 Publishing companies established by émigrés sprang up like mushrooms, e.g. *Helikon*, *Obrazovanye* (Education), *Skify* (Scythians), *Zarya* (Dawn) and many others. They sprang up and disappeared almost as soon as they were established.

Not only were there publishing companies established by the émigrés, but major German publishing houses maintained their own Russian subsidiaries.

With the introduction of the "New Economic Policy" after the end of the Civil War, Soviet Russia and Germany set out to establish trade relations which were to be of mutual advantage. This had a particular bearing on the production of books. Soviet Russia required books in all fields to fulfill, apart from everything else, the needs of a gigantic education program, but the wrecked country lacked paper, printers ink, and in fact everything else that was needed for producing books. On the other hand German publishing technology, one of the most advanced in the world, was in need of orders in the post-war reconstruction period, and paper was readily available. Thus agreements were concluded for Germany to supply books to Soviet Russia.

111 Petropolis had already been established there by the Blokhs. They had arrived in Berlin in 1921, about a year before my family. There was no sequel to the uncovering of their earlier attempt to leave Russia, when, if it had not been for Yenukidze's intervention, Blokh's wife and sister

were almost put before the firing squad. Lozinsky, who used to act as Chairman of Petropolis, had also left Petrograd before us. Blokh and Lozinsky re-established Petropolis in Berlin, together with Savely Isaakovich Grinberg, the brother of Blokh's wife. Abram Saulovich joined them upon his arrival.

Continuing its Petrograd practice, the Berlin publications by Petropolis were in the fields of poetry, art, and what can be described, in absence of an appropriate English word, as *belles lettres*.

The first book brought out by Petropolis in Berlin was a re-publication of Akhmatova's *Anno Domini*. To follow it, *Petropolis* re-published Gumilyov's *Ognenny Stolp* (*The Fiery Column*), *Kostior* (*Bonfire*) and *Child of Allah*. The last mentioned poem had been published earlier by Abram Saulovich in Petrograd. In 1923 Petropolis also brought out two works by Gumilyov, which had not been published before: his translation of French folk songs, and *K Siney Zvezde* (*To the Blue Star*), a collection of poems dating from 1918.

Petropolis cooperated with *Alkonost* in the publication of poems by Akhmatova and Kuzmin. – Also in 1923 Petropolis re-published Mandelstam's *Tristia*. In the same year it published Kuzmin's *Krylya* (*Wings*, a story in three parts), *Seti* (*The Net*, a book of poems), *Glinyanyye Golubki* (*Clay Pigeons*, another book of poems), and in 1924, *Tikhy Strazh* (*The Silent Guard*, a novel). – Petropolis published Russian translations of world literature: Samuel Coleridge's *Christabel* (translated by Georgy Ivanov), and Machiavelli's *Mandragora*, a comedy in five acts.

One of the first was a book about Natan Altman, published in 1924, written by an artist by the name of Aronson, who turned out to be a relative on Abram Saulovich's maternal side.

The book on Altman was published in a limited edition of 500 numbered copies. It compared favourably with the high quality artistic editions of books published by Petropolis in Petrograd. The printing was carried out by *Zinaburg & Co.*, Berlin, and was of the same excellence as that of the former printing house of *Golike & Vilborg* in Petrograd.

Another artist whose work was published by Petropolis was Dobuzhinsky. He had emigrated to Riga, and had come to Berlin on his way to Paris. While in Berlin, he arranged for Petropolis to publish a fairly voluminous book on his work. Another book in the artistic field, written in French, was Boris Grigoryev's *Bous-Bous au bord de la Mer*. Petropolis also took part in the publication of a book on the dancer Anna Pavlova. This book was financed by her husband, the former Mayor of St Petersburg. It proved a great success, but for the publishers it was more a matter of glory than of financial gain. Berberova's book on Tchaikovsky should also be mentioned among the publications in the field of the various arts. Actually, all these publications which were of an undisputed cultural value, did not bring in any profit.

All these publications came out as limited editions. Considering that the educated reading public among the Russian *émigrés* numbered some hundreds of thousands, these limited editions served only a very small section of the *émigré* market.

112 In Germany, "Kagan" was changed to "Kahan" to sound less Russian. Abram Saulovich intended to establish his own publishing firm, which would be independent of Petropolis. To do so required the necessary finance. He had brought only limited means with him from Russia, and it was also necessary for him to think of his family. Our relatives were very kind to him and promised to support his publishing venture. They were indeed very helpful in this respect, in spite of the palpable cultural difference that separated Abram Saulovich from them.

In contrast with the "emancipated" and "assimilated" Abram Saulovich, who identified himself with the progressive Russian intelligentsia of which he was part, and who was completely steeped in Russian culture and had devoted his publishing activity to its advancement, the Kagans of Berlin represented an altogether different culture, based on that assertion of Jewishness which evolved into Zionism. While Abram Saulovich dreamed of a democratic and socialist Russia, the Kagans of Berlin dreamed of a Jewish state in Palestine.

Our Berlin relations were all the three varieties in one: they advocated the establishment of a Jewish state in Palestine, they financed Jewish migration to Palestine and the planting of orange trees there, and some of the Kagans and their relatives settled there themselves.

113 As distinct from Petropolis, Obelisk was to follow the tradition of *Nauka i Shkola*.

114 To the above account should be added a revised edition of Lossky's *Loguika* (*Logic*), S.N. Prokopovich's *Ocherki Khozaistva Sovetskoy Rossii* (*Outlines of the Economy of Soviet Russia*) and the strangely omitted works by Kotlyarevsky and Karsavin (after all, they were Abram Saulovich's partners), namely: Kotlyarevsky's *Kholmy Rodiny* (*Hills of the Homeland*) and Karsavin's *Dialogui* (*Dialogues*), *Filosofia Istorii* (*Philosophy of History*) and *Giordano Bruno*. All the above were published in 1923, and copies of these works are contained in the Bakhmeteff Archive. Abram Saulovich could hardly be rebuked for this omission, for he was quoting from memory going back over half a century, while I was fortunate enough to make use of archival material.

According to Beyer, et al., *Obelisk* had published thirty-six titles by 1924. Of these, 14 were in the field of philosophy, 9 of exact science, 5 of social science, 4 of literature and 4 in the fields of history and geography.

A further work by Karsavin *O Nachalakh* (*On First Principles*), which was an essay on Christian metaphysics, was brought out in 1925. From then on Abram Saulovich no longer insisted on having his own publishing company, and all his publishing activity was devoted to Petropolis or to some of its alter egos. Thus the Russian translation of Carl Gustav Jung's *Psychological Types,* which would have belonged to the field of Obelisk publications, was brought out by Petropolis in 1929.

Among the many subjects dealt with in Abram Saulovich's publications, the subject of psychology in its various approaches had a particular fascination for him, although through circumstances, it was not until the end of his career as a publisher that he devoted himself almost exclusively to publications in this field. If William James' *Principles of Psychology,* published by *Naooka i Shkola* in Petrograd, was the first work of this kind, then Carl Jung's Psychological Types, published by Petropolis in Berlin, was the second, years before Freudian psychology became paramount among Abram Saulovich's publications in the United States.

115 The term "Eurasians" is used here as a cultural not a racial definition.

116 Ivan Petrunkevich, actually the stepfather of Countess Panina, was a founder of the Constitutional Democratic Party. He had been prominent in the first Duma, which the Tsar had agreed to establish in August 1905, as a purely consultative body elected on a limited franchise. Countess Panina had also been an active member of the Constitutional Democratic Party.

117 Russian for a small and secluded monastery

118 It is again the capital.

119 It is of interest to compare present-day conditions in Lithuania with Abram Saulovich's impression of that small country when it was an independent republic, and when its cultural life was the affair of Russians and Jews, but not of ethnic Lithuanians. Even the authority in the field of style and syntax of the Lithuanian language, its innovator, L.P. Karsavin, was a Russian.

120 Karsavin was the brother of the well-known ballet dancer. In his younger days Karsavin was a ballet dancer himself, while his father was a ballet producer. Karsavin died in the beginning of the occupation of Lithuania by Soviet troops. He fled to Vilnius where he was killed, but it is not clear whether this occurred at the end of the Second World War, or after the signing of the Stalin–Hitler Pact, when Lithuania was incorporated into the Soviet Union.

121 Hard to decipher in the manuscript.

122 As late as 1913, Mendel Beilis, a hapless Jew, was put on trial for murder. A journalist, who had investigated the case, produced evidence that the murder had been committed by a gang of thieves. But the then Minister of Justice, Shcheglovitov, an arch reactionary anti-Semite, was strenuously endeavouring to link the murder with ritual killings, allegedly perpetrated by the Jews. Beilis was acquitted, following the brilliant defence by Gruzenberg, but the Government had its revenge when the

journalist was jailed for twelve months for remaining seated while the Tsarist anthem happened to be played in a park, and V.D. Nabokov, the editor of the liberal newspaper *Rech* (*Speech*), the father of the writer and poet V.V. Nabokov was fined for expressing in his paper his determined opposition to official anti-Semitism.

123 Before the Revolution, which had abolished the rank of "Senator".

124 Name hardly legible in the manuscript.

125 Apart from Czechoslovakia, Poland, Lithuania, Latvia and Estonia, Abram Saulovich's business trips also included France and Italy. Thus he visited practically every European country where there was a demand for Russian books, and which was not sufficiently catered for by already existing publishing companies or firms importing Russian books. Hence his travels did not include those countries where the demand for Russian books was either negligible, or adequately provided for by already existing businesses. The latter case applied to Great Britain.

The question may be asked: how could Abram Saulovich travel all over Europe, with all its restrictions in respect of visas, while he still possessed a Soviet passport which had not been withdrawn since he had been exiled. Actually, the situation regarding his passport was rather odd. It was a proper Soviet passport, but in it was stated that the bearer had been exiled. However, the Soviet authorities kept on extending it. In addition, Abram Saulovich had a certificate issued by the international body, which provided so-called Nansen passports to stateless persons. This certificate was to the effect that Abram Saulovich could not be issued with a proper Nansen passport since the Soviet authorities continued to extend his Soviet passport and this being the only reason why he was still using that passport. It is not quite clear why Abram Saulovich did not simply let the Soviet passport lapse, and thus become stateless so as to be able to obtain a Nansen passport. Perhaps it was some kind of patriotism which stopped him from assuming the status of a stateless person. Perhaps there was some value in leaving things as they were, since in any case, no obstacles to the obtaining of visas etc. were encountered when producing an otherwise somewhat strange combination of documents. There was no problem in obtaining any relevant recommendations in order to obtain a visa: a friend, Goldenberg, worked at the French Consulate in Berlin; in Czechslovakia Abram Saulovich knew Vernadsky, Prokopovich and the rest of his friends who went to Prague; in Kovno he also had connections. The only problem which he imagined he might encounter, was that when crossing the border he could possibly be looked upon as a spy, or almost a spy.

Later on, under the Nazis, the possession of a Soviet passport had a definite advantage, putting us into the class of foreigners, and thus preserving us from any repression to which stateless persons could be subjected. But in time, this did not stop the German authorities from expelling us from the Third Reich before the beginning of the Second World War.

126 A phenomenon of the Russian Cultural life in Berlin in the early twenties, were the frequent visits to that *émigré* centre by Soviet writers and poets, who seemed to be able to travel abroad with comparative ease, which was no longer possible in later years. In Berlin they met up with those writers and poets who had fled after the Revolution, or who had been expelled. The contacts were at times friendly, while at other times a hostile attitude was displayed by the *émigrés* towards the visitors.

127 Vladimir Ivanovich Nemirovich-Danchenko (1858–1943) was a playwright and stage-director. He and Stanislavsky were the founders of the famous Moscow Art Theatre.

128 Ehrenburg was another prominent visitor to Petropolis mentioned earlier who, by contrast with the Meyerholds, was distinguished by his remarkable ability to survive the Stalin era. Ilya Grigoryevich Ehrenburg (1891–1967) was involved in revolutionary activity in his youth and had been arrested by the Tsarist authorities when only a teenager. For a while he settled in Paris, where he started his writing career as a poet. He returned to Russia during the Revolution, but subsequently vacillated for a number of years whether to stay in Russia, or in the West. He finally returned to Soviet Russia in 1924, and accommodated himself to the Stalinist line. Later he was to win two Stalin prizes for literature, the first one in 1942, for the novel *Fall of Paris*. After the death of Stalin he took a more critical view of the situation in the Soviet Union. In 1955 he wrote the novel *Ottepel (The Thaw)*, which gave a name to the liberal and critical trends which emerged in literature at that time, until these were again repressed in the Brezhnev era.

Abram Saulovich maintained friendly relations with most of the Soviet writers who called on him in Berlin, although he looked upon Ehrenburg with some suspicion.

Being a "completely unprincipled person" was the quality which enabled Ehrenburg to survive the Stalin era, while other writers who could not manage to develop sufficient flexibility in their spines, were dispatched to labour camps. The sway of Stalinism was only beginning at the time when Ehrenburg's books were published by Petropolis, although the case of Pilnyak (see below) had given an inkling of repressions to come. But since Ehrenburg, who was at his best as a satirist, directed his barbs against capitalist phenomena in various parts of the world e.g. *Fabrika Snov: Khronika Nashevo Vremeni (Factory of Dreams: Chronicle of Our Time*, dealing with the film industry), there were no grounds for any conflict with the super-arbiters of Soviet literature. But Ehrenburg, at times tried his luck too hard, for example, with his black humour in his *Priklyucheniya Lazika Roitshvanetza (The Adventures of Lazik Roitshvanets*), the story of a hapless Jew who escapes from Soviet Russia and, after a series of outrageous adventures, dies at the side of a road in *Palestine*.

Ehrenburg travelled widely outside the Soviet Union, and the Soviet authorities never curtailed his movements. He travelled more than possibly any other Soviet writer. Although he was aware of repressions against his fellow-writers, he always returned to his homeland after living abroad for lengthy periods. He did not feel that one day his turn would come, which, fortunately for him, it did not.

129 Abram Saulovich published Alexey Tolstoy's *Peter I* and his trilogy on the Civil War.

Alexey Nikolaevich Tolstoy (1883–1945) had begun his literary career in St Petersburg. In 1923 (i.e. a year after Abram Saulovich, his future publisher, had left Petrograd) Tolstoy began to write his novels Peter I and those comprising the trilogy of the Civil War *Khozhdeniye po Mookam* (*Walking on Torments*, translated into English as *Calvary*). In the years to come Tolstoy was to receive official approval, and became a prominent member of the literary establishment under Stalin.

Apart from Ehrenburg, who at times was wickedly satirical, there were, in particular, three authors whose works were published by Petropolis, and who were outstanding satirists: Mikhail Mikhailovich Zoshchenko (1895–1958), Ilya Ilf (Ilya Arnoldovich Fainsilberg, 1897–1937) and Yevgeny Petrov (Yevgeny Petrovich Katayev, 1903–1942). The last two collaborated on their novels *Dvenadtsat' stul'ev* (*The Twelve Chairs*) and *Zolotoy Tyelyonok* (*The Golden Calf*). The above works, after being published in the first place by Petropolis, found their widest distribution in their homeland, where many phrases of these novels became proverbial, and some of the characters came close to being included in folklore.

Zoshchenko, who survived Ilf and Petrov, was subject to vilification by the Stalinist machine in the period following the Second World War. He was attacked for his "thoroughly rotten and decayed socio-political and literary physiognomy", for being a "vile, lustful animal" and an "unprincipled and conscienceless literary hooligan". Together with Anna Akhmatova, Zoshchenko was excluded from the Union of Soviet Writers. But this was to be in the late forties, while in the twenties, Zoshchenko enjoyed immense popularity in Soviet Russia, and Petropolis played an important part in bringing this about.

130 In those years, Soviet Russia was not a signatory to the Berne Agreement, which governed copyrights for writers. On the other hand, a book published in Berlin automatically acquired copyrights for its author, and thus, possibly the greatest contribution towards Russian culture by Petropolis during its Berlin era, was the publication of books by practically all Soviet writers of that period.

131 Vsevolod Emilyevich Meyerhold (1874–1940) was, in the early twenties, at the peak of his career as an outstanding innovator of the theatre. But soon he was to be accused of "formalism" – an accusation levelled against avant-garde artists, poets, composers etc., by those in command of the Soviet cultural front.

In Testimony, the composer Shostakovich, himself accused of "formalism", tells that Meyerhold had dedicated one of his first stage plays to Trotsky. This came against Meyerhold when Stalin became the super-arbiter of Soviet arts. In the years before Stalin had risen to that position, Meyerhold's admirers, as reported by Shostakovich, also included Bukharin and Karl Radek.

Meyerhold was not the only one singled out in such a fashion, and further on in Testimony, Shostakovich characterises an artist's fate under Stalinist totalitarianism, as follows:

> "It did not matter how the audience reacted to your work or if the critics liked it. All that had no meaning in the final analysis. There was only one question of life or death: How did the leader like your opus? I stress: life or death, because we are talking about life and death here, literally, not figuratively. That is what you must understand."

And thus Meyerhold was arrested and his theatre was closed down. Like the record of historical facts and of people's lives, deposited into the "memory tube" in Orwell's *1984*, all further mention of Meyerhold was expunged as if he never existed.

132 A writer who also got into trouble was Evgeny Ivanovich Zamyatin (1884–1937) over the publication by Petropolis of his visionary fiction, *Muiy* (*We*). In *We*, Zamyatin had painted a picture of society in 2600 AD: People have lost their individuality, each one is known, not by name, but by number, the population is in the care of "guardians" presided over by the "benefactor". *Tribune*, 4 January 1946, had praised Zamyatin, claiming that Aldous Huxley had derived his *Brave New World* partly from Zamyatin's *We*, and Isaac Deutscher had pointed to the resemblance between Orwell's *1984* and Zamyatin's visionary fiction which preceded that of Orwell's. [154]. Of course Zamyatin's satire did not go down well with the Soviet rulers. The book was condemned as counter-revolutionary and was banned in the Soviet Union. Zamyatin, who earlier had been going through a period of indecision, decided not to return to his homeland in view of the violent campaign against him. He died in Paris.

133 Mayakovsky (1893–1930) wrote his first poems in 1912 at the age of nineteen, while he was a student at the Moscow College of Painting,

Sculpture and Architecture. He was then still undecided whether he should become a painter or a poet, but he was determined that his art should be a weapon in the struggle for a better social order. He was then still distant from Bolshevism which was an orientation hardly known before the Revolution.

Having decisively embraced the mission of a poet, Mayakovsky imparted to his verses a graphic imagery which had the blatant quality of a poster. At first Mayakovsky adhered to the "futurist" school which experienced its heyday in the years immediately preceding the First World War. The poets of that school, such as Khlebnikov and Mayakovsky himself, set out to restructure the Russian language and to generally break with accepted standards. One adherent of that school, Vasilisk Gnedov, even wrote a poem without words! The activities of the "futurists" often amounted to literary hooliganism.

The subjects of Mayakovsky's early poems comprised a condemnation of existing conditions. There was as yet no clearly defined political line in his poetry, but there was a foreboding of impending doom. Also, together with his fellow poets of the "futurist" school, he delighted in scandalizing respectable society.

Mayakovsky was twenty-four years old in 1917. He was one of the poets and artists inspired by the Revolution, which opened to them a new field of creative oportunities. If anyone could be called the "Bard of the Revolution", then Mayakovsky would have been worthy of that title. Some of his verses became akin to political slogans for the Bolshevik cause. His poems were addressed to the masses, and his poetry readings were equal to political meetings. It was not surprising that Abram Saulovich already disliked Mayakovsky's poetry on political grounds, apart from considering his verses to be "crude", compared with the refined style of the poets published by Petropolis like Akhmatova, Gumilyov or Mandelstam. Yet no lesser poet than Alexander Blok adopted Mayakovsky's style in his poem "Twelve". This too was the reason why Abram Saulovich disliked that famous poem by Blok.

Paradoxically, it was Anna Akhmatova who was one of the first to recognize in Mayakovsky what she thought to be a great poet, surprising as her assessment might have been, since her genre was altogether different, in fact, it was the very opposite to that of Mayakovsky's.

134   Lily Yurevna and Osip Maksimovich Brik, the couple who befriended Mayakovsky, lived in No.7 Zhukovskaya Street, practically opposite No.10, the building in which our apartment was located in St Petersburg. I can remember No.7 from my childhood days. Of course I knew nothing about its distinguished inhabitants, but I was fascinated by the sculptures of horses set into recesses flanking the entrance to the building. When, in 1968, I visited Leningrad for the first time after leaving it as a child, and walked the length of Zhukovskaya Street,

seeking out the remembered landmarks, I found to my disappointment that the horse sculptures had disappeared, while several floors had been added to what used to be a two-storey building, as I remembered it. I was informed that these regrettable changes had been carried out in the thirties, and that no photographs or other records of the original building had been preserved.

135 The idea underlying the subject of Mayakovsky's play, *The Bedbug*, was the unmasking of petty bourgeois Philistinism in Soviet Russia. Much in the play was left to the inventiveness on the part of actors and the director, giving much scope for improvisation.

136 Ironically, Mayakovsky had criticized the suicide of the poet Sergey Yesenin for giving up the struggle for a better social order, a struggle in which Mayakovsky considered himself to be involved with heart and soul. Mayakovsky's own suicide in 1930 at the age of thirty-seven, may well have been caused by the incurable venereal disease, as suggested by Abram Saulovich, but this may not have been the principal cause.

137 Shostakovich, intially fascinated by Mayakovsky's poetry, deemed he:

> was not a citizen, he was a lackey who served Stalin faithfully. He added his babble to the magnification of the immortal image of the leader and teacher. Of course, Mayakovsky wasn't alone in this unbecoming behaviour, he was one of a glorious cohort. There were many Russian creative artists who were infatuated by the person of our leader and teacher and who rushed to create works of praise for him. Besides Mayakovsky, I could mention Eisenstein and his *Ivan the Terrible*, with music by Prokofiev. Mayakovsky, turned from being a "Bard of the Revolution" to become, "a lead singer of the cult of personality", so as to be rewarded by Stalin with the title of "the best, the most talented".

138 Bukharin, who had spoken up for the Kronstadt sailors, and who had vouchsafed for Abram Saulovich in an attempt to achieve his release from jail, stood initially on the extreme Left of the Bolshevik Party.

After Lenin's death in 1924, Bukharin moved to the Right and allied himself with Stalin against Trotsky. It was in the beginning of this part of his political career (1925) that Bukharin commissioned Abram Saulovich with a translation of Keynes' treatise. This act was not politically motivated. Like Yenukidze, Bukharin had a compassionate nature, and would come to the assistance of people with whom he did not agree politically.

In 1926 Bukharin was appointed President of the *Comintern*, and as a co-leader of the Communist Party with Stalin, Bukharin became the ideologist of Stalin's then conservative policy, backing him against the Left Opposition. But when Stalin changed the direction of his policy towards industrialization and the forced collectivisation of agriculture, a policy which was a caricature of that advocated by the Left Opposition, Bukharin fell from grace, and although he had previously supported Stalin against the Opposition, he was arrested, put on trial as the main defendant in the Third Moscow Trial (1938), and was sentenced to death.

139 Neither was it for indulging another "political criminal", the poet Osip Mandelstam, some of whose poetry Abram Saulovich had published in the early days of Petropolis.

140 He was also seven years my senior, and was about to finish his course when I was just starting mine in 1932. Also, if according to Abram Saulovich, Sedov appeared to be 23–24 years old, this would make me 16–17 years old, i.e.when I was still at high school, the year being 1929 or 1930. What is relevant, of course, is the fact that it was published in 1930, two years before I started my studies at the *Technische Hochschule* where I was alleged to have made the acquaintance of Sedov.

While I knew that Sedov was a student at the *Technische Hochschule*, it was not until late in 1932 that I was made aware of it. I never had an occasion to meet him personally, much less to discuss the proposition he was to put before Abram Saulovich regarding the publication of *My Life*. But what particularly puzzled me in Abram Saulovich's account (both in the *Memoirs* and in the transcript of the Raeff interview) was the circumstance, that while he had informed me, at the time, about his involvement with Trotsky's books, and about the setting up of the publishing company Granit for the specific purpose of publishing these books, he never mentioned to me his meeting with Sedov, nor questioned me about the alleged exchange I was supposed to have had with the latter.

I believe that all these contradictions and "lapses of memory" can be explained within the context of the political situation in Germany in the late twenties and early thirties, and the conflicting reactions to that situation by Abram Saulovich and myself.

Further, while I was still at high school, I had a friend, Oscar Grossman, who was actually the nephew of a friend of Raissa Blokh. He and I were both members of a high school Left-wing students' club. Oscar was outspoken in voicing his opposition to the policy of the Communist Party, and he influenced me in this respect. He used to obtain the *Bulletin of the Opposition*, as well as other Trotskyist literature, and was active in the Communist Party, putting forward the Trotskyist line, according to which the Stalinist leadership was driving the Soviet Union and the Communist movement to ruin.

I avidly read the literature which Oscar used to give to me. I was particularly impressed by two of Trotsky's pamphlets: *Germany, The Key to the International Situation*, written in December 1931, i.e. a little more than a year before Hitler came to power, and *The Only Road for Germany*, which Trotsky finished writing in September 1932, i.e. only four months before Hitler became Reichs-Chancellor.

While Oscar was understandably discreet about his political contacts, he no doubt knew Trotsky's son Sedov, who was at that time studying in Berlin, and who had good cause for not becoming publicly known for obvious reasons of security. Oscar must have told Sedov about Abram Saulovich's publishing activity, and also that I was that publisher's son. Sedov, armed with that knowledge when meeting Abram Saulovich, could have claimed to be acquainted with me as an introductory gambit, before I ever became a student at the Technische Hochschule. Thus certain events and situations which were separated by time, have been telescoped in Abram Saulovich's memory.

Anyhow, all the above concerns only the circumstances of the publication of Trotsky's books by Abram Saulovich. The fact remains that by publishing, for whatever separate reasons, and under whatever circumstances, the writings of one of the towering and most controversial figures of the century, he made a very important contribution to mankind's treasury of thought.

141   It was clearly not advisable for Petropolis to publish books by authors, whose point of view was opposed to the Soviet regime, since the Soviet authorities, strange as it may seem, made unofficial use of Petropolis to bring about the publication of Soviet authors who would not be able to secure the copyright to their works, had those been brought out in their homeland. Hence Trotsky's works were published by Granit. But, Granit was not the only alter ego of Petropolis. Prior to the publication of Trotsky's works, Abram Saulovich published such books as Aleksandrov's *Kto otpravliaet Rossiei* (*Who Rules Russia?*), *Red Terror in Russia* by Aronson, *History of a Traitor* (*The Story of Azef*) by Nikolaevsky, a prominent Menshevik, and a book by Roman Gul, a White Guard, the title of which I cannot remember. These books were published by Parabola, another alter ego of Petropolis. Trotsky obviously did not want to be associated with the above authors, and thus Granit was created especially for the publication of his works. It can be seen that Abram Saulovich felt completely free to publish any author, no matter what his politics were, if, in his opinion, their respective work deserved some attention.

Petropolis had one more alter ego, *Nauchnoye Izdatelstevo* (Scientific Publishing Company) which published Russian translations of German popular books on mathematics, physics, chemistry etc. The translator was E.A. Rabinovich, who later became a specialist in nuclear physics. These books were published in association with the firm of Teubner of Leipzig. They were produced in large numbers, and all of them were exported to Soviet Russia. All arrangements were made quite officially and openly through the Soviet Trade Delegation, in contrast with the handling of the books brought out by Granit or Parabola, which reached Russia as contraband.

142   Apart from Trotsky's, Abram Saulovich also published the following works by this outstanding man: *The Permanent Revolution* – 1930, *History of the Russian Revolution* (3 volumes), 1931–1933 and *The Stalin School of Falsification*, 1932.

All these works, and were published by Granit, which was an alter ego (as Professor Raeff put it) of Petropolis for the publication of Trotsky's works, in accordance with the latter's own request, so as to be free from any implication arising from the publication of books by Petropolis of a differing ideological trend. This arrangement also suited Abram Saulovich.

143   The art historian Bernard Berenson was an American expatriate who had fallen in love with Italy. A few years before the First World War, he and his wife Mary had settled in a villa within sight of Florence. The villa, *I Tatti*, underwent alterations so as to accommodate the needs of the Berenson family. I remember reading somewhere that Cecil Pinsent and Geoffrey Scott, Berenson's architects, used to be referred to by him as "my artichokes".

144   Apart from the earlier mentioned authors from among the *émigrés*, Abram Saulovich published the works of many others who had left Russia, e.g. Nabokov, Krymov, Aldanov, Khodasevich, Bunin and others. He also maintained a personal friendship with some of these authors. Thus he had a long lasting and firm friendship with Bunin. He had published a complete collection of Bunin's works, for which the author was awarded the Nobel Prize. It seemed that Abram Saulovich had himself well established as a publisher of Russian books.

While in the early twenties there were more Russian than German books published in Germany, and although the Russian *émigrés* were largely of the educated classes and were avid readers, the quantity of production of Russian literature had brought about a glut on the literary market. Consequently Russian books had to be published in limited editions, e.g. not exceeding two thousand copies, and even then there were problems in finding customers. Thus Aldanov, who was a lightweight writer when compared with Nabokov, but who was more popular than the latter, was not accorded larger editions than of one thousand copies. It happened more and more frequently that unsold copies of Russian authors had to be pulped.

Abram Saulovich saw the need to change his publishing policy. The principal reason for that change, which amounted to the phasing out of Russian publications and switching over to those in German, was the setting in of the exodus of the *émigrés* from Berlin. The reasons for this exodus were, in the first place, economical. While in the very beginning of the twenties the sharp rise of the cost of living in France coinciding with the coming down of prices in Germany, had brought about a stream of émigrés from Paris to Berlin, that trend was now reversed under the impact of the inflation in Germany, which by 1923 had become catastrophic. The figures on the German bank notes assumed an astronomic magnitude. The mark, by the time it was revalued, equalled one billion inflationary marks; to be correct, what was called a billion in Germany was actually a billion multiplied by a thousand, a figure with twelve noughts: 1,000,000,000,000. The figure which elsewhere was called a "billion" was called a "milliarde" in Germany.

While the inflation had a ruinous effect, the revaluation of the mark meant a rise in the cost of living. The large Russian enclave in Berlin began shrinking. Those who were leaving went mainly to Paris, but others went to Prague. After the influx of émigrés into Berlin had peaked at several hundred thousand in the early twenties, it declined to some thirty thousand. By that time many émigrés had become culturally assimilated with the Germans and had lost interest in maintaining a Russian émigré culture.

The decline of the once flourishing Russian enclave was reflected, among other things, in the decline of the circulation of the Russian daily newspaper Rul. This daily, immediately after its establishment in 1921, when the number of Russians in Berlin had reached the first one hundred thousand, not only achieved the highest circulation in Germany, but had penetrated into all corners of the world. Its financial stability was assured by numerous columns of advertisements catering for the Russian population. With the exodus of the émigrés from Berlin, and the simultaneous increase in the cost of production following the stabilization of the mark, the circulation continued to drop until the paper, still prestigious in the émigré world, ceased publication in 1931.

145 Little was known (and still is) about Klyuchevsky outside of Russia. V.O. Klyuchevsky (1841–1911), became a Professor of History at the Moscow University in 1879. While his lectures attracted enthusiastic audiences, Klyuchevsky, because of the critical views which he held regarding the Tsarist regime, was unable to publish his research into Russian history until shortly before the First World War. It took him a number of years to complete the five volumes of his History of Russia. The reason why the Tsarist authorities were not kindly disposed towards him was that Klyuchevsky was one among those nineteenth century writers who had pointed to the image of a "dual Russia". Alan Bullock writes that Klyuchevsky:

> ...summed up the policy of the Tsars between the six-
> teenth and nineteenth centuries in the striking sentence:

"Exhausting the resources of the country, they only bolstered up the power of the State without elevating the self-confidence of the people... The State swelled up; the people grew lean".

146 To describe the translation of a classic of Russian historiography into German as "a major contribution to German science" might be considered as an exaggeration, but Abram Saulovich was certainly proud of his successful entry into the field of high-class German publications relating to other cultures. He had also marked for translation other books on history, Russian philosophy and literature.

147 When I visited Abram Saulovich in New York in 1977, I interviewed him regarding the many Russian writers whom he had an opportunity of knowing, both in Petrograd and in Berlin. His impressions of only one writer, namely Krymov, were singled out for tape-recording. What is written further in this Chapter about Pasternak and Nabokov is based upon my recollections of conversations which I had with Abram Saulovich.

148 The reason why "...it could not be said that he was generally accepted in society..." as Abram Saulovich expressed it, was Rozanov's principal characteristic, namely his ambivalence, a kind of intellectual schizophrenia. Rozanov used to express diametrically opposite opinions on the same subjects, and he often did so simultaneously. He was not only a contributor to Suvorin's *Novoye Vremya*, but also to the liberal *Russkoye Slovo* (*Russian Word*), in which he propounded ideas opposed to those in Suvorin's paper, but he did so under the pseudonym V. Varvarin, although the identity of the author hiding under this name was generally known.

Some of Rozanov's contemporaries in the literary world disliked him intensely. The writer and poet Vsevolod Sergeyevich Solovyov compared him with the same literary character, with whom Abram Saulovich compared Ehrenburg, namely Yudushka Golovyov. Among others, Rozanov's ambivalence produced corresponding ambivalent attitudes towards him. For example, this was demonstrated in Lydia Chukovskaya's Notes on Anna Akhmatova, in which Lydia Chukovskaya quotes a conversation about Rozanov, between herself and Anna Akhmatova. Lydia Chukovskaya begins the sentence: "I love him so much, except..." and Anna Akhmatova completes the sentence: "...except for anti-Semitism and the sexual problem".

149 Roman Gul was a well-known White Guard who fought against the Soviets, and whose books Abram Saulovich had published. Boris Ivanovich Nikolaevsky was an *émigré* Menshevik leader. Alexey Tolstoy was a prominent Soviet writer (not to be confused with Leo Tolstoy). Boris Pilnyak was another Soviet writer. Some Soviet writers had been introduced to Krymov by Abram Saulovich, these included Pilnyak, Vera

Inber, Solog. Abram Saulovich also introduced the *émigré* writer Dmitry Merezhkovsky to Krymov.

150 I did not enquire in what currency those cheques were written, and what effect inflation had on the amounts indicated. The fact was that Krymov grew wealthy.

151 Also in Berlin Abram Saulovich met the artist Leonid Pasternak and his son Boris Pasternak. Leonid was a friend of Alexander Eduardovich Kogan – Kogan, not Kagan – publisher of the Petersburg paper *Kopeika* (*Penny* – presumably that was its price). In Berlin Kogan published a very high-class art magazine, *Zhar-Ptitsa* (*Fire Bird*). He approached Petropolis with a view to partnership in the publication of that magazine. Abram Saulovich could not make up his mind, but he and Kogan ramained friends. It was through Kogan that he was introduced to Leonid Pasternak.

During my visit to Abram Saulovich in New York in 1977, we got talking about Boris Pasternak and, in particular, about *Doctor Zhivago*, which had been made into a film by David Lean. We both thought that the Doctor was not only glamourized as he was played by Omar Sharif, but was changed from someone who, in our opinion, had failed in his own personal relationships and his ability to measure up to the impact of historical events, into someone of almost heroic stature. The story in the novel had many allusions to Pasternak's life. But, in the film, certain episodes of his life received a completely different portrayal. A particular case was that of *Zhivago*, motivated by altruistic considerations, allowing Komarovsky to take Lara away from him so that she could start a new life abroad. The real life "Lara", Olga Ivinskaya, after being interrogated for a whole year by the NKVD, spent four years in a labour camp because of her relationship with Pasternak, while he lived comfortably in a dacha near Moscow with his wife and children. Stalin spared Pasternak in the hope that he, like other Soviet writers of that period, might still sing the dictator's praises. In return for Olga's martyrdom Pasternak sent her some poems, and made an entry in his diary expressing his regrets about her suffering.

It was also in Berlin that Abram Saulovich got to know Vladimir Nabokov (1899–1977) as a writer. Abram Saulovich was ten years his senior, so that while in Petrograd, he knew Nabokov only as a teenager. Nabokov had left Russia when he was twenty years old. Abram Saulovich had been friendly with Nabokov's father, Vladimir Dmitrievich. It was a personal friendship, for politically they were opponents. Vladimir Dmitrievich was a prominent member of the *Kadet* (Constitutional Democratic) Party, while Abram Saulovich was a Menshevik, but such political differences became of no account when confronted with Bolshevism.

According to Abram Saulovich, Nabokov junior, in contrast to his father, lacked all sense of social commitment. Born, as he was, to a very

279

wealthy family, he was, as a youngster, a "spoilt brat". As an example of such spoiling and the psychological effect it had on the youngster, Abram Saulovich mentioned how young Vladimir was taken to school (the prestigious *Tenishev Gimnaziya*) by one of the chauffeur-driven family cars (there were supposed to be at least three cars, a Benz, a Wolseley and an Opel). Such indulgence was rare in those days, even in the case of the wealthy.

Whatever effect the circumstances of his privileged existence had on the formation of Nabokov's consciousness, as a writer he was an accomplished stylist, whatever his choice of subject matter, and his heroes were often deviants of various kinds.

Abram Saulovich arrived in Berlin in November 1922, nine months after the assassination of Nabokov senior. By that time Nabokov junior had assumed the *nom de plume* of Sirin (in Russian folklore – a bird of paradise), and, writing under that name, had already acquired some reputation as a Russian *émigré* poet and writer. The erstwhile riches were gone, and writing almost exclusively for the *émigré* market was not a lucrative business. While in Europe, the Nabokov-Sirins suffered a life of penury, although shortly after leaving Russia the young poet and writer was able to devote himself to studies in Cambridge on the proceeds from his mother's jewellery. It was not until *Lolita*, written as a document of a different culture, that Nabokov would become a wealthy man.

Abram Saulovich admired Nabokov as a stylist but did not like his choice of subject matter. In particular this applied to two novels by Nabokov published by *Petropolis* in conjunction with the Paris based periodical *Sovremennye Zapisky* (*Contemporary Notes*), namely *Camera Obscura*, published in 1933, and *Otchayanie* (*Despair*) published in 1936.

152 Dr Heinrich Brüning, to whom the Social Democrats gave their support, became Chancellor in March 1930, and took recourse to the infamous Article 48 of the Weimar Constitution, which enabled the Chancellor to rule by decree, thus dispensing with parliamentary-democratic procedure. The policy of the "lesser evil" paved the way for Hitler. In 1932, the arch-conservative Field-Marshall Paul von Hindenburg was elected President with the support of Brüning and the Social Democrats, who, this time, called Hindenburg "the lesser evil" when compared with Hitler. Hindenburg's first presidential act was to sack Brüning, who was replaced by Franz von Papen, a representative of the East Prussian Junkers (the descendants of the feudal aristocracy who had large estates East of the river Elbe). Papen dissolved the Social Democratic State Government of Prussia and jailed its leaders. In December 1932, Kurt von Schleicher, the "strong man" of the German General Staff, who had been a member of the Brüning and then of the Papen cabinets, replaced Papen as Chancellor.

153 As for the coalition between the Social Democrats and the *Zentrum* which actually did come about, it meant, in reality, the support by the Social Democrats of Brüning as the "lesser evil" when compared with Hitler.

154 It may sound surprising that Abram Saulovich, whose political outlook was wedded to peaceful democratic concepts, should consider "the application of armed force" as part of the measures to resolve a political crisis. Yet the German Social Democrats, when raised to power after the overthrow of the Kaiser in 1918, used the army led by a reactionary officers' corps to crush revolutionary uprisings, eg. the Spartacus uprising in 1918, including the murder of Karl Liebknecht and Rosa Luxemburg. The overthrow of the Béla Kun regime in Hungary led to the establishment of a reactionary government there. By comparison, the suppression of the Hitler putsch in Munich, in 1923, was a relatively mild affair. After all, those on the opposite sides of the firing line, were politically and socially related, except that some had embarked prematurely on an adventure, the success of which was to be consummated ten years later when Hitler came into power. In the meantime, the Nazis could sport a martyr's halo. In the event, the conservative army offered no resistance to Hitler's assumption of power, and a year later became his support against the "populist" cadres of the Nazis.

155 By 1932, election results showed that the support for the Nazis had reached a peak and was beginning to decline. It was then that Papen advised Hindenburg to replace Schleicher with Hitler. Hindenburg followed Papen's advice and appointed Hitler as Chancellor in January 1933. The policy of the "lesser evil" had thus run its full course. The Reichstag was dissolved after Hitler had become Chancellor, and new elections were called, which took place under conditions of terror unleashed against the opposition. Even then, the Nazis did not manage to gain an absolute majority. It was only after they had made use of a half-witted arsonist, van der Lubbe, who set fire to the Reichstag, for which outrage the Nazi's put the blame on the Communists, that all opposition was effectively silenced.

Hitler became President after the death of Hindenburg. In June 1934, Hitler instituted a blood purge to rid himself of populist elements in the Nazi leadership, for after all, there were those who still harboured socialist ideas, as these were propounded in the early days of the movement. The "crime" of some of the leaders was their homosexuality. Some other individuals who could have proved troublesome were also disposed of, including the former Chancellor Schleicher. The army became Hitler's power base, and he could start preparing for the forthcoming war.

German Capitalism had used Hitler to crush the powerful but dis-united workers' movement in Germany. This, the first objective, had been achieved. Now the second objective, to gain dominance in Europe, could be tackled by preparing for the war which was to bring this about.

156   Right-wing conservatives.

157   Many Russian *émigrés* were Jewish, if not by religion then by descent. By and large they did not identify themselves with the German Jews, on whom they looked not so much as Jews but as Germans, while the bulk of the German Jews considered themselves Germans in the first place. It was mainly with the coming into power of the Nazis that the German Jews became aware of being in a rather nasty way, the "chosen people". The indigenous population, where it was inclined to anti-Semitism, a phenomenon which was by no means all pervasive, looked at the Russian Jewish *émigrés* simply as foreigners. In fact, many of them had foreign citizenship or Nansen ("stateless") passports, and, thanks to this, were not discriminated against as were the German Jews in whatever field discrimination occurred.

Of importance was the political reaction of the *émigrés* to the establishment of the Nazi power. The political Left-wing among the émigrés which was comprised by those who had maintained their sympathies with the pre-revolutionary parties such as the Constitutional Democrats, the Social Revolutionaries and the Mensheviks, or continued active work in those organizations, as they were reconstituted in emigration, as well as those who had integrated themselves into the German Social Democratic and even the Communist Party – this section of the *émigrés* fell silent, while those who were not mere sympathisers but who had been active politically, hastened to leave Germany, or went underground, at least temporarily.

In 1936 Jews were not only dismissed from government jobs, but generally from all places of employment, except where a business was owned by Jews. They were excluded from all organizations and generally subjected to conditions similar to those of the blacks in South Africa in the days of apartheid, except that the German Jews were over-whelmingly middle class economically, and were strongly represented in the professions such as doctors, lawyers, as well as in academic professions. There were a number of organized acts of terrorism, e.g. the boycott of Jewish businesses on 1 April 1934, but there was nothing yet on the scale approximating the *Kristallnacht* in November 1938.

158   Bunin's Berlin sojourn as he returned from Stockholm to Paris via Berlin in December 1933, deserves some attention, apart from the reception arranged by Cassirer. The Union of Russian Writers arranged a function in honour of Bunin at which Yosif Gessen, the publisher of *Rul* was to preside, while Fyodor Stepoon and Vladimir Nabokov were to talk about different aspects of Bunin's work. Hitler had been in power for almost a year, and, as mentioned, there were among the Russian *émigrés*, those who had espoused the Nazi ideology. As Gessen

relates in his memoirs *Gody Izgnaniya* (*Years of Exile*), he had been warned against allowing "a *Yid* and a half-*Yid*" to give addresses at the function. The "Yid" in question was Gessen, and the "half-Yid" Nabokov, who actually was a Gentile married to a Jewess. The warning came from Paramonov, a well-heeled member of the Russian *émigré* community, the owner of several large garages in Berlin. Paramonov was also a contributor to *émigré* culture as a publisher, although it is not clear what the contents of that culture was. The function nevertheless went ahead and proved a great success. Although the exodus of the Russian *émigré* intelligentsia had already started before Hitler had gained power and had been accelerated since then, the attendance was much larger than expected, and there were no hostile demonstrations.

Bunin returned to Paris, but not without being involved in an incident reported in Brian Boyd's book on Nabokov, *The Russian Years*. Nabokov had met Bunin in Paris where the latter

> ...a brilliant raconteur, told him that as he left Berlin he had been stopped by the Gestapo, interrogated, searched for smuggled jewels, stripped and searched again. Nobel Prize or not, he had to swallow a strong dose of castor oil, squat over an empty bucket until the treatment had its effect, then be searched again, naked, by the *Gestapo* agent who wiped him.

159 Petropolis continued to function. The Staatsbibliothek (State Library) in Berlin contains works published by Petropolis in 1936, 1937 and 1938, which was the year in which Abram Saulovich was expelled from Germany.

Actually, one of the first books published by Petropolis under the Third Reich was Nabokov's *Camera Obscura*, brought out in 1933 (the year in which Hitler came to power) in conjunction with the Paris based publishing company *Sovremennye Zapiski* (*Contemporary Notes*).

In 1934 Petropolis commenced the publication of a twelve-volume edition of the collected works of Ivan Bunin. The twelfth volume was not completed until 1939, and was published by Abram Saulovich in Brussels after his expulsion from Germany.

In 1936 Petropolis published another novel by Nabokov – *Otchayanie* (*Despair*).

Also in 1936 Petropolis published Gumilyov's dramatic poem "Gondola", fifteen years after the shooting of the poet by the GPU. In the same year Petropolis published an anthology of *émigré* poetry, under the title *Yakor* (Anchor), compiled by G.V. Adamovich (a prominent *émigré* literary critic) and L.M. Kantor. Also a work by Dmitry Merezhkovsky, an *émigré* writer who specialized in historical subjects, and, in this particular case, with a leaning towards the mystical. The work was entitled *Litsa Svyatykh ot Issoussa k nam* (*Faces of the Saints from Jesus to Our Times*). The respective saints comprised St Paul, St Augustin, St Francis of Assisi and Joan of Arc.

Parabola also continued to operate, bringing out Gladishchev's *Snyi na Yavoo* (*Waking Dreams*) in 1933, and Mandelstam's collection of poems *Tretiy Chas* (*The Third Hour*) in 1935.

Thus there was quite a variegated production of books in these harrowing years without any interference by the Nazi authorities.

160 While the time of the notice was extended, it was clearly impossible, in those days, to leave Germany for any other country without a visa which would assure that the applicant would not be stranded in the host-country, but either return, or proceed further.

161 The authorities agreed to issue us a return visa to Germany, on the understanding that it would not be used. This was therefore quite a smart move by the German authorities to ensure a painless process of expulsion, and this is what Kreutzburg convinced the authorities to do.

162 Yakov Frumkin and Natasha Tumarkina were friends of our family. Frumkin was connected with HIAS, an organization set up to aid Jewish refugees, and based mainly in New York. Frumkin was also a friend of Nabokov senior, and in 1940 helped Nabokov junior and his family to leave Paris a month before the German army marched into the French capital.

The obtaining of a visa to England was not entirely due to Frumkin's efforts on my behalf, for the German authorities "cooperated" in their own manner, as was indicateed above.

I am not sure what part Natasha Tumarkina played in obtaining my visa to England. My only recollection of her is that she was one of the young ladies whom my parents considered to be eligible to become their daughter-in-law (unbeknown to her), while I had already made a different commitment. Thus she became Natasha Frank, completely unaware of the fate from which she had escaped.

Anyhow, I left Germany for Belgium and England in March 1938, one week before my parents, and quite unsuspecting of the trauma to which they were subjected during that week.

163 Petropolis now became *Les Editions Petropolis, Bruxelles*. One of the books published in 1939 was *Zavety* (*Behests*), a collection of poems by Raissa Blokh and Mira Borodina.

164 The work was published in 1940 under the title *Le Répertoire Biographique des Francs – Maçons Russes, XVIII-XIX siècles*.

Abram Saulovich writes that he never suspected that there had been such a number of Masons in Russia, even among those in power, but he would have been even more surprised at recent *Glasnost*-induced "revelations" regarding the dominance of Masons in all Russian corridors of power, not only before the Revolution, but even in the course of it. At least, this is what can be gathered from two articles by Victor Brachev, who claims that, according to the reckoning of Soviet historians (he does not name which ones), at least half the membership of the first Provisional Government consisted of Masons, and that according to N.N. Berberova, who published a book entitled *People and Lodges*, in New York, as recently as 1986, all the ministers of the Provisional Government (with exception of Milyukov) were Masons. Also that it was on the request of its French "Brothers" that the Provisional Government refused to consider a separate peace with Germany, and "…ignoring the national interest of the country, drove tens of thousands of Russian soldiers into the offensive in the summer of 1917". According to Brachev, it was not only that the bourgeois Provisional Government was ruled by Masons, but the Petrograd Soviet of Workers and Soldiers Deputies also happened to be under the influence of the Masons, for the Menshevik Chkheidse (who, at one stage, had entrusted his official stamp to Abram Saulovich) was a Mason.

If that was not enough for the "Brothers" to establish their sway over Russian affairs in 1917 which, according to Brachev, was an "indubitable fact", he cites some "information" from a book by V.F. Ivanov, *Secret Diplomacy*, published in Harbin in 1937, according to which the most prominent Bolsheviks were Masons, namely: Lenin, Trotsky, Sverdlov, Zinoviev, Kamenev, Rakovsky and Radek. The name of Stalin is "characteristically" missing. Brachev does not explain what is meant by "characteristically", but then he becomes less assertive and claims that, so far, only the names of three well known Bolsheviks can be listed among the "Brothers", namely: Skvortsov-Stepanov, Sereda and Radek. The last named Bolshevik is referred to as "K.B. Radek (Sobelson)". Why that "precision" in mentioning the original name following the historically known *nom-de-guerre*? After all, Brachev does not refer to Stalin as "Stalin (Dzhugashvili)". The mention of the obviously Jewish original name when referring to an opponent, is the hallmark of a "genuine Russian" anti-Semite. And would Radek not be an apt exponent of the "Judeo-Masonic Conspiracy against the Russian People", a notion espoused by reactionary forces emerging in Russia?

165 My first wife.

166 Neither did the majority of the Germans, for that matter.

167 While the Second World War had already begun in 1939, it had been a "phoney war" as far as Western Europe was concerned. In May 1940 the armed forces of the Third Reich started their onslaught on the West. This turn of events frustrated the publication of two works by Nabokov: *Dar (The Gift)* and *Volshebnik (The Enchanter)*.

Abram Saulovich had agreed to publish *Dar* after Nabokov had run into trouble with the editor of *Sovremennye Zapiski*, the Paris based *émigré* journal which had undertaken to publish *Dar* in a series of instalments.

Dar was Nabokov's most significant work, and one of his last before he migrated to the United States. It is largely autobiographical, although there are differences between Nabokov and Fyodor, the central character of the novel, and the circumstances surrounding their lives. Fyodor who undertakes the "original investigation of the relation between art and life" which brought about the refusal by Vadim Rudnev, the editor of *Sovremennye Zapiski*, to publish this particular part of the novel, since in it Nabokov, as Fyodor, had subjected Chernyshevsky whom the radical Russian intelligentsia considered as holy, to a scathing criticism and which appeared as nothing short of blasphemous to *Sovremennye Zapiski*, even though that journal had established for itself a reputation of broadmindedness.

The first instalment of *Dar* comprising the first chapter, was published in *Sovremennye Zapiski* in the first half of 1937, followed by four more chapters, but Nabokov felt that the second chapter required some amending before it could be published in the next issue of the journal. As a substitute, Nabokov sent the publisher the fourth chapter, which contained the *Life of Chernyshevsky*, completed two years earlier. Nabokov felt it could be read as an independent treatise. Vadim Rudnev, was not pleased with the proposed substitution of the second chapter by the fourth chapter, before he had even become cognisant of what the fourth chapter contained. After having read it, he refused to publish something which seemed sacrilege with respect to Chernyshevsky *Sovremennye Zapiski* was established by a group of Social Revolutionary *émigrés*, for whom the name of Chernyshevsky was sacrosanct. The name of the journal alluded to the two 19th-century organs of Russia's radical intelligentsia: *Otechestvennye Zapiski* (*Annals of the Fatherland*) and *Sovremennik* (*The Contemporary*), with both of which, and especially with the latter, Chernyshevsky had been associated.

Eventually *Sovremennye Zapiski* still published the other chapters, omitting the offending fourth chapter, but in view of the attitude taken by Vadim Rudnev in refusing to publish the chapter which contained the Life of Chernyshevsky, Nabokov, as Brian Boyd writes,

> had been delighted the previous October [1938] when Abram Kagan, who had run Petropolis in Berlin until Hitler squeezed him out, had agreed to publish *The Gift*, including the unpublished chapter four. By December Nabokov hoped that the novel might already be at the printers. Whatever happened to the projected edition remains unclear.

What actually happened was the invasion of Belgium by the armies of the Third Reich. It caused Abram Saulovich to flee from Brussels. *The Gift* was not published in its entirety until fifteen years later.

Another work by Nabokov, which Abram Saulovich considered for publication, was *Volshebnik* (*The Enchanter*), offered by Nabokov after *Sovremennye Zapiski* had rejected it. Again the war interfered. *Volshebnik* was not published until 1986, in French translation, nine years after Nabokov's death.

Volshebnik was the precursor of *Lolita*. It concerns a pederast and his love for a twelve-year-old girl, but the story is less complex *Lolita,* which is told in the first person. *Volshebnik* is told in the third, and is a late work written by Nabokov in his native Russian, whereas *Lolita* is not only written in English but is also a document of a different culture.

168 My sister Irene gave me a different version of the effect of the bombardment of the escape route. According to her, there was a "direct hit": a bullet (possibly a shell splinter) went right through the door of the car near Sonya, narrowly missing her. How is it that Abram Saulovich took no notice of this, he who had such a good memory?

I suggest the following explanation: Abram Saulovich was not so much brave as, at times, utterly oblivious of danger. He was scared of bees, and his fastidiousness was often based on fear of vermin. But when the *Cheka* confronted him with the verdict: either expulsion from the country, or the death sentence, he described his reaction as being merely "in a depressed condition". To him, the bullet or shell splinter penetrating the door of the car was just one of the incidentals of the escape from Belgium, which he decribes without the slightest air of panic. Apparently a "direct hit" had at least to cause some fatalities to become noteworthy, while a projectile that narrowly missed, was not worthy of note.

169 There is a minor, but somewhat puzzling detail in Abram Saulovich's account regarding that "boiling water". Did he mean "boiled water", since it was possibly not safe to drink any other, or perhaps the boiling water was for tea making? But then there was no mention of any provisions carried by my parents. They are no longer here to resolve that mystery. But then they were undergoing quite an ordeal, and the query regarding the "boiling water" would border on inappropriate facetiousness.

170 A leading Menshevik.

171 Abram Saulovich did not want to disclose the name.

172 *or* = French for gold; *mont* = French for mountain, *Berg"* in German.

173 It seems rather odd that a pre-revolutionary Russian Consulate could still function in Marseille, or anywhere for that matter, especially in a host country which, until recently, had a military alliance with the Soviet Union. Actually, when France had eventually recognized the Soviet Government, the French authorities allowed the former Russian ambassador and consuls to become the directors of the *Office des Réfugiés Russes*, which was empowered to issue certain documents (birth certificates, Nansen passports, schooling certificates, etc.) and exercise some functions of consular authorities with respect to Russian *émigrés*.

174 There is some disagreement here between this account of the journey, and that given by my sister, who denies having been either sea sick or emaciated. She only thought, before the voyage, that she might be seasick. But Abram Saulovich was so proud of being a good sailor, that anyone who even entertained the thought of possibly becoming sea sick, would not measure up as fit for the sea voyage.

175 Here again my sister begs to differ. According to her, the British treated the children to a "god-awful-picnic in the blazing sun". It was "beastly hot", and she would gladly have relinquished the sweets that were distributed in exchange for a swim in the ocean. Abram Saulovich, in the meantime, was looking longingly at the Bermuda Islands from the *Serpapinto*, where the heat was unbearable while the ship was stationary, and thus came to the conclusion that the children had the better part of the deal.

176 My sister disagrees with the description of that urban environment as "peaceful", for she claims that she was terrorised by pugnacious black youngsters. Abram Saulovich does not mention this. For his part, he was not easily terrorised (his marksmanship with an inkwell, as a youngster, may be recalled!), but it did not occur to him that a girl, at a still tender age, did not possess the retaliatory capacity which he possessed at that age.

177 Abram Saulovich mentioned her earlier in connection with her refusal to give him an affidavit.

178 There is no religious connotation in Abram Saulovich invoking Allah.

179 Presumably in camps in Germany, or in German-occupied territories accessible to the Red Cross. The United States were not as yet involved in the Second World War.

180 Initially, the company's name was International University Press.

181 The last three preceding paragraphs constitute the last entry (31 July 1975) in Abram Saulovich's *Memoirs* dealing with the establishment of his publishing venture in New York.

182 When visiting Abram in 1977 I asked him for more details about that venture, and about its further progress. I recorded on tape the respective interviews, and below is the translation of the transcript of the tape and comments relevant to the interviews.

183 1929.

184 Back in Petrograd, Abram Saulovich had also published the first Russian translation of William James' *Principles of Psychology*.

185 While the involvement of psychoanalysts as holders of "preferred stock" did not establish a financial base for the company, such involvement was nevertheless an important financial contribution. Incidentally, a privilege enjoyed by all stockholders was that, for many years, they received gratis, copies of all books published by the company.

186 At that time, the Association used to publish the *Bulletin of the American Psychoanalytic Association*. Abram Saulovich took over that publication

with, I believe, some financial loss, in order to cement his relation with the Association, and in the hope of eventually publishing the *Journal* which also encompassed the *Bulletin*.

187 It should be mentioned that while The American Psychoanalytic Association comprised the majority of psychoanalysts in the USA there was also, and still is, an International Psychoanalytical Association, to which the Americans and the rest of the world belong.

Although Abram Saulovich, together with Frosch, was instrumental in bringing about the establishment of the *Journal*, he was at no time in charge of determining what material was to be published. From its inception, the *Journal* had an Editorial Board which evaluated what was to be published, and an Editor who made the final decisions.

The Journal of the American Psychoanalytic Association, which was founded in 1953, continues to this day. At the time of writing (1995) the *Journal* was, under the editorship of Theodore Shapiro, while my sister Irene was the Manuscript Editor. She has held that position for 14 years. Beginning with 1994, the *Journal* will be under the editorship of Arnold D. Richards.

188 The Institute referred to was the New York Psychoanalytic Institute. Abram Saulovich also published a very distinguished lecture series: the *Freud Anniversary Lectures* of the Institute, and a few brief works dealing with the history of the Institute.

189 *The International Journal of Group Psychotherapy*, which was begun in 1950, was continued after the death of A. Slavson. It was published on a quarterly basis, and its last editor was Robert R. Dies, but there have been several editors in between. The publication of that journal was discontinued in 1993.

190 The publication of *Psychological Issues* still continues. Initially it was under the editorship of George S. Klein, and was a quarterly monograph series. At present it is being edited by Herbert J. Schlesinger, but is no longer a quarterly. It is published at irregular intervals, and consists of book-length monographs. Here again, my sister was Manuscript Editor. The last monograph (1993) was No.61.

191 Actually, such an Index had been put together by Alexander Grinstein, but he had run out of funds, and Abram Saulovich undertook its publication.

192 In the interviews which I had with Abram Saulovich in 1977, he added some more information on his contribution to the propagation of Psychoanalysis.

193 It should be mentioned that while in the past Abram Saulovich's publishing activities involved him in extensive travelling in Europe, this was not the case in connection with IUP. All his travelling was confined to the United States, except on one occasion in 1971, when he attended an international congress of psychoanalysts in Vienna, and had one of his meetings with Anna Freud.

194 This was, according to Abram Saulovich, the situation of *International Universities Press* in 1977.

195 While publishing always constituted Abram Saulovich's principal interest and activity, it was never all-absorbing. He devoted much of his energy to activities arising from his sense of social commitment. This was also the case when he came to the United States.

I am quoting from the transcript of his remarks made in Russian a tape-recorded conversation which I had with him in 1977, during one of my visits to New York.

196 Another incident occurred much later, after the war, arising from the disagreements within the organization over the interpretation of alarming developments in the Soviet Union, where a new wave of repressions took place, directed this time mainly against members of the intelligentsia who happened to be Jews, euphemistically called "rootless cosmopolitans". This latest turn arose from Stalin's paranoia about alleged Jewish plots, and culmitated in the trial, in 1953, of a number of doctors, dubbed "assassins in white coats", most of whom were Jews, and who were said to have confessed to murdering, back in 1949, Zhdanov – Stalin's lieutenant in charge of cultural affairs, and were now planning to assassinate other Soviet leaders. Stalin also sought to implicate Lavrentiy Beriya, the Chief of the NKVD in this "Doctor's Plot", but died before succeeding in achieving this. Stalin based his suspicion of Beriya on the fact that during the war Beriya had been instrumental in organizing the Jewish Anti-Fascist Committee in the United States, to win Jewish public opinion there in the struggle against Nazi Germany. The Chairman of the Jewish Anti-Fascist Committee was the well-known actor Solomon Mikhailovich Mikhoels, the founder of the Jewish Theatre in Moscow. Mikhoels had come to the United States in 1943 on the invitation of Albert Einstein, where, among other activities, he addressed a meeting of fifty thousand people in the New York Polo Ground. After the war, Stalin disbanded the Jewish Anti-Fascist Committee, and in January 1948, Mikhoels was found brutally murdered, officially by hooligans, but, as it transpired later, the murder had been ordered by Stalin. As the campaign against the "rootless cosmopolitans" gained momentum, Mikhoels was accused of having been an agent of US Intelligence.

197 Lieutenant General Andrey A. Vlasov made common cause with the Nazis justifying his betrayal by denouncing the Soviet regime "...as a tyrannical perversion of the October Revolution".

198 Abram Saulovich kept up his friendship with his old Menshevik comrades while they were still about. Basically he did not change the political beliefs which he had held as a young man, but became more tolerant of opposing views. He would have welcomed *Perestroika* had he lived to the launching of that attempt at reform, although I am not at all sure that he would have welcomed the introduction of a "market

economy", a euphemism for the restoration of Capitalism. It is true that in 1917 the Mensheviks believed that Russia should pass through a capitalist phase before even considering Socialism, but the further development of Capitalism in the world since those days, gave Abram Saulovich pause to reconsider the implications of the capitalist perspective for Russia, as I could gather from some of my conversations with him.

Abram Saulovich's political interests were not confined to his old homeland, but extended also to the new. He considered American politics to be rather primitive by European concepts, purely pragmatic, lacking in ideology and easily subject to corruption. He pointed to the immaturity of the labor movement which was not sufficiently politically advanced to establish a Labor Party. Nevertheless he took an interest in American politics. He always voted for the Democrats, and I believe that he was registered as one, but he considered that some Democrats were more Right-wing than the Republicans and sometimes downright reactionary, while some Republicans held progressive views. He professed some admiration for John F. Kennedy, but had only contempt for Richard Nixon.

On 14 July 1972, Abram Saulovich Kagan wrote: "The whole week beginning with Monday, I watched the Democratic Party Convention, from early evening until the early hours of the morning, on TV. How much demagogy, trivial foppery, straight out dishonesty! What a low cultural level! There is no respect for the individual, for whom "dignity" should be re-established. The opponent is guilty just by being the opponent, and he is accused of all deadly sins. They shout about democratic reforms yet on the spot abandon democratic principles. The elections of the members of the Convention is most undemocratic. The Vice-President is only fictitiously elected. The political division into Democrats and Republicans is an anachronism which is only of historical significance. In the Democratic Party there is a sufficient number of deep-rooted Conservatives, and in the Republican Party there are progressive people. In the Congress the voting of the Republicans and Democrats is determined by the most diverse questions. All Congressional Committees are definitely formed undemocratically: at the head stand Congressmen and Senators, but not really in accordance with seniority. One cannot honestly say that the Republican Party is the party of the "Haves", while the Democratic Party defends the interests of the "People". In each there are some of both.

Regarding Abram Saulovich's opinion of the American people, living in cosmopolitan New York, he had accepted the multi-national composition of the population in that metropolis, and the resulting tensions between the various ethnic groups as a given fact. The milieu in which he moved was white and to a large extent Jewish; this applied in particular to his circle of friends among the psychoanalysts. He never felt himself to be a foreigner in New York, as had been the case in Germany. His reasoning went something like this:

The only original Americans are the Red Indians. All the others are of alien origin, and an alien among aliens feels at home.

199 To the uninitiated reader, Tulchinsky's article expressed respect and admiration for Abram Saulovich. But, unfortunately, this well-intended contribution to literary journalism was an amalgam of fact and fiction, and was full of inaccuracies. It was hardly suitable as source material for serious research.

Above all, Abram Saulovich loved precision and could become very intolerant of someone who had made the slightest slip-up in this respect, in an otherwise irreproachable case. He was equally intolerant of any exaggeration, undue embellishment or stretching of the truth, not to mention the reference to anything that was not true.

200 Abram Saulovich had an amazing memory for names. Russians, as a rule, use the patronymic in addition to the first name, and his memory was faultless when remembering these. He had not much regard for those who were not thus endowed, and did not tolerate any misspelling.

201 Incidentally, the above statement that Abram Saulovich "did not immediately agree to enter into yet another company..." since he was overloaded by work, being " already the head of a number of major publishing companies", bears out the point made in Chapter Twelve, that Petropolis became a publishing company in 1920, when Abram Saulovich's reputation as a publisher had already been well established, and not in 1917, the year of the Revolution. As for Freud's dream book, which Abram Saulovich denied ever publishing, it was actually titled *The Interpretation of Dreams*, and not *The Psychology of Dreams*.

202 The Nabokov mentioned in the beginning of the above paragraph is Nabokov senior, the father of the poet and writer. Clearly, the Nabokovs were used to better conditions before the Revolution. The Nabokov-Sirins referred to are Nabokov junior, the writer, and to his wife.